CHRISTIANITY IN ANCIENT ROME: THE FIRST THREE CENTURIES

CHRISTIANITY IN ANCIENT ROME: THE FIRST THREE CENTURIES

BERNARD GREEN

t&t clark

Published by T&T Clark International
A Continuum Imprint
The Tower Building, 11 York Road, London SE1 7NX
80 Maiden Lane, Suite 704, New York NY 10038

www.continuumbooks.com

First published 2010
Reprinted 2011

Bernard Green has asserted his right under the Copyright, Designs and Patents
Act, 1988, to be identified as the Auther of this work

British Library Cataloguing-in-Publication Data
A catalogue record for this book is available from the British Library.

ISBN : 978-0-567-03249-2 (Hardback)
          978-0-567-03250-8 (Paperback)

Typeset by Fakenham Photosetting, Fakenham, Norfolk
Printed and bound in the United States of America

For David Morland OSB,
who took me back to Rome.

CONTENTS

PREFACE

This book grew out of lectures that, for several years, I have given at Oxford on early Christianity in Rome. It owes a good deal to tutorial discussions with undergraduates where questions and ideas raised in the text were first explored. I am grateful to friends and colleagues for their help and expert advice, particularly Dr Mark Edwards and Ian Boxall, Dr Morwenna Ludlow and Professor Norman Tanner and Professor Timothy Barnes. I am grateful too to Rupert Allen and Tom Harrison, who read parts of the manuscript, and especially to Triona Adams, who read the whole of the text with rare diligence and generosity. They helped purge it of unnecessary obscurity and mistakes. I appreciate the help of Mrs Anna Mayer, whose gift of a laptop allowed me to write this book in the Bodleian and Sackler Libraries in Oxford. I owe a particular debt of gratitude to the British Academy, who gave me a grant to pursue research in Rome. I dedicate the book to a member of my monastic community at Ampleforth, Fr David Morland, who first opened my eyes as an adult to the wonder and beauty of the city of Rome.

Bernard Green OSB
St Benet's Hall, Oxford
Feast of Saints Peter and Paul, 29 June 2009

ABBREVIATIONS

AJ	Josephus, *Antiquities of the Jews*
ANRW	*Aufstieg und Niedergang der römischen Welt*
BJ	Josephus, *Jewish War*
CUP	Cambridge University Press
HE	Eusebius *Ecclesiastical History*
ICUR	Angelo Silvagni, Antonio Ferrua, Danilo Mazzoleni and Carlo Carletti *Inscriptiones Christianae Urbis Romae septimo saeculo antiquiores, nova series*, vols I–X, (Civitas Vaticana: Pontificium Institutum Archaeologiae Christianae, 1922–92)
JECS	*Journal of Early Christian Studies*
JEH	*Journal of Ecclesiastical History*
JRS	*Journal of Roman Studies*
JTS	*Journal of Theological Studies*
LP	Louis Duchesne *Le Liber Pontificalis: Texte, introduction et commentaire* I–II Paris, 1886–92
LTUR	Eva Margareta Steinby *Lexicon Topographicum Urbis Romae* 6 vols (Rome: Edizioni Quasar, 1993–9)
LTUR Sub	Adriano La Regina *Lexicon Topographicum Urbis Romae Suburbium* 5 vols (Rome: Edizioni Quasar, 2001–8)
MGH Cron Min	Theodore Mommsen *Monumenta Germaniae Historica: Auctorum Antiquissorum IX: Chronicorum Minorum Saec. IV, V, VI, VII* vol. 1 (Berlin: Weidmann, 1891)
OUP	Oxford University Press
TDAR	Samuel B. Platner and Thomas Ashby *A Topographical Dictionary of Ancient Rome* (Oxford: OUP, 1929)
ZPE	*Zeitschrift für Papyrologie und Epigraphik*

Chapter 1

ORIGINS

The Acts of the Apostles opens in Jerusalem and ends in Rome. The book's architecture is presumably deliberate: to show how a Jewish sect spread from the city which was the heart of their faith to the city which was the political capital of their world. The earliest travellers who brought to Rome the belief that Jesus of Nazareth had risen from the dead were Jews. They must have reached the city about a decade after his crucifixion in Jerusalem. In Rome, they found a long-established Jewish community with its own distinctive traditions; but Christianity was not to take root and grow among the Roman Jews. Whereas elsewhere in the diaspora Christianity remained a Jewish sect for generations, even while drawing in gentile converts, in Rome Christianity became something separate with a clearly distinct identity. The Christians there were thought of as Jews by the imperial authorities in 49; by 64 they were recognised as a new and foreign religion. When they were blamed by Nero for the great fire of 64, they were a separate and readily recognised group. One of the great strengths of the early Roman church was that it had counted both Peter and Paul in its membership; what impact their presence had on the community can only be a matter of conjecture but the confident claim that they both died in Rome as martyrs gave the Roman church a distinct prestige. The persecution of 64 must have been devastating for the early Christian community but they had recovered by the beginning of the second century, when they could speak with confidence of their position in the Christian world.

THE JEWS OF ROME

The economic and political power of Rome drew to the city vast numbers of immigrants not only from Italy but from the whole expanse of the empire.[1] Roman attitudes to the foreigners in their

---

[1] See David Noy, *Foreigners at Rome: Citizens and Strangers* (London: Duckworth, 2000).

1

midst were, unsurprisingly, complex and contradictory.[2] Distaste and contempt were probably common enough. Juvenal, writing in about 130 AD, put the most notorious statement of loathing for foreigners into the mouth of his preposterous character Umbricius in his *Satires*:

> My fellow citizens, I cannot bear the city being Greek, but what proportion of the dregs really is Greek? For a long time now, the Syrian Orontes has poured into the Tiber and dumps in it its language and customs, its slanting strings, horns and foreign drums and the girls who are sent to sell themselves by the Circus.[3]

As with all effective satire, the joke cuts several ways — readers are expected to laugh at Umbricius's old-fashioned prejudices but at the same time to recognise how far they share them. Speaking of the early Christians in Rome at the time of Nero, Tacitus casually observed that it was no surprise to find them there as 'every sort of crime and shameful activity flows from everywhere else into the city and is practised there'.[4] Elsewhere, Tacitus recorded a speech to the Senate in the time of Nero which reveals bewilderment and fear on the part of owners surrounded by households of slaves made up of 'entire nations with customs alien to ours, practising different cults and foreign rites or none at all', a situation very different from the old days when slaves shared their masters' language and religious assumptions.[5] On the other hand, the presence in Rome of people from all over the empire could be a matter of pride. They showed that the city was 'a single fatherland of all the nations of the world'[6] and that, whereas other people had a delimited territory, in Rome 'the city and the world are the same'.[7]

Inevitably, from the second century BC Rome had a significant Jewish community.[8] The earliest evidence for their presence was in 139 BC. Their numbers were swollen in the aftermath of Pompey the Great's capture of Jerusalem, when he brought back large numbers of Jewish slaves in 61 BC. Only two years later, Cicero commented on the

---

[2] Noy *Foreigners* pp. 31–52.

[3] Juvenal *Satires* 3.62–65.

[4] Tacitus *Annals* 15.44.3.

[5] *Ann.* 14.44.3.

[6] Pliny the Elder *Natural History* 3.5.39.

[7] Ovid *Fasti* 683–84.

[8] See Harry J. Leon, *The Jews of Ancient Rome* (Peabody, Mass: Hendrickson, 2nd ed, 1995); for the Roman Jews down to 70, see Erich S. Gruen, *Diaspora: Jews amidst Greeks and Romans* (Cambridge, Mass: Harvard University Press, 2002) pp. 15–53.

presence of many Jews at the trial in Rome of the former governor of Asia, Flaccus, accused among other things of confiscating the gold sent each year by the Jewish community of Rome for the upkeep of the Jerusalem Temple. He depicted the Roman Jews as a large body, closely united and influential in public meetings.[9] The community was repeatedly refreshed by further immigration from elsewhere in the diaspora and from Judaea itself.[10] Two pieces of information allow for some estimate of their numbers. On the death of Herod the Great in 4 BC, about eight thousand Roman Jews turned out to support a delegation from Judaea calling for an end to the rule of his dynasty.[11] In 19 AD, four thousand were conscripted for military service in Sardinia.[12] These figures have led historians to estimate that there were probably between forty and fifty thousand Jews in Rome by that period.[13]

The fullest account of Jewish faith and practice from a Roman point of view was provided in about 110 AD by the historian Tacitus. Here we can see what a highly educated, sophisticated Roman made of this oriental religion. Having speculated about the origins and history of the Jewish people, he offered various pieces of information which were a strange mix of the well and badly informed. He correctly informed his readers that Jews abstained from pork, kept certain fasts, ate unleavened bread and observed the Sabbath — offering his own curious reasons for these practices — but he also believed that they had a shrine where they had the statue of an ass to commemorate finding water in the wilderness by following a herd of wild asses. He then went on to offer a description of the Jews not in Jerusalem but in the diaspora, in other words in Rome:

These rituals, in whatever way they originated, are observed on account of their antiquity. The other customs, which are sinister and base, survive because of their depravity. For the worst people [converts outside Judaea], renouncing their ancestral religions, kept sending tribute and contributions there, so that the wealth of the Jews mounted up. Among themselves, the Jews are extremely loyal and quick to show compassion, but towards everyone else they show hate and hostility. They eat separately and keep to their own beds, for although as a people they are very prone to be libidinous they abstain from sex with foreign women. Among themselves, however, nothing is illicit. They insti-

[9] Cicero *Pro Flacco* 66.
[10] Noy *Foreigners* pp. 255–67.
[11] Josephus *The Jewish War* [*BJ*] 2.80; *Antiquities of the Jews* [*AJ*] 17.300–3.
[12] Josephus *AJ* 18.84; Tacitus *Ann.* 2.85; Suetonius *Tiberius* 36; Dio Cassius *Roman History* 57.18.5.
[13] Leon *Jews of Ancient Rome* pp. 135–36.

tuted circumcision to distinguish themselves from other peoples. Those who are converted [to Judaism] follow the same customs and the first lesson they are taught is to despise the gods, to disown their country and to regard their parents, children and brothers as of little account. But they look to increase their numbers for they regard killing an unwanted child as a crime and they believe that the souls of those killed in battle or by execution are immortal, from which comes their love of having children and their contempt of dying. They bury bodies rather than cremate them, in the Egyptian manner, and they show the same care for the dead and belief about the world below [as the Egyptians]; but about heavenly things they have the opposite belief. Whereas the Egyptians worship many animals and images they have made, the Jews, purely mentally, think there is only one God. They regard as impious those who make images of gods out of corruptible material in the likeness of men and women. They believe the supreme and eternal God is incapable of representation and without end. Therefore they do not set up any statues in their cities, still less in their temples. They do not give that flattery to kings or such honour to the Caesars.[14]

Try as he might, even when he is at his most scornful, Tacitus cannot quite suppress a note of respect for a brave and defiant people, fearless in battle, utterly loyal and generous to each other, with their austere conception of the absolute, eternal and invisible God. They differed from others because of their large families and their opposition to abortion and infanticide, but Tacitus's hostility mainly derives from the way the Jews are so self-contained, unassimilated into society, separated off by marriage and dietary customs and religious belief. Anyone joining them, and there are clearly enough of them to be worthy of comment, have to cut themselves off from the society of which they were formerly a part.

That description of diaspora Judaism occurs in the middle of Tacitus's account of the Jewish War of 66–73 AD. The fortunes of the Jews throughout the diaspora were, of course, always bound up with the history of Judaea. It was ruled by the Hasmonaean royal family from 142 to 63 BC but passed decisively under indirect Roman control as a result of the third Mithradatic War. Mithradates was Rome's most dangerous foe in the first century BC. King of Pontus, the kingdom to the south of the Black Sea, he had survived two previous attempts on the part of the Romans to suppress his power but he was finally destroyed by Rome's most brilliant general, Pompey the Great, in a devastatingly effective campaign which was to transform the Near East decisively and permanently. It was a region of unstable states and ambitious rulers which presented a risk of future conflict. Pompey seized the opportunity to lay down a new settlement and ensure the

---

[14] Tacitus *Histories* 5.5.

security of Roman rule in the eastern Mediterranean. He annexed Bithynia and Pontus, thereby establishing Roman control of Asia Minor, and also annexed Syria, which was politically unstable. He made Armenia a client kingdom and went on to do the same with Judaea. There the succession to the throne was disputed between two brothers, Hyrcanus and Aristobulus. Pompey intervened in favour of Hyrcanus, capturing Jerusalem in 63 BC at the end of a siege that cost twelve thousand Jewish lives. He set up Hyrcanus as king and re-drew the boundaries of the country. From now on, decisions concerning the rulers and borders of Judaea would be made in Rome.

The slaves Pompey brought to Rome for his triumph in 61 BC had seen Jerusalem sacked and the Temple desecrated. Pompey had entered the Holy of Holies and was amazed to find that it contained no image of God.[15] The Jewish historian Josephus, with studied ambiguity, reported the event both as a grave sin which shocked the Jewish nation but also as a sign of his clemency as he left the Temple treasures untouched.[16] It is more than likely that the gravity of the sin rather than the clemency coloured Pompey's reputation among Jews throughout the diaspora as well as in Judaea. Eventually he and Julius Caesar became rivals for power in Rome. Caesar challenged him in 49 BC by crossing the Rubicon into Italy with his legions from Gaul. As the civil war spread across the Mediterranean, it is highly likely that Caesar could rely on Jewish support. Pompey was dead the following year, murdered as he attempted to land in Egypt after his defeat by Caesar at Pharsalus in Greece. Caesar was ruler of the Roman world until his own assassination in 44 BC.

In what looked like a reward for support across the empire in the civil war, Caesar bestowed special privileges upon the Jews. His decrees gave them freedom of worship and association, permission to raise money to support the Temple in Jerusalem, exemption from military service (which would have been incompatible with Sabbath observance) and the right to adjudicate legal cases between Jews without having to refer to the civil courts.[17] It is no surprise that, when Caesar was assassinated, crowds of Jews came for days to mourn at his tomb.[18] After his death, these legal privileges were renewed

---

[15] Tacitus *Hist.* 5.9.
[16] Josephus *BJ* 1.152; *AJ* 14.71.
[17] *AJ* 14.185–216.
[18] Suetonius *Divine Julius* 84.5.

in the city of Rome and throughout the Roman empire.[19] Jewish communities were a substantial presence in many cities and the different contenders for Caesar's legacy, Mark Antony and Octavian, were more than ready to court their support. Furthermore, control of Judaea remained a vital part of Roman policy in the East. The Parthians invaded the country and took Jerusalem in 40 BC, forcing the Romans to besiege the city again and take it back. A new ruler, Herod, was chosen to maintain Roman interests. He was proclaimed King of Judaea by the Roman Senate and escorted by Mark Antony and Octavian to the Capitol where the decree of his appointment was deposited and a sacrifice offered on his behalf.[20] Three years later, he was firmly in the saddle in Judaea and was rewarded with considerably expanded frontiers.

Herod the Great proved a very astute choice. A ruthless despot determined both to retain the confidence of Rome and to modernise his country, he was indispensable. When Mark Antony's and Cleopatra's fleet was defeated by Octavian at the great naval battle at Actium in 31 BC, he switched sides painlessly and joined Octavian, who sealed his rise to power by taking the name Augustus. Herod's greatest achievement was intended to have been the massive enlargement of the Temple in Jerusalem, a vast project which was still uncompleted when it was destroyed by the Romans in 70 AD. Herod's one major weakness, however, was his failure to produce an heir of comparable stature to succeed him. He had too many wives and too many sons and, despite his grim readiness to thin out their ranks by judicial murder, he left three sons at his death in 4 BC among whom his territories were partitioned: Archelaus, Herod Antipas and Philip. It is striking that all three sons were in Rome when Herod died and the division of the territory was presided over and sanctioned by Augustus. Herod's long reign of thirty-three years had brought stability to the region but these three pocket states were inherently unviable. Within a decade, Augustus had taken one of them — Archelaus's share, Judaea, Samaria and Idumaea — under direct rule as part of the province of Syria, ruled on behalf of the governor of Syria by a procurator (the most famous of whom was Pontius Pilate, 26–36 AD). A further slice of Herod's kingdom was also taken over by Tiberius, Augustus's successor, on the death of another of Herod's sons, Philip, in 34 AD.

---

[19] *AJ* 14.217–67.
[20] *AJ* 14.387–89.

It is clear, however, that Rome had no desire to take responsibility for ruling this difficult kingdom if someone else could be found to act as a vassal ruler. When Tiberius died in 37, one of the first acts of his successor, Gaius (commonly known as Caligula), was to allocate Philip's share of the inheritance to an able grandson of Herod the Great, Herod Agrippa. Two years later, Agrippa was given Herod Antipas's territory of Galilee and Peraea — which did not prevent his spending a great deal of his time in Rome. By 41, Caligula was showing alarming signs of insanity — one of the most dangerous of which was his determination to have a statue of himself erected in the Jerusalem Temple, an instruction which the governor of Syria was wisely delaying putting into effect. Agrippa intervened to dissuade him from what would have been a disastrous move.[21] When Caligula was then assassinated by exasperated members of his own staff, Agrippa played a major part in the selection of his uncle, Claudius, to replace him.[22] For this he was rewarded with the territories of Judaea and Samaria, thereby endowing him with the whole kingdom of his grandfather. Agrippa could have been the client king the Romans needed to bring stability to the region but for his premature death in 44. This forced the Romans to resume direct control of his kingdom, which they mismanaged so badly that it flared up in a revolt that became a hideously bitter war in 66.

Rome's Jewish policy from the time that they became the major player in the Near East after Pompey's victories down to the outbreak of the Jewish War in 66, a period of 130 years, was therefore reasonably consistent, though not always effectively pursued. Among the Jewish communities in the diaspora right across the empire, especially in great cities such as Rome and Alexandria, the Romans wanted peace and secured it by granting extensive legal privileges by which Jews could not only practise their own religion but also enjoy considerable autonomy in daily life. In the kingdom of Judaea, the Romans wanted a loyal government that could resist Parthian power. They preferred a strong vassal king when they could find one but, if necessary, were willing to exercise direct control. All of this was imperilled in 41 by the mad behaviour of Caligula and by riots in Alexandria.

[21] The story is vividly told by Philo *Embassy to Gaius* 261–333 and Josephus *AJ* 18.289–309.

[22] *BJ* 2.206–10; *AJ* 19.236–47.

The Jewish community in Alexandria was large, well organised and violent.[23] Philo,[24] the brilliant Jewish philosopher and biblical theologian, estimated that there were a million Jews in the whole of Egypt,[25] when the total population of Egypt apart from Alexandria was about seven and a half million.[26] Josephus, another cosmopolitan Jewish aristocrat and intellectual, believed that the Jewish community in Alexandria had been brought there as slaves from Judaea and Samaria several hundred years before his time and that 120,000 had been liberated by Ptolemy II.[27] According to him, there had been incessant strife between the native inhabitants and the Jews since the time when they had been given civil rights and a district of the city as their own.[28] The Jews thus had a considerable degree of autonomy within the city, which caused resentment, while at the same time aspiring to full rights as Alexandrian citizens, which was steadfastly resisted by the Alexandrian political elite.

The Alexandrian Jews were engulfed in a pogrom after the visit of Agrippa in 38 AD,[29] described in two books by Philo which were both vindications of the Alexandrian Jews, the *In Flaccum* and the *Embassy to Gaius*. Having been granted the tetrarchy of his late uncle Philip by Caligula and thus acceding to the whole of his grandfather's kingdom, Agrippa was travelling across the Mediterranean to claim his territory. He passed through Alexandria at a time of prolonged and intense dispute about the civil rights of the Jewish community; the Jews wanted to use his presence, as a Jewish king and a friend of the emperor, to promote their cause. This was seen as politically provocative[30] and it led to attacks on synagogues which were either destroyed or else defiled by the clever tactic of the erection within

---

[23] See John M. G. Barclay, *Jews in the Mediterranean Diaspora from Alexander to Trajan (323 BCE to 117 AD)* (Edinburgh: T&T Clark, 1996); Christopher Haas, *Alexandria in Late Antiquity: Topography and Social Conflict* (Baltimore: Johns Hopkins University Press, 1997) pp. 91–109; for the period down to 70, and stressing the broadly constructive relations between Jews and Greeks in the city, see Gruen *Diaspora* pp. 54–83.

[24] Erwin R. Goodenough, *An Introduction to Philo Judaeus* (Oxford: Blackwell, 2nd ed, 1962).

[25] Philo *In Flaccum* 43.

[26] An estimate for a few years later: *BJ* 2.385.

[27] *AJ* 12.7–11.

[28] *BJ* 2.487.

[29] E. Mary Smallwood, *The Jews under Roman Rule from Pompey to Diocletian: a Study in Political Relations* (Leiden: Brill, 2nd ed, 1981) pp. 235–50; Dorothy I. Sly, *Philo's Alexandria* (London: Routledge, 1996) pp. 167–80.

[30] Philo *In Flacc.* 30–31.

them of images of Caligula — the Jews could not remove them without offence to the imperial dignity but their presence prevented the Jews from worshipping in the synagogues.[31] The Alexandrian authorities attempted to restrict Jewish rights and to force them to live in the one quarter of the city which had been made over to them; this gave licence to the mob to evict Jews from other parts of the city and in the process to plunder over four hundred houses[32] as well as shops and warehouses. Jews were brutally murdered and outrages of all kinds were inflicted on them.[33] Jews were tortured in the theatre — scourged, hanged, turned on the wheel and impaled while dancers, mime artists and flute players performed[34] — and Jewish women were forced to eat pork and tortured if they refused.[35] It was in an attempt to reach a resolution of the political and religious deadlock after these appalling events that Philo took part in the embassy to Caligula which brought him to Rome in 41.

When Philo wrote an account of his embassy to the court of Caligula, it was in large part an apologia for his claim that the Alexandrian Jews should both retain their special privileges but also enjoy full Alexandrian citizenship. With that aim in view, he described the Jewish community he encountered in Rome:

> He [Augustus] was not unaware that the large section of Rome across the River Tiber is owned and inhabited by Jews. Most of them were Romans, having been emancipated. They had been brought to Italy as captives and were liberated by their owners, without having been forced to violate any of the observances of their native land. He knew that they have synagogues (*proseuchai*) and meet together in them, especially on the holy Sabbaths when as a people they are taught the wisdom of their fathers. He also knew that they collect money for sacred purposes from their first-fruits and send it to Jerusalem with people who would offer the sacrifices. But he neither expelled them from Rome nor deprived them of Roman citizenship for being careful to preserve their Jewishness nor attacked their synagogues nor stopped them from meeting to be instructed in the Law nor opposed their offering of the first-fruits … Furthermore, in the monthly distribution in his own city when all the people in turn receive money or corn, he never put the Jews at a disadvantage in sharing this favour. Even if the distributions happened on the Sabbath when no one is permitted to receive or give anything or transact any of the business of ordinary life, he ordered the officials responsible for the distribution to keep for the Jews their share of the common largesse till the following day.[36]

[31] Philo *Emb.* 20.

[32] *In Flacc.* 94.

[33] *In Flacc.* 55–72; *Emb.* 16–20.

[34] *In Flacc.* 83–85.

[35] *In Flacc.* 95–96.

[36] *Emb.* 155–58; see E. Mary Smallwood, *Philonis Alexandrini Legatio ad Gaium, Edited with an Introduction, Translation and Commentary* (Leiden: Brill, 1961) pp. 233–42.

According to Philo, the collection of the Temple tax, the teaching in the synagogues, the strict observance of the Law, especially of the Sabbath, and the long memory of their origins marked out the Jewish community in Trastevere, across the Tiber from the main part of the city, as a proud and closely-knit group. But it would be naïve to read Philo's account as though it were the pure and simple truth. Philo was writing not to inform but to persuade.

This is not the unvarnished report of a curious traveller but rather a carefully calculated description of a community that has all the rights which the Alexandrian Jews want to claim. By highlighting the wise policy of Augustus, it emphasises the madness of Caligula. The Roman Jews, like the Alexandrians, are depicted as occupying a particular district of the city (from Philo, the reader might imagine that no one but Jews lived in Trastevere and that Jews lived nowhere else) but that this is the cause of no tension or dispute. In the pogrom in 38, the Alexandrian authorities had attempted to force the Jews to withdraw into their own quarter, with terrible consequences. In Trastevere, the Roman Jews have synagogues which are respected by the authorities. In the Alexandrian riots, synagogues in particular had been targeted — some destroyed, others desecrated. Finally, and for Philo most importantly, the Jews are Roman citizens, recipients of the corn dole, while also being loyal to their Jewishness and paying a tax to support the Jerusalem Temple. The real aim of Philo's mission was to win full citizenship of the *polis* of Alexandria for Jews while allowing them to retain their distinctive privileges. Thus, every detail of his description of the Roman Jews was carefully chosen because of its bearing on the situation in Alexandria.

Philo says that the Jews were Roman citizens: they were Romans, having been given their freedom, and Augustus never sought to deprive them of their Roman citizenship (*tēn Rōmaikēn ... politeian*). He ignores the large numbers of Jews who cannot have been Roman citizens, slaves or immigrants who had the status of resident aliens. It would not have suited his purpose to mention them. He stresses the corn dole and the respect shown to the Jews by allowing them to collect it the following day should the distribution date fall on the Sabbath. The free corn supply was an important feature of the Roman administration of the city. It should not, however, be envisaged as poor relief staving off starvation from the huddled masses. It was not available to the really poor. Only citizens were eligible to receive it, though not of course of the richer classes; it was something of a status symbol to possess the *tessera frumentaria*, the corn token, which was shown each month to receive the dole. It was regarded as sufficiently prestigious for people to record that they had been recipients in their epitaphs. The quantities handed out did not provide enough food to supply people's needs; it was, rather, a supplement to their income. It was, in other words, a way by which the government could not only hold the allegiance of the solid lower-middle classes but even define their status in relation to the Roman state.[37] For Philo, the fact that they were recipients of the corn dole and yet could receive it on a different day from everyone else in recognition of their religious observance sums up everything he wants to say about the status of the Roman Jews as citizens with a dual nationality, observant of two laws and obedient to two allegiances.

It would be a mistake to think of the Roman Jews as a bourgeois, well-instructed, synagogue-attending single community of conformists. Evidence from before and after Philo's time suggests that there were plenty of Jews who sought to disguise their Jewish identity and also poor, uneducated and unassimilated Jews in Rome. Three of Horace's satires, written about 35 BC, were rounded off with a reference to Jews. They are presented as odd and alien. One depicts Jews as notorious for pressing people to join their ranks — in other words, they were regarded as a separate group standing over and against society.[38] Another, the 'Journey to Brundisium', depicts Jews as superstitious or gullible — in other words, irrational and uneducated.[39] In the third, the fact that it is the 'thirtieth Sabbath' is taken as an excuse to terminate the conversation, with the proposal that they should go and mock the circumcised Jews.[40] Again, they are presented as alien and comic. These three brief passages suggest that Jews would have been a familiar sight to Horace's readers but they do not sound like the well-instructed and respectable citizens portrayed by Philo eighty years later.

Martial, writing in about 80, also observed poor Jews — one was taught by his mother to beg[41] and another was a slave.[42] But he also

---

[37] Geoffrey Rickman, *The Corn Supply of Ancient Rome* (Oxford: Clarendon Press, 1980) pp. 156–209; Paul Veyne, *Bread and Circuses: Historical Sociology and Political Pluralism* (abridged with an introduction by Oswyn Murray; Brian Pearce (trans); Penguin History; London: Allen Lane, 1990) pp. 236–45.

[38] Horace *Satires* 1.4.140–43; 1.5.100.

[39] *Sat.* 1.5.100.

[40] 9.69–70.

[41] Martial *Epigrammata* 12.57.

[42] *Epig.* 7.35.

refers to a circumcised poet born in Jerusalem who criticised and yet plagiarised his poems. What infuriates him most was that he sodomised Martial's slave boy, the implication being that reminding him of his Jewish ancestry was a rebuke for such behaviour.[43] He also refers to an actor whose jock-strap came off while playing a game revealing, to his shame, that he was circumcised.[44] This suggests that there were educated Jews who were trying to forget their Jewish heritage.

Writing in about 130, Juvenal includes Jews among the gallery of grotesques who are the objects of his mockery. In his third satire, the one which savagely laments the eclipse of old Roman virtues in a city full of bizarre immigrants, Umbricius and Juvenal leave the city by the southern gate, the Porta Capena, but find the grove of Numa has been taken over by Jews who are distinguished by their hay-lined boxes (which were designed to keep food warm for the Sabbath). They are depicted as beggars — the wood is so full of beggars that it has become a beggar itself. His point is that one simply cannot escape the foreigners who have even spilled over beyond the city walls.[45] In another satire, he depicts a poor woman, again equipped with a hay-lined box, begging and offering to work as a soothsayer.[46] In a third, a Syrian Jew from the Idumaean Gate (a satirical reference to the Porta Capena), drenched in perfume, is running an all-night bistro.[47] For Juvenal, Jews are foreign and distasteful, either poor and superstitious or oleaginous and unpleasant. Though Juvenal is often a writer whom it is not difficult to dislike, the force of his satire always depends on some basis of fact. There must have been a significant Jewish presence near the Porta Capena; there must have been poor and uneducated Jews and recent immigrants running small businesses. Philo's picture is a corrective to these satirical accounts but it clearly cannot have been the whole truth in his day. There is no reason to suppose that between the time of Horace and the time of Juvenal there was a period when there were no poor or uneducated Jews or recent immigrants who had still not adapted to Roman ways.

Two features of Judaism stand out for the Roman writers: circumcision and the Sabbath. Petronius, writing in the time of Nero,

[43] *Epig.* 11.94.
[44] *Epig.* 7.82.
[45] Juvenal *Satires* 3.12–16.
[46] *Sat.* 6.543–47.
[47] *Sat.* 8.158–62.

thought circumcision was entirely distinctive of Jews.[48] Martial repeatedly remarked upon it. The Sabbath, however, seemed to have been not only a sign of Jewish identity — Juvenal talked of hay-lined boxes as though they were a standard appurtenance of any Jew — but also of something which affected non-Jews. Many people seem to have been intrigued by the Jewish Sabbath observance[49] and even to have copied it. Persius, who died tragically young in the time of Nero, ended one of his satires with reference to the Sabbath, with its lights and its special meal.[50] A lost work of Seneca on superstition known to Augustine,[51] criticised the Sabbath and its lights but noted its attractiveness to non-Jews. Ovid remarked that the Sabbath was a good day to take your girlfriend out as the shops would be shut.[52] According to Josephus, there was not a town in the Roman Empire where people had not imitated Jewish Sabbath observance along with other religious practices such as lighting lamps and fasting or charitable giving, hard work and endurance.[53]

Josephus was exaggerating the degree of respect in which Jews were held. He straddled the worlds of Jewish religion, Greek culture and Roman politics in the closing decades of the first century with complex and at times conflicting allegiances.[54] For Jews, he was Yosef ben Mattityahu; in Rome, he adopted the name of his imperial patrons and was Flavius Josephus. His book, *Against Apion*, was an apologia for Judaism addressed to an educated Greek readership he well understood. There were certainly admirers of Judaism who supported it like a buttress from the outside rather than like a pillar from within and who adopted some Jewish customs without fully embracing the Law, but it seems that making the Sabbath a holiday reached beyond their ranks to a wider society. There is little sign in the pages of Horace, Ovid or Juvenal that the religious beliefs and practices of Judaism were well understood. Tacitus, as we have seen, offered a better-informed account,[55] though one coloured by his repeated attempt to

---

[48] Petronius *Satyricon* 102.14.

[49] Horace *Sat.* 1.9.69–70; Ovid *Ars Amatoria* 1.76.

[50] Persius *Satires* 5.176–84.

[51] Augustine *City of God* 6.11.

[52] Ovid *Ars Amatoria* 1.415–16.

[53] *Against Apion* 2.282.

[54] Tessa Rajak, *Josephus: the Historian and his Society* (London: Duckworth, 2nd ed, 2002); Per Bilde *Flavius Josephus between Jerusalem and Rome: his Life, his Works, and their Importance* (Sheffield: Sheffield Academic Press, 1988).

[55] *Hist.* 5.3–5.

explain the uniqueness of Judaism in terms of more familiar religious or cultural influences. Sabbath observance, when Jewish businesses were closed, was apparent enough to any curious observer but what was taught in the synagogues or practised in the home was not. It is striking that Augustus, for instance, believed that Jews fasted on the Sabbath, remarking in a letter that no Jew could have kept the Sabbath fast as strictly as he had on a day when he did not eat before sunset.[56] Similarly, for all his apparent acquaintance with Jews, Martial imagined that the Sabbath was a fast day.[57] Everyone could see that they abstained from work, but could then only guess what they did at home.

For all the hostility or ignorance or indifference displayed by many Romans towards the Jews, there is good reason to believe that Judaism did attract converts.[58] The Jews recognised a special status for gentiles who did not embrace the Law in its fullness but who could share in the hope of salvation; behind the covenant with Moses, when God gave the Law to his people, there was the covenant with Noah. These gentiles were called 'Godfearers'; they were expected not to sacrifice to idols or eat blood, not to commit incest, not to work on the Sabbath or to eat leavened bread during Passover. The evidence, insofar as it exists, that the Roman community included Godfearers comes of course largely from the ranks of the upper classes. Josephus reported a scandal which occurred in 19 AD in which Fulvia, the wife of the senator Saturninus who was a friend of the emperor Tiberius, had become a convert to Judaism. She used to have regular meetings with four Jews who persuaded her to make a major gift of purple and gold to the Jerusalem Temple; they pocketed the money and Saturninus informed Tiberius of the fraud. This was the occasion when the emperor conscripted four thousand Jews for military service in Sardinia.[59] It was the embezzlement that caused outrage, not Fulvia's conversion. Forty years later, in 57, Pomponia Graecina, the wife of the general who conquered Britain, Aulus Plautius, was accused of 'foreign superstition' and tried and acquitted by her

---

[56] Suetonius *Augustus* 76.

[57] *Epig.* 4.4.

[58] For a very full survey of Jewish-gentile relations in the ancient world and the appeal of Judaism, see Louis H. Feldman, *Jew and Gentile in the Ancient World: Attitudes and Interactions from Alexander to Justinian* (Princeton: Princeton University Press, 1993).

[59] *AJ* 18.81–84.

husband.[60] It is plausible, though not certain, that this meant that she had adopted Judaism.

Josephus also described a mission he undertook, travelling from Judaea to Rome in 64 to intercede on behalf of some Jewish priests who had been sent there as prisoners for trial. He used an actor of Jewish origin, Aliturus, who was a favourite of Nero's, to make the acquaintance of Nero's wife, Poppaea Sabina. Josephus describes her as a Godfearer who had already intervened on behalf of the Temple authorities in Jerusalem who sent an embassy to Rome to prevent a wall they had built being knocked down.[61] Through her intervention on Josephus's behalf, the priests were released.[62] Thus within the space of two years, she used her influence with Nero twice for the sake of Jerusalem Jews. What is most striking about this is that without Josephus's references to Poppaea her involvement with Judaism would be unknown. She was portrayed by Tacitus as a promiscuous and scheming woman, who had everything except good character, who succeeded in becoming Nero's mistress and then his wife, but who also proved hard and vengeful.[63] But nowhere does Tacitus or Suetonius refer to her Jewish sympathies. In 65, the year after Josephus's mission, Nero, furious that she rebuked him for getting back late from the games, kicked her to death while she was pregnant.[64]

These fragmentary pieces of evidence show that there were women of very high rank with connections at court who were attracted to Jewish belief. How Judaism penetrated these exalted circles cannot be known. Members of the Herod family lived in Rome. Though they might well not have been the most convincing advocates of the Jewish faith, they did influence court circles. The daughter of Herod Agrippa, Drusilla, married Antonius Felix, the brother of Antonius Pallas who was the most powerful civil servant in the service of the emperor Claudius. Drusilla and Felix had a son whom they named

---

[60] Tacitus *Ann.* 13.32.

[61] *AJ* 20.195; it makes little sense, in the light of the role she played in his mission in 64, to read this as simply meaning that she was a devout woman — an opinion of her shared by no other commentator.

[62] Josephus *Life* 16; Rajak *Josephus* pp. 42–44; Bilde *Flavius Josephus* 31.

[63] *Ann.* 13.45; 14.61: a description colourful enough for Monteverdi to make her the subject of the first historical opera on a non-biblical theme, *L'Incoronazione di Poppea*, in 1642.

[64] Suetonius *Nero* 35; Tacitus *Ann.* 16.6.

Agrippa and who was killed in the eruption of Vesuvius.[65] Felix had earlier married another Drusilla, the granddaughter of Antony and Cleopatra; since Claudius was the grandson of Antony, this made them remote cousins by marriage.[66] He married the second Drusilla when he was procurator in Judaea, where he imprisoned the apostle Paul.[67] In other words, Judaism must have been seen as eminently respectable in certain elite circles. It also seems likely that there were members of the Roman Jewish community well enough educated and sufficiently sympathetic to upper-class Roman attitudes to be able to present Judaism in a way that won the allegiance of some very distinguished people. Josephus wrote his apologia for Judaism, *Against Apion*, which demonstrated its antiquity compared with Greek culture. There must have been other cultured Jews in Rome who could also present persuasive accounts of the Jewish Law.

Jewish influence in the political and social elite of Rome survived the calamity of the Jewish War of 66–73. The corruption and misman-agement of Roman direct rule in Judaea following the death of Herod Agrippa in 44 fed the long-standing desire for religious and political independence. A revolt erupted in 66 which turned into a full-scale war. The Romans suppressed Jewish opposition with their usual brutal efficiency. They besieged Jerusalem and finally destroyed the city and the Temple in 70. The war finally ended in 73 with the heroic but doomed defence of Masada. The Romans succeeded in prosecuting the war despite the political turmoil following Nero's suicide in 68. A year of civil war followed out of which Vespasian, the general commanding the Roman forces in the first phase of the war, emerged as the new emperor in 69. His son Titus took over in Judaea and brought the war to its conclusion, succeeding his father as emperor in 79. His mistress for many years had been Bernice, the daughter of Herod Agrippa, but he had to end the relationship when he became emperor.[68] He in turn was succeeded by his brother, Domitian, in 81. The Jewish War therefore saw the rise to power of a new dynasty, the Flavians, whose lasting monument is the Flavian amphitheatre, better known as the Colosseum. Perhaps it might be

---

[65] *AJ* 20.137–44.

[66] Tacitus *Hist.* 5.9.

[67] Acts 24.24.

[68] One of the great love affairs of antiquity celebrated in two plays staged in 1670, Corneille's *Tite et Bérénice* and Racine's *Bérénice*, the triumph of Racine's play eclipsed the talent of Corneille.

considered the lasting monument to the fall of Jerusalem and the destruction of the Temple.

Yet, only twenty-five years after the fall of Jerusalem and the destruction of the Temple, people at the highest level of society were again showing a strong interest in Judaism. In 95, Domitian executed his cousin Flavius Clemens, the consul, who was married to another of his relatives, Flavia Domitilla, whom he banished to the island of Pandateria. Domitian made a habit of executing members of the elite — he disposed of a dozen ex-consuls during his reign — but to kill a consul in office to whom he was closely related and whose sons he had nominated as his heirs was memorable even by his standards. Flavius Clemens and his wife were charged with 'atheism', 'a charge on which many others who drifted into Jewish ways were condemned; some of these were put to death and the rest were at least deprived of their property'.[69] To have had any credibility, the accusation must have been based on the reality of Jewish influence among the aristocracy.

It is unsurprising that there is less evidence of the lives and beliefs of people below the level of the upper nobility but it is extremely likely that Godfearers and full converts to Judaism could be found among people of less exalted degree. One example comes from the pen of Juvenal, who reported with disgust the case of a man who observed the Sabbath, which led to his son getting circumcised and despising the Roman laws.[70] In other words, the father was a Godfearer and his son became a full proselyte, accepting circumcision and the full observance of the Law.

One of the bitterest consequences of the Jewish defeat in the war of 66–73 was the diversion of the Jewish Temple Tax to the restoration of the Temple of Jupiter in Rome.[71] The Temple of Jupiter had been badly damaged in the fighting that engulfed the city in the struggle for power after the deposition of Nero in 68. To take the money Jews devoutly collected for the upkeep of God's Temple in Jerusalem and allocate to the rebuilding of a pagan shrine was an insidious violation of their faith.[72] Domitian made the collection of the Temple Tax more stringent. Suetonius described how, when young, he had been

[69] Dio Cassius *Roman History* 67.14.1–2; Suetonius reports the execution of Flavius Clemens with puzzlement as he was contemptibly lazy *Domitian* 15.

[70] *Sat.* 14.96–106.

[71] *BJ* 7.218; Dio Cassius *Rom. Hist.* 66.7.2.

[72] And regarded as something of a just retribution by Martial *Epig.* 7.55.

in a crowded court room when the procurator had had a ninety-year-old man undressed to see whether he had been circumcised.[73] It is not unlikely that the persecution of Romans sympathetic to Judaism was connected with the stridently anti-Jewish policy expressed in the heightened severity of the tax. After Domitian's inevitable assassination in 96, his successor Nerva prohibited accusations of adopting Jewish ways[74] and relieved the burden of the Temple tax, issuing coins with the inscription *Fisci Iudaici Calumnia Sublata* (the malicious charge of the Jewish tax has been lifted).[75]

Not only was the persistent influence of Judaism in the upper reaches of Roman society remarkable, so too was the peaceful stability of the Jewish community in Rome. The Arch of Titus in the Roman Forum commemorated the Jewish defeat, with the sacred vessels of the Temple being carried in procession. Titus was Domitian's elder brother, whose glory it was to have pillaged and destroyed the Temple in Jerusalem in 70. The scenes on his arch depicted his triumph, when the sacred vessels were paraded through the streets of Rome, of which Josephus left a detailed account.[76] Though the Jewish community of Rome must have seen this as a profound affront and humiliation, there was no sign of any unrest. Protestors would have had to have been fools to have raised a voice against the victorious general and his army, but fanatics can often be fools. What is striking about the Jewish community in Rome is that they were not fanatics. They had long been a peaceful community. Four thousand Jews had been conscripted for military service in Sardinia after the Fulvia scandal in 19 AD. The fact that it was so regularly remembered but so little understood in the historical record[77] indicates how exceptional that punitive measure was. In 41, Claudius succeeded Caligula in the middle of a crisis in Jewish affairs occasioned by his lunatic nephew's plan to install a statue of himself in the Jerusalem Temple and with the aftermath of the pogrom of 38 in Alexandria still unresolved. Dio Cassius recorded that he forbade the Roman Jews

[73] *Domitian* 12.2.

[74] Dio Cassius *Rom. Hist.* 68.1.2.

[75] Harold Mattingly, *Coins of the Roman Empire in the British Museum vol.* 3 (London: Trustees of the British Museum, 1936) p. 15; Plate 4, 7.

[76] *BJ* 7.118–57.

[77] *AJ* 18.65–84; Tacitus *Ann.* 2.85; Suetonius *Tiberius* 36; Dio Cassius *Rom. Hist.* 57.18.5; Josephus attributes the conscription, improbably, to the Fulvia affair, while Tacitus associates it with a crack down on Egyptian and Jewish religious rites and Dio says it was due to the growth in Jewish numbers and their success in proselytising.

to meet — presumably closing the synagogues — because they were too numerous to expel from the city.[78] This looks like a precautionary measure to forestall any disturbances while he found a satisfactory way out of the problems he had inherited. There is no hint in any of the detailed accounts of the accession of Claudius that he faced unrest from the Jews of Rome at an extremely sensitive time.[79]

The Jewish community in Rome was therefore quiet at the two most troublesome times in the first century, the end of the reign of Caligula (38–41) and the Jewish War and its aftermath (66–73). It was very different in Alexandria. Though the culprits for the pogrom in 38 were the city authorities and the mob of Alexandria, when the Jewish War broke out in 66, the Alexandrian Jews themselves rose in revolt.[80] According to Josephus, fifty thousand Jews were killed by Roman troops in the massacres that followed.[81] However inflated a figure, it does indicate very heavy casualties. In the course of the war, the Jewish population of the cities of Syria were slaughtered; eighteen thousand were killed in Damascus and perhaps more than sixty thousand in all Egypt.[82] Even more dramatic and cataclysmic was the great revolt of 115–17, when a messianic campaign to liberate the Jews and re-establish an independent kingdom engulfed Alexandria along with the rest of Egypt and Cyrenaica.[83] The bloodshed, both gentile and Jewish, was enormous. Jewish communities across Cyrenaica were smashed by Roman force and the Jewish community in Alexandria seems to have been eclipsed for two centuries.

Yet, during all these tumults, the Roman community was peaceful. No doubt, many factors heightened tension in Alexandria and Egypt which did not pertain in Rome but one factor above others, about which Philo was deliberately silent in his portrayal of the Roman community, seems to have distinguished the Jews of Alexandria from those of Rome. Not only did Philo report that there were Jews and synagogues in all parts of Alexandria,[84] but also that of the

[78] Dio Cassius *Rom. Hist.* 60.6.6.

[79] For a review of these expulsions, see L. V. Rutgers, 'Roman Policy toward the Jews: Expulsions from the City of Rome during the First Century CE' Karl P. Donfried and Peter Richardson (eds), *Judaism and Christianity in First-Century Rome* (Grand Rapids, Michigan: Eerdmans, 1998) pp. 93–116.

[80] Smallwood *Jews under Roman Rule* pp. 364–68.

[81] *BJ* 2.490–8.

[82] *BJ* 7.367–9.

[83] Smallwood *Jews under Roman Rule* pp. 389–412; Haas *Alexandria* pp. 99–103.

[84] *Emb.* 132.

five districts of the city two had a heavy concentration of Jewish occupation.[85] These quarters were named after the first five letters of the Greek alphabet and it was the Delta district above all,[86] alongside the sea-front and the most desirable residential area,[87] which belonged to the Jews. Philo, of course, wanted to depict Trastevere as the Roman equivalent. But furthermore the Alexandrian Jews had a system of self-government with a council of elders, the *gerousia*,[88] which amounted to a city within the city, a *politeuma*. There was an official called the *Hazzan* who managed the daily administration of Jewish affairs in the city who also played a liturgical role in the great synagogue, the largest of the synagogues, which was so big that more distant members of the congregation could not hear the words of the prayers. The *Hazzan* waved a brightly coloured scarf at the end of a Benediction to signal the people to respond with Amen.[89] Josephus described the scale of autonomy enjoyed by the Alexandrian Jews:

> In Egypt, there is territory designated as a settlement for the Jews and a great part of the city of the Alexandrians has been allocated to this people. An ethnarch of their own has been put in place who governs the people and judges law cases and supervises contracts and decrees, just as if he were the ruler of an independent city.[90]

In other words, the Jewish community in Alexandria had a centralised authority which gave them considerable autonomy in their affairs. This clearly caused great resentment and it is not unlikely that it also politicised and united the Jewish reaction to the wider issues in Jewish-Roman relations. How far the centralising structures of Alexandrian Judaism were intended to promote a vision of salvation which would ultimately liberate the Promised Land and restore Jewish self-government as the fulfilment of the covenant can only be a matter of speculation but that such hopes long persisted in the diaspora can be seen in the crises of 66–73, 115–17 and 132–35. Neither Philo nor Josephus suggests that the members of the Alexandrian *gerousia* orchestrated anti-Roman activity but it seems not unlikely that they did little to try and prevent it. Significantly, in the aftermath of the defeat in 70, the Jewish leadership in Alexandria marginalised the extremists and mobilised the people against them. The extremists,

---

[85] *In Flacc.* 55.
[86] *BJ* 2.494–95.
[87] Josephus *Against Apion* 2.33–36.
[88] Philo *In Flacc.* 74; Josephus *BJ* 7.412.
[89] Haas *Alexandria* 96–97.
[90] *AJ* 14.117.

the *sicarii*, had murdered several of the leading Jews in Alexandria for opposing them. The leaders of the *gerousia* called a public assembly and persuaded the people to seize the *sicarii* and hand them over to the Roman authorities.[91]

There was nothing like this in Rome. There is no sign anywhere in the ancient literature or the inscriptions surviving from the Jewish catacombs that the Jews there had any over-arching system of self-government;[92] had there been, Philo could not have failed to mention it as it would have perfected the parallel he wanted to draw with Alexandria. Tacitus too, in his description of diaspora Judaism which presumably owed much to his observation of Roman Jewry would have made mention of a feature which would have illustrated his point about Jewish separateness. Perhaps the Roman Jews did not feel the need of a governing council; neither in governing internal affairs nor, more significantly, in messianic hope did they show any interest in establishing structures by which they could govern themselves and aspire to concerted political action. Perhaps the real reason was that they lacked the means of forming them. The Alexandrian *gerousia* was, presumably, drawn from the senior membership of the synagogues; its *Hazzan* was an official in the great synagogue. In other words, it is plausible to suggest that the Alexandrian community was organised around the life and leadership of synagogues. It is arguable that the Roman Jews did not set up a similar central governing council in the time of Augustus and Tiberius because synagogue life in Rome was less fully developed.

It is unwise to assume that all Jewish communities in the diaspora were defined by synagogue membership.[93] There is considerable uncertainty about the development and use of synagogues in the

---

[91] *BJ* 7.412.

[92] Leon *Jews of Ancient Rome* pp. 167–94; the existence of some form of over-arching council in Rome is defended by Margaret Williams, 'The Structure of the Jewish Community in Rome' in Martin Goodman (ed), *Jews in a Graeco-Roman World* (Oxford: Clarendon Press, 1998) pp. 215–28; her case is based on the fact that the Jews formed one community and that an inscription using the title 'archgerousiarch' has been found.

[93] Magnus Zetterholm, *The Formation of Christianity in Antioch: A Social-Scientific Approach to the Separation between Judaism and Christianity* (London: Routledge, 2003) pp. 37–39 claims that, though there is only evidence for the existence of three synagogues in Antioch in c 20–30 AD, there must have been more for a community estimated to have been about 20,000 strong and that the organisation of the community known in Alexandria must have existed also in Antioch, though again there is no evidence for it.

ancient world and it is almost certain that they appeared in some places long before others. The uniquely rich epigraphic evidence of the Roman Jewish community reveals that they had at least eleven synagogues.[94] The inscriptions largely come from the catacombs and reflect the situation in the third and fourth centuries;[95] it is surprising that for a community that might still have numbered tens of thousands of people there were not more. The names of a few suggest that they dated from the period described by Philo. The synagogue of the Augustiales, for instance, might have owed its name to the emperor Augustus. That of the Agrippeans might have been named after Vipsanius Agrippa, Augustus's closest lieutenant, who died in 12 BC, or perhaps after Herod Agrippa (who was named after him) who died in 44 AD. That of the Hebrews might have taken its name from its liturgical use of the Hebrew language, which might indicate that its roots lay in the early settlement of Judaean captives in Rome. Though some others might have existed in Philo's time but had closed by the time of the catacombs, what is most striking is how few synagogues seem to have existed in Rome at the time of his visit. Four or five synagogues could not have played a central role in the life of a community of 40,000 people. Philo's careful phrase — that Augustus knew that the Jews in Trastevere had synagogues and met in them, especially on the Sabbath, when as a people they were taught the wisdom of the fathers — must therefore be read with the same caution as the rest of the passage. He simply wants to assert that synagogues were respected by Augustus, whereas they had been attacked in Alexandria, and is careful to avoid admitting how many there were[96] whereas he is keen to emphasise the large number that existed in Alexandria. It is striking that the mockery and the criticisms of Jews found in the pages of Horace, Seneca, Petronius,

[94] Leon *Jews of Rome* pp. 135–66; the existence of four others has been suggested but cannot be proved; the eleven might not all have existed simultaneously.

[95] For the dating of the Jewish catacombs, see L. V. Rutgers, *The Hidden Heritage of Diaspora Judaism* (Leuven: Peeters, 1998) pp. 45–71; for a full review of the evidence for first-century synagogues in Rome, see Peter Richardson, 'Augustan-Era Synagogues in Rome' in Donfried and Richardson *Judaism and Christianity* pp. 17–29; for a cautious assessment of the evidence, see Lee I. Levine, *The Ancient Synagogue: The First Thousand Years* (New Haven: Yale University Press, 2nd ed, 2005) pp. 283–86.

[96] Margaret H. Williams, 'The Structure of Roman Jewry Re-Considered — Were the Synagogues of Ancient Rome Entirely Homogeneous?' *ZPE* 104 (1994) pp. 129–41 discusses the titles attributed to officials in the different synagogues; on p. 130 she says that Philo said there were 'numerous *proseuchai*' in Transtiberinum — in fact, Philo carefully does not claim they were numerous.

Persius, Martial and Juvenal make no reference to synagogues; Jews are distinguished from ordinary Romans by circumcision and the Sabbath. Even more striking, in his account of diaspora Judaism, Tacitus makes no reference to synagogue membership or worship. He defines the Jews by the ritual observances of the home rather than by any organisation to which they belonged. This must have reflected his knowledge of the Jews in Rome in about 110; had he had direct knowledge of the Jews in Alexandria, his description would have been different.

Jews were seen, and saw themselves, as one people. In Rome, they could gather at times as a Jewish crowd. A large and conservative community, they embraced the very rich and the very poor and regularly welcomed new immigrants into their ranks. Some, perhaps many, had citizens' rights. They made converts among the members of the high nobility and, no doubt, at every other level of society. They were regarded with admiration by some and scorn by others. They preserved their religious and cultural identity for centuries, as the evidence of the epigraphs in the catacombs shows. They paid the Temple Tax, whether for the maintenance of Herod's Temple in Jerusalem or, after its destruction, the restoration of the Temple of Jupiter in Rome. But they were not defined by allegiance to a formal leadership. They were not organised for self-protection or self-promotion as a community. They showed no sign of political messianism. They did not put over-arching governing structures in place because the majority of them probably did not have any kind of synagogue membership. In other words, Jewishness in ancient Rome was not defined by attendance at or involvement in a synagogue. Rather, observance of the Law was primarily a religion of the home, of the customary prayers, Sabbath observance, dietary regulations and the keeping of the commandments. This was to have profound effects on the genesis in the Jewish community of early Roman Christianity.

THE GENESIS OF CHRISTIANITY IN ROME

The first Christians in ancient Rome about whom very much can be known were Jewish tentmakers, a married couple called Aquila and Priscilla (often known as Prisca). Paul met them in Corinth, probably in the summer of 50 AD:

> Paul left Athens and travelled to Corinth. There he found a Jew called Aquila, whose family came from Pontus. He had recently left Italy along with his wife Priscilla because Claudius had issued a decree that all the Jews should leave

Rome. Paul went to them and, on account of having the same trade, for they
were tentmakers, he lived and worked with them. He used to argue in the
synagogue every Sabbath, trying to persuade both Jews and Greeks. (Acts 18.
1–4)[97]

Paul's efforts in the synagogue did not meet with success. After a row,
he moved to the house next door which belonged to a Godfearer
called Justus and in due course won over many people whom he
baptised, including the president of the synagogue, Crispus, and his
whole household. After eighteen months, the Jews of the synagogue
brought a case against Paul before Gallio, the proconsul of Achaia,[98]
who threw it out as a religious issue beyond his competence or
authority. The synagogue president Sosthenes, presumably Crispus's
successor, was beaten up by his furious congregation outside the
court house.[99] Paul moved on and sailed with Aquila and Priscilla to
Ephesus, where he left them having debated in the synagogue again.
Aquila and Priscilla continued to attend the synagogue. When Paul
returned to Ephesus, he preached and argued in the synagogue
for about three months until he met with too much resistance and
moved to a lecture hall to continue his teaching. He taught there for
two years until a riot among the silversmiths, whose trade in souvenirs
of the goddess Diana was threatened by his success, forced him to
leave. From Ephesus, he wrote a letter to the Corinthian Christians
in which he sent greetings from the church which met in the house
of Prisca and Aquila (1 Cor. 16.19).

Here we have a glimpse of the mobile, urban, synagogue-based
Judaism of the cities of the eastern Mediterranean which looked
back to Judaea and was influenced by the teaching of both John
the Baptist[100] and Jesus, but also reached out to gentile worshippers
and expected a sympathetic hearing from Roman magistrates. It
was a world in which a couple from Pontus could befriend a fellow
tentmaker and believer in Jesus from Tarsus when they met in

---

[97] The use of the Acts of the Apostles as an historical source is not, of course,
without its problems; one of the best commentaries is C. K. Barrett, *A Critical and
Exegetical Commentary on the Acts of the Apostles* (International Critical Commentary on
the Holy Scriptures of the Old and New Testaments; 2 vols; Edinburgh: T&T Clark,
1994–8).

[98] Gallio was the elder brother of the Stoic philosopher, Seneca; since he was
proconsul in 50–51 or 51–52, the date of Paul's visit to Corinth can be established as
within the years 50–52.

[99] This is presumably the same man who features along with Paul as sending the first
letter to the Corinthians: 1 Cor. 1.1.

[100] Acts 18.24–26; 19.1–7.

Corinth, a world united by a common Greek language and cultural assumptions as well as trade and business links that must have made those Jewish communities open and permeable to Jewish travellers and settlers.

Why had Aquila and Priscilla left Rome? Acts refers to a decree of Claudius evicting all the Jews from the city. This cannot be the same as Claudius's ban on Jewish meetings in 41, recorded by Dio Cassius; he explicitly said that Claudius could not expel the Jews from Rome as they were too numerous.[101] Had Dio Cassius reported this wrongly and Claudius had expelled the Jews from Rome in 41, it is likely that such a significant event would have been recorded in the detailed accounts of that remarkable year left by Josephus and Tacitus. Instead, a modest precautionary measure, closing the synagogues for a time while Claudius resolved the tensions in Roman-Jewish relations that he inherited from the recently assassinated Caligula, makes perfect sense. Suetonius, however, does record that Claudius expelled Jews from Rome, though he does not give any date. Commenting on this passage in Suetonius, Orosius, writing in the early-fifth century, provides one. He says that Josephus reported an expulsion in 49 AD, though whether only of the Jews or of the Christians too, no one can now discern.[102] Unfortunately, there is no trace in Josephus's writings of any reference to an expulsion of the Roman Jews in 49 AD, but that date does fit the reference in Acts very neatly. Orosius had been commissioned by Augustine of Hippo to produce a history which would supply him with material for his *City of God.* This section of Orosius's history is arranged chronologically, events reported by the year in which they took place. Orosius refers to the expulsion briefly; he attributes no larger significance to it; he does not connect it with Aquila and Priscilla. Even if he attributes the event to the wrong source, Orosius seems to be guilelessly reporting an event of which he had some record.[103]

In a section of his life of Claudius where Suetonius records a long list of his acts and decrees, slipped in between giving Ilium (Troy) perpetual exemption from tribute and allowing the German envoys to sit in the prestigious seats in the orchestra in the theatre, he

---

[101] Dio Cassius *Rom. Hist.* 60.6.6.

[102] Orosius *Against the Pagans* 7.6.15–16.

[103] There is an extensive bibliography of works arguing about the dating and significance of this expulsion; see for instance Peter Lampe *From Paul to Valentinus: Christians at Rome in the First Two Centuries* (Michael Steinhauser (trans.); London: T & T Clark, 2003) pp. 11–16.

reported: 'He [Claudius] expelled from Rome the Jews who were constantly making disturbances at the instigation of Chrestus.'[104] The Latin, *Iudaeos impulsore Chresto assidue tumultuantes Roma expulit*, might be rendered differently. Another translation could be, 'Claudius expelled the Jews from Rome because they were constantly making disturbances at the instigation of Chrestus.'[105] Both translations attribute the disturbances to Chrestus, but the second version suggests that all the Jews were causing trouble and all were expelled whereas the first suggests that Chrestus was only affecting some and that only those who were causing trouble were expelled. Despite the fact that Acts 18.2 says, 'Claudius had issued a decree that all the Jews should leave Rome', it is effectively impossible that he could have expelled the whole Jewish community. Dio Cassius observed that it had been impossible to do so in 41; had there been any mass expulsion later, it would have received more attention from Suetonius and would certainly have been recorded by Josephus and Tacitus. Consequently, this must have been a fairly small event, the expulsion of a group of Jews who were constantly causing trouble at the instigation of Chrestus.

Chrestus is a common enough name for a slave, meaning 'useful' or 'good', but Suetonius writes as though he expects his readers to know who he is talking about. The most plausible interpretation is that it is a misspelling of Christus[106] and that it means Christians. In other words, Suetonius was reporting the expulsion of Jews who had accepted Jesus as the Messiah, such as Aquila and Priscilla, and who were responsible for tumults within the Jewish community.[107] The imperial government would not, presumably, have wanted to get

---

[104] *Claudius* 25.4.

[105] A third translation could be, 'Claudius, at the instigation of Chrestus, expelled from Rome the Jews who were constantly making disturbances.' Here, Chrestus would be the instigator of Claudius's action while the Jewish disturbances remain unexplained, but this translation is unlikely on the grounds of word order.

[106] Christus and Chrestus were often confused: Tertullian *Apology* 3.5; Lactantius *Divine Institutes* 4.7; or else a pun was made upon their similarity: Justin *1 Apology* 4.

[107] An alternative interpretation would be that the dispute was caused by Jewish Christians such as Aquila and Priscilla arguing for a 'Law-free Gospel', in which case only some of the Jewish Christians would have been expelled; disputes between those who did not embrace a 'Law-free Gospel', who had remained in Rome, and those teaching a 'Law-free Gospel', Jews or gentiles, would then be the cause of the letter to the Romans. But the tumults were caused by 'Chrestus', suggesting it was the Messiahship of Jesus that was at issue, and according to Acts 18.2 'all' the Jews had been expelled.

drawn into a Jewish theological dispute but they might easily have acted to keep the peace when there was rioting or disturbances. Local authorities had repeatedly acted against Paul in Asia Minor and Greece. He made a habit of stirring up trouble in the synagogues of the towns and cities he visited. He and Barnabas were expelled from Antioch in Pisidia when their opponents among the Jews persuaded leading citizens to act against them, but their disciples were not (Acts 13.44–52); they moved on to Iconium but were driven out again after the intervention of the town authorities (Acts 14.4–5), they later revisited Iconium and Antioch and appointed elders to preside over the communities they had founded (Acts 14.21–23). Paul faced similar problems in Thessalonika (Acts 17.5–9) and Beroea (Acts 17.13–35) where Jewish opponents turned the city authorities and the people against them.

In those towns and cities, it is the civic authorities who intervened to move Paul on. In Corinth, however, leading members of the synagogue asked the Roman imperial authorities to intervene in 51, bringing a case against Paul before Gallio, Proconsul of Achaia, in Acts 18.12–17. They failed; Gallio, unsurprisingly, was not willing to be drawn into a matter that he depicted as purely to do with the interpretation of the Jewish Law. But an expulsion of Jewish Christians from Rome in 49, including Aquila and Priscilla now resident in Corinth and probably attending the synagogue, would make sense of their hope that Gallio might have judged in their favour. They had a precedent of imperial intervention and wrongly hoped that Gallio would follow it.

What was striking about the 49 expulsion, if this interpretation of the evidence is correct, is that it was not just one or two troublemakers (as when Paul and Barnabas were expelled from the cities of Asia Minor) but the whole Jewish Christian group who were driven out. In Asia and Greece, Paul was repeatedly forced to move on but left disciples behind with whom he kept in touch. In Rome, it was the *Iudaeos impulsore Chresto assidue tumultuantes* who were expelled. The expulsion of the whole Jewish Christian group, not just the leadership, was notable and presumably accounts for the reference in Acts to 'all the Jews' being exiled by Claudius — all, not just the leaders.

As late as 53 or 54, Aquila and Priscilla were still in Ephesus, hosting a church that met in their house (1 Cor. 16.19). There is no reason to suppose that they had stopped attending the synagogue. Just three or four years later, they were back in Rome, again providing a house in which a church met (Rom 16.3–4). They were away from Rome for between four and six years in all. It is impossible to know whether all the Jewish Christians stayed away for that length of time but a plausible point at which the decree could have been regarded as having fallen into abeyance was 54, with the death of Claudius.

This reading of Acts 18.2 and Suetonius's *Claudius* 25.4 is based on a series of probabilities. Though it must remain uncertain, it allows a hypothetical reconstruction of Christian origins in which the first Christians in Rome were Jewish immigrants, coming from the eastern Mediterranean, Priscilla and Aquila among them. Their belief that Jesus was the Messiah provoked unrest in Rome and led to their expulsion by the Roman authorities in 49 AD.

It is not unlikely that the Christian community in 49 already included some non-Jews, whether Godfearers or converts from paganism. Given the significant number of gentiles among the Roman Christians about eight years later, it is highly plausible that there were already gentile converts to Christianity before 49. If that were so, and the Jewish Christians were expelled for several years, then during that time, perhaps for even as long as four or six years, the Christian Church in Rome was substantially gentile. Under those circumstances, gentiles would have assumed positions of leadership and, presumably, found a confident voice evangelising fellow gentiles. When Jewish Christians such as Aquila and Priscilla returned, probably after 54, they would have found that the Christian community was no longer theirs but was equally that of the gentiles. They did not feel any less Jewish — after all, in Rome being a Jew was not defined by synagogue membership — but they would have been painfully aware of a rift with the Jewish community and perhaps felt the challenge of the new strength of non-Jewish Christianity.

THE LETTER TO THE ROMANS

It was to this community that Paul addressed one of the greatest works of Christian thought, the Letter to the Romans, in the winter of 55–56 or 56–57.[108] For centuries, certainly from the time of Luther, it was read as a treatise in systematic theology, the great summation of Paul's thought, with the opposition of faith and works as its main theme. Paul was understood to be urging his readers to abandon a

---

[108] There are several excellent commentaries; the most recent is Robert Jewett, *Romans: A Commentary* (Hermeneia; Minneapolis: Fortress Press, 2006).

religion in which they tried to win God's favour by their works and instead accept Christ in faith. It is impossible to read the letter that way now.[109] It is not a summary of the great themes of Paul's thought; it omits too much. When compared with the letters to the Corinthians, it can be seen to neglect or even ignore totally major issues in Paul's theology: the Resurrection of Christ, the expected resurrection of believers, the Church understood as the Body of Christ, the eucharist, spiritual gifts.

Furthermore, it is a letter, not a treatise. Paul was in Greece, presumably in Corinth (Acts 20.3; Rom. 16.23 cf. 1 Cor. 1.14), and seized the opportunity of sending it by the hand of Phoebe, deacon of the church at Cenchreae, which was the eastern port of Corinth on the Saronic Gulf. He described her as a 'benefactor of many, including myself' — the word for benefactor, *prostasis* carrying strong connotations of patronage and leadership — and asks that they give her whatever help she might require, which suggests that she was travelling to Rome on business. In other words, the decision to write it might have been determined by the mundane fact that a distinguished church official happened to be about to make the journey to Rome. Paul can contrive to be a very unclear writer at the best of times but he surpasses himself in the Letter to the Romans. This is largely because the letter has aims which are specific to its time, determined by the situation in which both Paul and his Roman audience found themselves. Paul wanted to introduce himself formally to a Roman community, some of whom he knew, which he longed to visit (Rom 1.13; 15.22–23). His immediate plan was to visit Jerusalem with the collection he had raised from the churches in Macedonia and Achaia, then he intended to travel to the West, to Spain, to preach the Gospel and he wanted to visit Rome on the way (Rom 15.22–29). He was worried about his opponents in Jerusalem and wanted the prayers of the Roman community (Rom 15.31) and perhaps any more concrete support they could give. It is likely that the letter was intended to begin negotiations towards asking for their eventual help for his mission to Spain. He was keen also to clear himself of the accusation that he was an antinomian, indifferent to law, teaching that it was permissible to do evil so that God could bring about the good. He was well aware of the accusation (Rom 3.8). All of these played their part in his decision to write the letter but its main aim was

---

[109] The reading of the letter has been transformed by the 'new perspective' built upon E. P. Sanders, *Paul and Palestinian Judaism* (London: SCM, 1977).

to address disputes that existed in the Roman Christian community concerning the significance of the Jewish Law and the relationship between Jewish and gentile Christians.

Towards the end of the letter, Paul provides a list of people to whom greetings are sent.[110] It is the earliest roll-call of Christian Rome.

> Greet Prisca and Aquila, my fellow workers in Christ Jesus, who risked their necks for my life, to whom not only I give thanks but all the churches of the gentiles, and [greet] also the church in their house. Greet my beloved Epaenetus, who was the first convert in Asia for Christ. Greet Mary, who has worked very hard among you. Greet Andronicus and Junia, my compatriots and fellow prisoners who are prominent among the apostles and became Christians before I did. Greet Ampliatus, my beloved in the Lord. Greet Urbanus, our fellow worker in Christ and Stachys, my beloved. Greet Apelles, who is approved in Christ. Greet those who belong to the household of Aristobulus. Greet my compatriot Herodion. Greet those in the Lord who belong to the household of Narcissus. Greet those workers in the Lord, Tryphaena and Tryphosa. Greet the beloved Persis, who has worked hard in the Lord. Greet Rufus, chosen in the Lord, and greet his mother, a mother to me also. Greet Asyncritus, Phlegon, Hermes, Patrobas, Hermas and the brothers who are with them. Greet Philologus and Julia, Nereus and his sister and Olympas and all the saints who are with them. Greet one another with a holy kiss. All the churches of Christ greet you. (Rom 16.3–16)

It is a remarkable list. Paul has personal links with several of them — Aquila and Priscilla, of course; Epaenetus, his first convert (first fruit) in Asia; Andronicus and Junia, converts before him and outstanding among the apostles; Rufus's mother who has been a mother to him also; presumably Urbanus, whom he describes as a fellow-worker. Three are identified as Jews (taking the word *syngeneis* to mean compatriots) — Andronicus, Junia and Herodion. Priscilla and Aquila are also Jews. It is likely that Mary and Rufus and his mother are also Jews. Rufus might well be the son of Simon of Cyrene, described in Mark's gospel as the man who carried Christ's cross and was the father of Alexander and Rufus (Mk 15.21). Most of the rest are probably gentiles. The prominence given to women is noticeable. Priscilla, as well as her husband, is his fellow worker. Junia, as well as Andronicus (probably her husband), has been a fellow prisoner and prominent among the apostles. Four people are commended for hard work, all of them women: Mary, Tryphaena, Tryphosa and Persis. Aquila and Priscilla are business people with interests that range across the

---

[110] Many early manuscripts omit chapter 16, but it is more likely that it was omitted by copyists than that it was a later addition.

Mediterranean. Herodion was probably a freedman of the Herod family. Many of the names are typical of slaves — Persis, Ampliatus, Urbanus and Stachys, Asyncritus, Phlegon, Hermes, Patrobas, Hermas. In every respect, this is a very diverse community — men and women, gentiles and Jews, slaves and middle-class business people, Romans and immigrants, people who have been Christians from the early days and, presumably, recent converts.[111]

It is a diverse community, but is it one community at all? The standard reading is that the Roman Christians were distributed between five or more house churches which did not constitute one community and whose divisions might well have been perpetuated for generations. Though widely held, this view depends on surprisingly thin arguments.[112] First, does Paul address one community, one *ekklēsia*? Much is made of the fact that Paul does not address the letter to the church in Rome, in the way he addresses the church in Corinth (1 Cor. 1.2; 2 Cor. 1.1) and Thessalonica (1 Thess 1.1; 2 Thess 1.1), which are written to the *ekklēsia* in Corinth or in Thessalonica. This has been taken to mean that he did not regard the Romans as one community (*ekklēsia*). This might be expecting too much consistency from Paul. The letter to the Philippians, for instance, is not addressed to the church in Philippi, though he describes them later in the letter as the only church who helped him with gifts of money (Phil. 4.15). It does seem as though he used the word *ekklēsia* to mean a Christian body who could meet as one assembly (1 Cor. 11.18; 14.23) and could therefore speak of churches in the plural in Galatia (1 Cor. 16.1), Asia (1 Cor. 16.19), Macedonia (2 Cor. 8.1) and Judaea (Gal. 1.22). He addressed his letter to the Galatians to the churches of Galatia (Gal. 1.2). If the Roman Christians met as multiple communities, why not address them as churches in the plural? Does the fact that they live in one city rather than in a province matter, if the definition of church is a group which assembles together? Furthermore, it is extremely odd that he should address the group which meets in the house of Aquila and Prisca as a church but not the others. Writing to the Romans, it is therefore just as striking that Paul did not address them as churches

[111] For an immensely thorough analysis of what these names might reveal, see Lampe *From Paul to Valentinus* pp. 164–83.

[112] For an effective demolition of the view that the Roman Christian community was a loose federation of house churches, see Chrys C. Caragounis, 'From Obscurity to Prominence: The Development of the Roman Church between Romans and *1 Clement*' in Donfried and Richardson *Judaism and Christianity* pp. 245–79 at pp. 252–60.

in the plural as that he failed to address them as a church in the singular.

The assumption that the Christians not only met as separate assemblies but that they were only loosely federated is based on the lack of an over-arching governing structure of the Jewish synagogues. This, it has been suggested, set out a pattern of organisation which lasted among the Roman Christians for centuries.[113] Apart from the obvious objections that there is no proof that the Christians modelled their organisation on synagogues[114] and that Nero's persecution of 64 probably uprooted whatever organisation the early Christians had, this claim is open to the criticism that it assumes that the Jewish community was organised as synagogues, the evidence for which is not compelling.

Many readers have detected in the list, in addition to the house church of Priscilla and Aquila, a series of others. One reading[115] would suggest that there were five house churches: in addition to the church of Prisca and Aquila, there are the household of Aristobulus, the household of Narcissus, the people mentioned in association with Asyncritus and the brothers who are with them and the people mentioned along with Philologus and the saints who are with them. Another reading has identified six house churches,[116] while another[117] has detected seven and believes that Paul's arrival in the city later formed an eighth. This way of reading the text is now standard orthodoxy but it is open to several objections. The first is that the text makes no suggestion at all that 'those who belong to the household of Aristobulos', for instance, meet as a group. It simply does not say that there are five, six or seven churches in Rome; it merely lists names. The second objection is that one group, but only one group, is addressed as a church — those meeting in the house of Aquila and Prisca. The mention of one church makes

---

[113] Lampe *From Paul to Valentinus* pp. 364–65; 431–32.

[114] Indeed the argument is placed the other way around by Wolfgang Wiefel, 'The Jewish Community in Ancient Rome and the Origins of Roman Christianity' in Karl P. Donfried (ed), *The Romans Debate* (Edinburgh: T&T Clark, rev ed, 1991) pp. 85–101, who argues that the expulsion of Jewish Christians from the synagogues by Claudius (necessitated by the lack of a ruling Jewish council who could have resolved the disputes in separate synagogues) left the gentile Christians to establish an entirely different system of assembly, their house churches.

[115] For instance Jewett *Romans* p. 953.

[116] Paul S. Minear, *The Obedience of Faith: The Purposes of Paul in the Letter to the Romans* (London: SCM, 1971) p. 7.

[117] Lampe *From Paul to Valentinus* p. 359.

the failure to refer to the other four, five or six groups as churches quite odd. If there are seven house churches, why does Paul not call them churches? The third objection is revealed by the uncertainty of these scripture scholars about how many churches they can find in the passage. The expansion of the number of churches found in the list of names from five to six and to seven shows the there are too many other unaffiliated names mentioned by Paul which cannot be compressed into these groups. To which church, for instance, does Herodion belong, or Rufus and his mother? In other words, it is not at all obvious that this is a list of groups; what it does look like is a rather random list of names, with allusions to some people of whose existence Paul is aware but whose name he does not know.

One thing is very striking: that the text singles out for special greeting those who are the members of the church who meet in Prisca's and Aquila's house. The imperative form of greeting used throughout the passage as Paul asks the Romans to greet each other is unusual. He does not employ it elsewhere in his letters. At first, 'greet the church in their house', sounds as though he is asking people who are not members of that church to greet those who are. The list continues, somewhat strangely, to keep inviting the Romans to greet each other. If it were read, however, to mean, 'greet each other, all you who are members of the church in Prisca's and Aquila's house', it would be wholly reasonable for Paul to follow that with as full a list of the members of the church as he could muster. One could imagine a letter that bore the injunction, 'greet the family' or 'greet the college', which carried no implication that the recipient was not a member of the family or the college. This reading is consonant with the list's conclusion: 'greet one another with a holy kiss', which is plainly addressed to everyone named. Thus the list could be read as opening and closing with a general call to greet everyone in the church and in between listing all the names Paul knew. In other words, this list of names could be the membership of the one church in Rome, consisting of twenty-eight people whom Paul can name and several others whom he does not — the members of the households of Aristobulus and Narcissus, those who are with Hermas and those who are with Olympas. It seems much more realistic to expect that the Roman Christians amounted to several dozen in the mid-50s than a much bigger number distributed around five, six or seven house churches.[118]

---

[118] The objection that sixty people could not meet in one house is easily countered by the observation that Prisca and Aquila ran a business — tent making — and might have had a warehouse or workshop where a large group could convene.

Few people read the ending of the letter in this way. But even those who discover multiple groups in the final chapter have no reason to think of them as groups with a fixed membership which could not move from one to another.[119] Paul is clearly concerned about the unity of the Roman community in the letter but nowhere does he indicate that they were broken up into discrete groups with no interchange between them. In fact, the opposite seems to be the case in Rom. 14.1–15.13, where the problems of the Roman community arise precisely when they do sit down and eat together. It is worth remembering that the Corinthian church could include a recognisable group such as 'the household of Stephanas' (1 Cor. 1.16 — why is this different from the groups noted in the list of names in Rom. 16 such as 'those who belong to the household of Aristobulus?). The Corinthians were also divided, into factions appealing to Paul or Peter or Apollos (1 Cor. 1.12) and apparently also by social class (1 Cor. 11: 18–22), yet they assembled as one church (1 Cor. 11.20) and all met in the one house of Gaius (Rom. 16.23). In fact, it was because they met as one assembly that their divisions became apparent. The simple fact is that, if the Roman Christians were not one community, Paul would not have addressed them one letter; if they did not meet together, he would not have suggested they greet each other; if they did not eat together, there would have been no problem for Paul to try and resolve between Christians who observed the Jewish Law and those who did not.

There is thus no reason to envisage the Roman Christians addressed by Paul as a cluster of separate communities, a federation of distinct assemblies, but they were certainly a community that experienced tension. He was writing within a year or two, presumably, of the return of Jewish Christians to the city. Other Jewish Christians might have settled in Rome in the early 50s, but the gentile Christians must have been unusually important. That meant that instead of seeing gentile Christians as having the status of Godfearers, people supporting the Jewish community and ultimately saved by it but outsiders nevertheless, they had to be seen in Rome as fully the equal of Jewish Christians. That raised questions about the significance and value of

---

[119] Fanciful notions of Phoebe carrying the letter from one community to another and waiting while it was read out (taking between sixty and ninety minutes) and then expounding its meaning have been proposed, for instance by Philip F. Esler, *Conflict and Identity in Romans: The Social Setting of Paul's Letter* (Minneapolis: Fortress Press, 2003) p. 117.

the Jewish Law, which also had a bearing on the position in God's plan about the non-Christian Jewish people. Jews did not think that keeping the Law won God's favour and was their means of salvation; rather they believed that God established a covenant of mercy with his people and gave them the Law as the framework of their response to his mercy and the means of atonement for transgression.[120] In other words, it was the essential sign of belonging to God's chosen people. The question was, of course, who was God's chosen people?

The Letter to the Romans is notoriously difficult to interpret.[121] The text does not speak for itself. Too much depends upon the way Paul's overall theology is understood and the way the community he is addressing is portrayed. Too many words such as *nomos* (law)[122] or Israel[123] might not have one consistent meaning and are difficult to translate. At different points in the letter, Paul appears to be speaking to, or at least conscious of, different constituencies — Jewish Christians, non-Jewish Christians and Law-observing Christians. It is noticeable, for instance, how the density of scriptural reference intensifies in chapters 9–11. Overall in Paul's letters, there are about ninety or a hundred quotations from scripture; over fifty of them feature in the Letter to the Romans alone and, of them, about twenty-eight occur in those three chapters. Addressing the Roman community, at that delicate point in his argument in chapters 9–11, Paul had readers in mind who would be very well versed in and impressed by a

---

[120] Sanders *Paul and Palestinian Judaism* calls this view of the Law 'covenantal nomism'.

[121] Good accounts of the purpose and meaning of the letter are A. J. M. Wedderburn, *The Reasons for Romans* (Edinburgh: T&T Clark, 1988) and Francis Watson, *Paul, Judaism and the Gentiles: Beyond the New Perspective* (Grand Rapids, Michigan: Eerdmans, 2nd ed, 2007); other interpretations include Mark D. Nanos, *The Mystery of Romans: The Jewish Context of Paul's Letter* (Minneapolis: Fortress Press, 1996), which claims that Paul is himself a Law-observant Jew and aims at the restoration of Israel under Christ, so it is the gentile Christians who are the problem and they must learn respect for the Law; Stanley K. Stowers, *A Rereading of Romans: Justice, Jews, and Gentiles* (New Haven: Yale University Press, 1994) and Andrew A. Das, *Solving the Romans Debate* (Minneapolis: Fortress Press, 2007), which claim Paul's audience is entirely gentile; Steve Mason, *Josephus, Judea, and Christian Origins: Methods and Categories* (Peabody, Mass: Hendrickson, 2009) pp. 303–28 argues the audience is overwhelmingly Jewish.

[122] Particularly difficult passages are Rom. 3.27–31; 7.23; 8.2; 9.31 and 10.4.

[123] Compare Rom. 9.6 with 11.25–26.

great range of scriptural references.[124] Yet other passages in the letter are explicitly addressed to gentile readers.[125]

Furthermore, Paul avoids the kind of invective which, in other letters, achieves a sharper definition of what is at issue. His colourful account of the disputes in the church he knew so well in Corinth or the savagery of his language speaking to the Galatians allow the reader to form a clearer view of what the problems were in those churches. His unusually conciliatory tone in the letter to the Romans leaves the reader unsure in many places what the difficulties are that he is addressing. This is partly because he had not founded the Roman church (Rom 15.20) and so does not adopt the same paternal, authoritarian voice he uses when addressing others. Instead, he praises them in almost deferential terms (Rom 1.8; 16.19). His major aim in writing to the Romans was to achieve reconciliation within the community. That is why the people listed at the end of the letter are instructed to greet each other, rather than receive his greetings. Immediately after that affectionate roll-call of the saints of Rome, Paul urges unity, for the first time in the letter, in the strongest possible terms (Rom 16.17–20). What, then, was the problem in Rome? The problem was the relationship between Roman Christians who did not keep the Jewish Law and those who did.

As with so much of Paul's thinking, this letter is dominated by the question of Jewish — gentile relations (e.g. Rom. 1.16; 11.17–24). One large early section is devoted to establishing that the Gospel is no longer limited to Jews (chapters 2–5); another to defending this claim as being faithful to the message of Judaism, which forces him into a lengthy and anguished consideration of the status of Israel as God's chosen people (Chapters 9–11). At the heart of his message is the belief that it is through faith in Christ, not by doing the works of the Law, that people are now constituted God's righteous covenant people (Rom. 3.21–8 cf. Gal. 2.16). Since the standard Jewish view at this time seems to have been that keeping the Law was a response to receiving God's mercy, a sign of membership of the covenant people of Israel, Paul is not attacking the claim that performing the works of the Law made people righteous before God. Paul is, rather, attacking

[124] The sheer weight of scriptural reference here is quite different from the passages in Galatians, addressed to gentile Christians, who are adopting circumcision; though Paul's argument made a strong appeal to scripture, his readers need only have been familiar with the story of Abraham for it to have had real force.

[125] He explicitly turns to his gentile readers at Rom. 11.13; see also 1.5–7, 12–14; 15.16.

the belief that the only members of God's covenantal people, the true Israel, are circumcised Jews who keep the dietary laws and other requirements of the Mosaic Law. In other words, it is role of the Law as a boundary marker, signifying not just the Jewish people but the true Israel, that he criticises.[126]

Paul is critical of the Law when it is deployed to separate Jews from gentiles, whether in terms of superior moral knowledge (Rom. 2.12–14); or ethnic pride, which is in fact hypocritical (Rom. 2.17–23); or circumcision, which is merely an external sign of what ought to be an inward fidelity (Rom. 2.25–29). He says that the Law cannot solve the problem of sin (Rom. 7.7–12) and indeed in some sense promotes sin (Rom. 5.20). What Paul offers as a positive evaluation of the Law is less clear. Having asserted that it cannot solve the problem of sin, he still insists that the Law is holy, but he appears finally to relegate it to a very secondary level. He says that no one can be justified by the Law but only by faith (Rom. 3.27–31) and that the Law has come to its fulfilment, or even an end, with Christ and that everyone who has faith may be justified (Rom. 9.30–10.4).

A major theme of the letter is that Christ reconciled both Jew and gentile to God by the sacrifice of his death (Rom. 3.24; 5.1–2; 5.6–11). Alongside sacrificial and redemption language to account for the saving power of the crucifixion (e.g. Rom. 3.24–25), he uses the language of participation, which might be regarded as more central to his thought. Christ shares in the common fate of humanity, accepting death, so that people can become a new creation in him by sharing in his resurrection. The phrase 'in Christ' is distinctively Pauline — used widely in his letters and scarcely anywhere else in the New Testament. It is 'in Christ' that Jew and gentile are made one. The evidence that people are incorporated into Christ is the gift of the Holy Spirit. The love of God has been poured into the hearts of Christians by the Holy Spirit who has been given to them (Rom. 5.5). The Spirit of God has made his home in them and will raise their mortal bodies (Rom. 8.9–11), making them co-heirs with Christ and sons of God (Rom. 8.14–7), so that those who possess the first fruits of the Spirit groan to be set free (Rom. 8.23) and their inexpressible prayers are uttered by the Spirit (Rom. 8.26–27). The Kingdom of God is not about food and drink, the dietary rules of the Law, but rather the joy and peace given by the Holy Spirit (Rom. 14.17).

[126] See James D. G. Dunn, *Jesus, Paul and the Law* (London: SPCK, 1990); *The Theology of Paul the Apostle* (Edinburgh: T&T Clark, 1998).

Here, the similarities with the letter to the Galatians are very apparent. Paul insists to the Galatians that the Law cannot justify people and that if it could Christ's death would have been pointless (Gal. 2.15–21) but that the proof that they have been redeemed by Christ and become sons of God is the Spirit crying in their hearts 'Abba Father' (Gal. 4.4–7). He asks baldly, 'Was it because you kept the Law that you received the Spirit?' (Gal. 3.2). Whatever respect Paul shows to Israel in the letter to the Romans (e.g. Rom. 9.1–5; 11.16–24), it is clear enough that he believes that the true Israel is the people redeemed by Christ and filled with the Holy Spirit. At the heart of the message of the letters to the Galatians, Corinthians and Romans is that the Spirit is re-creating God's people and that this cannot be achieved by the Law but only by Christ.

What is less clear is the relationship of the 'true Israel' to the people conventionally recognised as Israel (the Jews). This is the issue Paul discusses in Chapter 11. He seems to present the 'true Israel' as the faithful remnant, a familiar theme in the scriptures, who prepare the way for the conversion of the rest. In this context, the gentiles who accept Christ are a stimulation to the Jews who have not, rousing them to envy (Rom. 11.13–15): in other words, the conversion of the gentiles is at the service of the whole Jewish people. The gentiles are grafted on to the root of Israel (Rom. 11.16–24). They are saved because God is faithful to his covenant with the Jews. But alongside this passage, there are the places where Paul speaks strongly of the equality of Jew and gentile in Christ (Rom. 3.24; 5.1–2; 5.6–11) and is plainly impatient with legal observance as a visible expression of God's covenant people. Instead, Christians are constituted as the Body of Christ by the Holy Spirit (e.g. 1 Cor. 12) through baptism (Rom. 6.1–11) and the eucharist (1 Cor. 11.17–33).

Much of what Paul says about Judaism and the Law concerns those Jews who have not accepted Jesus. Does that mean that the problems in Rome are only about the relationship of the Christian community to non-Christian Jews? The passage on which the whole interpretation of the letter depends is Rom. 14.1–15.13. Here Paul contrasts the weak and the strong. The weak are those who keep some days as holier than others and observe dietary regulations so strictly that they are vegetarians. The strong are those who feel free to eat any sort of meat and regard all days as equally holy. Paul takes a very irenic line and says that neither should condemn the other (14.13) and that they should accept each other (15.7) for Christ's ministry benefited both the circumcised and the gentiles (15.8–9). The most plausible reading of the passage is that Paul is talking about disputes between Law-observant Christians, predominantly Jews but perhaps including some gentile converts who had embraced the Law, and the non-observant, presumably predominantly gentiles but including also Jews who had abandoned strict legal observance, such as Paul himself or close associates of his such as Aquila and Priscilla. Vegetarianism was adopted by Jews who had good reason to doubt the purity of the meat available to them in a non-Jewish environment.[127] That suggests that the observant Christians were refusing to eat meat when dining with non-observant Christians. They might, for instance, have feared that the meat had come from a pagan temple, where it had been sacrificed to the pagan gods.[128]

The tone of the whole letter is different from the letter to the Galatians, where Paul warns gentile Christians against accepting circumcision. The problem in Rome is not that the non-observant Christians are being persuaded into observance of the Law but rather the co-existence and relationship between Law-observant and non-observant Christians. In urging mutual toleration and encouraging fellowship between the observant Jewish Christians and the rest, he is in fact undermining the position of those who observe the Law. By implication, he is asking them to compromise their fidelity to ritual observance.

The letter therefore addresses the single most important question early Christianity faced: was Christianity to remain Jewish? Its answer is to respond with another question: what is the true Israel? There is no such thing as an uncontroversial reading of Paul — opinions about his theology are very varied and it is far from easy to present a single, coherent account of what he thought — but it could be said that by excluding ancestry, circumcision, observance of dietary regulations and holy days from the definition of what constitutes the true Israel and defining it instead as the community united by the gift of the Spirit, through baptism and the eucharist, in the death and resurrection of Christ to form the Body of Christ, Paul had given his answer.

---

[127] Dan. 1.8–16; Judith 12.1–4; Josephus says that the priests living as prisoners in Rome were mindful of their religion and ate figs and nuts, *Life* 3.

[128] 1 Cor. 8 also talks about weak believers whose conscience demands that they avoid meat sacrificed to idols; Paul says their weakness must be respected and he will never eat meat to avoid causing one of them to fall.

PAUL AND PETER IN ROME

For a man who might so often have felt thwarted in his missionary endeavours by the intervention of political officials, driving him out of towns where his teaching had provoked offence, Paul expressed surprising approval of governing authorities. He told the Roman Christians, 'Let everyone be subject to the governing powers, for there is no power except from God and those that exist have been instituted by God.' (Rom. 13.1) This was a strong statement of his belief that all that had happened to him from the hands of civil authority had been not only for his own good but had been part of God's providential design. His audience in Rome needed to accept the same message for they too had met the sharp edge of political power in the expulsion of Jewish Christians in 49, which, in the event, might well have been recognised as a blessing in disguise.

Within about three years of writing those words, Paul found himself travelling to Rome under the constraints of Roman power.[129] He fulfilled his intention of travelling to Jerusalem where the fears he had voiced (Rom. 15.31) were realised. The story is told in Acts 20–28. Having run into trouble in the Temple, he was taken into protective custody by the Roman authorities and then moved to the Roman administrative capital, Caesarea. There he was held for two years by the procurator, Felix, who was contending with extremist groups, messianic claimants, assassinations, riots and violence in Jerusalem and Galilee.[130] Felix's response was brutal as well as venal, earning the Tacitean epigram that he 'wielded the power of a king with all the instincts of a slave'.[131] His successor, Porcius Festus, offered to try Paul in Jerusalem himself but Paul invoked his rights as a Roman citizen to be tried in Rome. Before he left, he met Herod Agrippa II, son of Agrippa I, who ruled over the northern part of his late father's territories, and his sister Bernice. They were the siblings of Drusilla, who had married Festus's predecessor, Felix. Bernice was later to be the mistress of Titus until he became emperor in 79. These encounters with high Roman officials and Jewish royalty provided Paul with a glimpse into the world of the imperial court.

The description of Paul's voyage to Rome (Acts 27.1–28.13) is one of the most vivid in ancient literature. After a very difficult voyage,

---

[129] For a full survey of all the evidence, see Hermann Lichtenberger, 'Jews and Christians in Rome in the Time of Nero: Josephus and Paul in Rome' *ANRW* 2.26.3 (1996) 2142–76.

[130] *BJ* 2.253–70; *AJ* 20.137–81 *passim*.

[131] *Hist.* 5.9.

they landed at Puteoli in the bay of Naples. As they sailed towards the harbour, they must have gazed at the towns lining the bay — Misenum, Baiae, Herculaneum, Pompeii, Stabiae and Surrentum — and, towering above the eastern horizon, the brooding silence of Vesuvius. Puteoli was the main port of western Italy. Despite Claudius's opening up of the harbour of Ostia, Portus, it remained the usual landing point for travellers to Rome. Josephus was to land there on his trip to Rome in 64.[132] The grain fleets were only re-directed to Portus in the time of the emperor Commodus (180–92). Puteoli had a flourishing Greek community and strong contacts with Asia, so it was no surprise that Paul met Christians there:

> On the second day, we came to Puteoli. We found brothers there and were invited to stay with them for seven days. And thus we came to Rome. The brothers from there, when they heard of us, came as far as the Forum of Appius and Three Taverns to meet us. On seeing them, Paul gave thanks to God and took courage. When we came to Rome, Paul was allowed to live by himself with the soldier who was guarding him. (Acts 28.13–16)

The details are telling: the presence of Christians in Puteoli, their contacts with Christians in Rome, the binding sense of fellowship that united them with Paul. The week's stay at Puteoli was long enough for Christians to get from there to Rome with the news of Paul's arrival. The groups meeting him as he travelled up the Appian Way, at the Forum of Appius forty-three miles from Rome and Three Taverns thirty-three miles from Rome, are, strikingly, the only reference to the Roman Christians in Acts. This is because Acts does not want the climax of the book to be Paul's sojourn with the Roman church but rather his bringing the Gospel from Jerusalem to Rome. Instead of the Christians, it is the Jews of Rome whom Paul is now described as meeting.

Three days after his arrival, Paul called together the leaders of the Jews. He told them that he had been arrested in Jerusalem, though he had done nothing against the Jewish people or the customs of their ancestors, and been handed over to the Romans; they had wanted to release him but, when the Jews objected, he had appealed to the emperor. The Jewish leaders replied that they had received no letters from Judaea about him and that none of the brothers coming to Rome had reported anything evil about him, but that they would like to hear what he had to say, 'for with regard to this sect, we know that everywhere it is spoken against'. They fixed a day and

---

[132] *Life* 3.

then came back to his lodgings in great numbers. Paul spoke from morning till evening, testifying to the Kingdom of God and trying to convince them about Jesus from the Law of Moses and the prophets. Some were convinced by what he said, others refused to believe. They disagreed with each other and as they were leaving Paul quoted Isaiah 6.9–10, warning that this people's heart has grown dull so that they might not look with their eyes or listen with their ears or understand with their heart. Instead, 'the salvation of God has been sent to the gentiles who will listen.'

This passage has been constructed to make a point, that Paul regularly started his preaching with the Jews until he was rejected and then moved on to speak to the gentiles (e.g. in Antioch in Pisidia, Acts 13.16–52). The book ends, not with Paul consolidating his efforts to unite the Christian church in Rome as he must have tried to do, but for two years welcoming all who came to him and proclaiming the Kingdom of God and teaching about Christ. It may seem an odd ending, requiring a sequel, but in fact it is a very pointed conclusion. Acts begins with the Ascension of Christ in Jerusalem and ends with Paul's proclaiming him in Rome. Its message is a demonstration of how the Holy Spirit continues Christ's work through Christians, often using vicissitudes such as persecution as a means of spreading the Gospel, taking the news of Christ from Jerusalem to the political capital of the Roman world.

Even though the account of Paul's time in Rome given by the Acts of the Apostles is carefully presented to make a theological point, some of the details remain very telling. Most important is the failure of Paul to make any significant impact on the non-Christian Jews. The reader is left with the impression that Christianity in Rome is going to become a substantially gentile church. Already, the Jewish leaders speak as though Christians are alien to them, a sect about which they have only heard ill. If Paul arrived in Rome in about 60, then it would have been over ten years since the Jewish Christians had been expelled from the city. The impression given by Acts is that even on returning they did not re-integrate into the Jewish community.

While in captivity in Rome,[133] Paul wrote the letter to the Philippians. It is a letter full of reassurance to a church which was clearly dismayed by his imprisonment. He described himself dramatically as being poured out as a libation over the sacrifice and the offering of their

---

[133] Other dates have been suggested: when Paul was a captive in Caesarea before coming to Rome or an earlier, possible captivity in Ephesus.

faith, suffering the loss of everything for the sake of Christ and now pressing on to reach the goal for the prize of the heavenly call of God in Christ Jesus.

> I want you to know, brethren, that what has happened to me has helped to spread the Gospel. It has become known thoughout the whole praetorium and to everyone else that my imprisonment is for Christ. Most of the brethren, having been made confident in the LORD by my imprisonment, dare to speak the word with greater boldness and without fear. (Phil. 1.12–14)

The praetorium could either be a governor's palace (Mt. 27.27) or the imperial guard. The latter is the more likely reading; given that it is followed by 'and to everyone else', praetorium seems to be referring to people. The fact that the letter ends with greetings especially 'from those of the emperor's household' (Phil. 4.21) does suggest that Paul is in Rome and has begun to make contacts among the troops and converts among the staff in the imperial service. He also wrote the letter to Philemon, a touching little appeal for the forgiveness of a runaway slave, Onesimus, who had joined Paul. Surprisingly, Paul hopes to be restored to Philemon and asks him to have a room ready for him (Philemon 22). This is a hint that Paul sees some end to his captivity. He says something similar to the Philippians, trusting in his deliverance (Phil. 1.19) and promising to send Timothy with news of how things went and trusting that he would come soon himself (Phil. 2.23–24).

What finally happened to Paul? It is inconceivable that the early Christians did not know. The letter to the Philippians is evidence enough of communication across the Mediterranean about his welfare. It is possible that he was released and succeeded in his ambition of preaching in Spain before his death. It is also possible that he was never released and died in Rome.[134] The earliest evidence after the New Testament comes from a Roman letter addressed to the church in Corinth, dated perhaps to about the year 97, named *1 Clement*:

> Because of jealousy and strife, Paul showed the way to the prize for patient endurance. After he had been in chains seven times and driven into exile and been stoned and had become a preacher in the east and in the west, he received the noble renown of his faith, having taught righteousness to the

---

[134] The Pastoral Letters addressed to Timothy and Titus are seldom regarded as works of Paul himself; they indicate Paul's presence in various places — Macedonia (1 Tim. 1.3), Corinth and Miletus (2 Tim. 4.20), Crete (Tit. 1.5), Nicopolis (Tit. 3.12) — which might be evidence of actual travels after the end of a first captivity of Rome or might refer to earlier travels.

whole world and having reached the extreme west. And having borne witness
before the rulers, he left the world and went to the holy place, having become
a great example of endurance.[135]

The passage has no need to be more explicit; both writer and
recipients knew the story of Paul's life and death. It certainly gives
the impression that Paul did reach Spain — the extreme west — but
also that he died a martyr's death. The phrase 'having borne witness'
(*marturēsas*) could be translated 'having been martyred'; the word
certainly carried that connotation in Christian circles already by the
end of the first century[136] and the form of the verb, an aorist parti-
ciple, suggests completeness and finality.

At the other extreme is a highly detailed novella, the *Martyrdom of
Paul*, part of the collection of stories about him which make up the
Acts of Paul,[137] the earliest version of which probably dates from the
end of the second century. The text has much of the atmosphere of
the novels which were made into Hollywood biblical epics. Readers
knew that they were not strictly true but enjoyed pondering what
might, or ought to have, happened. Real and fictional people rub
shoulders in these stories but it might be naïve to suppose that the
reader could not distinguish between them. Speeches, characters
and incidents were tolerated as inventions, but inventions that were
probably understood to illuminate and enrich an accepted historical
core. To be effective, these stories have to be embroidered onto some
substance of universally known truth. The *Martyrdom of Paul* describes
Paul's beheading in Rome on the orders of Nero, in an atmosphere
of miracles and conversions for which the Acts of the Apostles had
already given warrant. Four facts stand out as probably having some
historical basis: that Paul was executed in Rome; that he died in the
reign of Nero; that he was beheaded; and that his death had nothing
to do with the execution of Christians by Nero after the great fire in
Rome in 64.

Peter's association with Rome is quite another matter. There
is evidence in the New Testament that Peter, like Paul, was a
travelling missionary. Paul reveals that Peter took his wife around

[135] 1 Clement 5.5–7.
[136] See Acts 22.20 (Stephen); Rev. 2.13 (Antipas); 1 Tim. 6.13; Rev. 1.5, 3.14
(Christ).
[137] J. K. Elliott, *The Apocryphal New Testament: A Collection of Apocryphal Christian
Literature in an English Translation* (Oxford: Clarendon Press, 1993) pp. 350–89; the
Martyrdom is on pp. 385–88.

with him on his journeys (1 Cor. 9.5),[138] and encountered him in Antioch (Gal. 2.11). Since there were Christians in Corinth who described themselves as belonging to Paul or Apollos or Cephas (and Paul and Apollos had preached in Corinth), then it also seems likely that Peter had been there. But these pieces of evidence are fragmentary and the New Testament offers no account of Peter's life after a persecution of the Jerusalem church by Herod Agrippa I in his brief reign 42–4. Having described his deliverance from prison, Acts remarks enigmatically, 'Then he left and went to another place.' (Acts 12.17). Apart from his participation in the Council of Jerusalem (Acts 15.6–21), Peter vanishes from the biblical record.[139]

Later tradition is again unanimous that Peter went to Rome and was martyred there. Early evidence would include Ignatius of Antioch, writing to the Romans in about 107, who says, 'I do not give you orders like Peter and Paul: they were apostles, I am a prisoner; they were free but even now I am still a slave.'[140] This could most naturally be read as saying that Peter and Paul had taught the Roman church. This view received much firmer expression from Irenaeus of Lyons, writing in the 170s, who attributed the foundation of the Roman church to Peter and Paul.[141] Such a claim could only be made — and it was an important plank in his argument against his opponents — if there was universal agreement that Peter as well as Paul had visited Rome. Irenaeus's view was shared by the Christians in both Corinth and Rome as can been seen from a letter written in about 170 from Dionysius of Corinth to the church in Rome remarking that Peter and Paul had founded both the churches in Corinth and Rome.[142] It is hardly likely that such claims could be made

---

[138] 'Do we not have the right to lead about a sister wife in the same way as the other apostles and the brothers of the LORD and Cephas?' The term 'sister wife' probably means a wife who is a believer.

[139] Some scholars have therefore preferred to look at Petrine influences in the early church, as in Terence V. Smith, *Petrine Controversies in Early Christianity: Attitudes towards Peter in Christian Writings of the First Two Centuries* (Tübingen: Mohr, 1985), or at the different ways that Peter was presented in the early literature, as in Christian Grappe, *Images de Pierre aux deux premiers siècles* (Paris: Presses Universitaires de France, 1995).

[140] *Romans* 4.3.

[141] *Adversus Haereses* 3.3.2.

[142] Eusebius *HE* 2.25.8.

without fear of contradiction a hundred years after the death of Peter and Paul.[143]

Further evidence that Peter spent time in Rome is the First Letter of Peter, written to the churches in Asia Minor from Babylon (1 Pet. 5.13), which cannot be anywhere other than Rome.[144] It describes itself as a letter from Peter (1 Pet. 1.1), though it says he has written it through Silvanus (1 Pet. 5.12), which might account for a letter in decent Greek being produced by a Galilean fisherman. Though there are the inevitable and inconclusive arguments about its authorship from different scholars and its Petrine authorship must stand at the very least open to serious doubt, it affords striking evidence that it was assumed in the first century that Peter had been in Rome. Furthermore, there was an early tradition that Mark's Gospel was produced in Rome at the behest of Peter.[145] If that were the case, then Rome would have seen the writing of the first gospel. If that remarkable document, the first attempt to convey the meaning of Jesus's Messiahship in the new form of a gospel, was composed in Rome, it would be powerful testimony to the vigour of the Roman church — before the persecution of 64, or after it.

It was also an early belief that Peter, like Paul, was martyred in Rome. The letter of Clement to the Corinthians says of Peter, as it does of Paul, that he 'bore witness', *marturēsas*, and then went to his appointed place of glory.[146] At the start of the fourth century, Eusebius of Caesarea reported:

> It is said that under [Nero's] reign Paul was beheaded in Rome and that apparently Peter was crucified. This account is confirmed by the naming of the

[143] For full reviews of the evidence, see Oscar Cullmann *Peter, Disciple, Apostle, Martyr: A Historical and Theological Study* (London: SCM, 2nd ed, 1962) and D. W. O'Connor *Peter in Rome: The Literary, Liturgical and Archaeological Evidence* (New York: Columbia University Press, 1969). Nevertheless Peter's visit to Rome and death there are still contested by Michael D. Goulder, 'Did Peter ever go to Rome?' *Scottish Journal of Theology* 57 (2004) pp. 377–96, which provoked a response from Markus Bockmuehl, 'Peter's Death in Rome? Back to Front and Upside Down' *Scottish Journal of Theology* 60 (2007) pp. 1–23.

[144] As used, for instance, in the Book of Revelation: 14.8; 16.19; 17.5; 18.2; 10.21.

[145] Mark ('my son') is mentioned as sending greetings at the end of 1 Peter (5.13). Eusebius *HE* 2.15.2 quotes Clement of Alexandria, writing at the very beginning of the third century, to this effect, though he quotes him also saying that Paul wrote the Letter to the Hebrews in Hebrew and it was translated into Greek by Luke *HE* 6.14.2; he also quotes Papias, writing at the beginning of the second century, to say that Mark was the interpreter of Peter and wrote down accurately but not in order what he could remember of the sayings and deeds of the LORD *HE* 3.39.15.

[146] 1 Clement 5.4.

cemeteries of Peter and of Paul down until today. This is what an ecclesiastic called Gaius, who lived under Zephyrinus, Bishop of the Romans [198–217] ... he said about these places where the holy remains of the aforementioned apostles were buried: 'I can point out the monuments of the apostles. If you want to go to the Vatican or on the road to Ostia, you will find the monuments of those who founded this church.'[147]

The statement about the *tropaion* or monument of Peter on the Vatican received striking archaeological verification from excavations conducted under the present St Peter's Basilica between 1940 and 1949. Directly below the high altar, what was clearly the *tropaion* referred to by Gaius at the start of the third century was found. The whereabouts of Peter's bones, however, remain a matter of dispute.[148]

Closely related to the apocryphal *Acts of Paul* is a similar novella, the *Acts of Peter*,[149] which includes the *Martyrdom of Peter*.[150] These also date from the end of the second century. The *Acts* describe Paul's departure from Rome for Spain, whereupon Simon Magus (Acts 8.9–24) tries to become the main teacher of the Christians, claiming to be the power of God. Peter, in Jerusalem, has a vision of Christ, sending him to Rome. When he gets there, he becomes involved in a magic competition with Simon — Peter makes a dog speak, brings a tuna fish to life and makes an infant speak with a man's voice. The climax comes with a public confrontation in the Forum when Peter raises a young man from the dead and Simon pretends to emulate him but is exposed as having performed a magic trick. Simon flies over the city but Peter brings him down, asking the LORD to let him fall and break his leg in three places, which he does. Peter converts a woman called Xanthippe, the wife of a friend of the emperor called Albinus. Peter exhorts her to chastity and Albinus, angry that she will not sleep with him any more, engineers Peter's death. Warned by Xanthippe, Peter leaves Rome but meets Christ on the road — the Quo Vadis incident. Peter returns to face martyrdom and is sentenced to be crucified for 'godlessness'. He asks to be crucified upside down and is then buried in a converted senator's marble

[147] *HE* 2.25.5–7.

[148] J. M. C. Toynbee and J. B. Ward-Perkins *The Shrine of St Peter and the Vatican Excavations* (London: Longmans and Green, 1956).

[149] Elliott *Apocryphal New Testament* pp. 399–426; for thorough studies of the history of these texts, see Jan N. Bremmer, *The Apocryphal Acts of Peter: Magic, Miracles and Gnosticism* (Leuven: Peeters, 1998) and Christine M. Thomas *The Acts of Peter, Gospel Literature, and the Ancient Novel* (Oxford: OUP, 2003).

[150] Elliott *Apocryphal New Testament* pp. 421–26.

tomb. Nero is angry when he hears of the execution. Though much of the story told by the *Acts of Peter* is quite fantastical, it might contain a kernel of truth.

That Peter was crucified is not inherently unlikely. It was a common enough form of execution for slaves and non-Romans. John's Gospel records Jesus predicting Peter's death in terms that have often been read as a reference to crucifixion (Jn. 21.18). Writing shortly after 200, Tertullian spoke of the happy church of Rome on which the apostles poured out the whole of their teaching in their blood, with Peter suffering a passion like Christ's and Paul being crowned with the death of John the Baptist (i.e. crucifixion and beheading). Unfortunately, he rather spoils this elegant account by then referring to the legend of the apostle John's painless immersion in boiling oil in Rome.[151] That Peter was crucified upside down must remain open to doubt. The *Martyrdom* says that he asked to be crucified upside down but the descripion of the burial leaves the reader uncertain of its reliability. It says that he was buried in a senator's marble tomb — echoing the burial of Christ in the tomb of Nicodemus — but, not only does that lack plausibility, it stands in apparent contradiction to the archaeological evidence of the Vatican excavation. Eusebius quotes Origen (c 230) to say that Peter was crucified upside down in Rome,[152] but it cannot be ruled out that Origen derived this from an apocryphal source such as the *Martyrdom*. There is nothing implausible about the story but the evidence for it is not compelling.

Several other points about the *Acts of Peter* are of interest and might claim some historical plausibility. Peter's visit to Rome is located between Paul's departure for Spain and Paul's own eventual death, which is not referred to. Peter's death is ascribed to the reign of Nero but not linked to the persecution of Christians in 64 or even to Nero himself. Readers of the *Acts of Paul* and the *Acts of Peter* would therefore find a picture in which Paul was released from prison and went off on his long-hoped for missionary journey to Spain; in his absence, the Roman church needed help and was visited by Peter, who was executed there. Paul later returned and was also executed, though once again not in the persecution of 64.

Though the evidence is fragmentary, it does make Peter's having been in Rome and dying there look a virtual certainty. What remains

---

[151] *De Praescriptione Haereticorum* 36; he offers a similarly elegant reference to their deaths by crucifixion and decapitation about ten years later in *Scorpiace* 15.

[152] *HE* 3.1.2.

perplexing is his motive for going to Rome. The *Acts of Peter* is unusual in offering one: to rescue the Roman church in Paul's absence by doing battle with Simon Magus. This is interesting because it clearly indicates that the historical memory of Peter's aims in going to Rome had been lost. Whatever they were, they did not fit into the expectations and assumptions of the late second century. The other late-second century claim (found in Irenaeus,[153]), that Peter went to Rome to found the church there, can be discounted. Irenaeus also describes Paul as the founder of the Roman church, but he plainly did not found the church to which he addressed his letter. It is extremely unlikely that Peter had been to Rome before Paul's letter. Paul does refer to not wanting to build on someone else's foundations in Rome (Rom. 15.20) but he could not have written to the Romans without making any reference to Peter if their church had been founded by him and, above all, if Peter was either still with them in 55 or 56 or else had been martyred by then. It therefore seems very likely that Peter went to Rome after Paul had been taken there as a prisoner in about 60.

Two obvious possible motives for Peter's visit might be considered. He might have journeyed to Rome in the aftermath of the persecution of 64 in order to bring comfort or even effectively re-found the church. That could explain the belief that he was the church's founder reported by Irenaeus and in all tradition afterwards. The other is that, as the *Acts of Peter* indicate, he went to resolve a crisis in the Roman church following the departure (or death) of Paul. The crisis would have to be one that lapsed from later memory. The most plausible candidate for such a crisis would have been continuing disputes between Law-observant Jewish Christians and Christians who did not observe the Law. Paul addressed the issue in an irenic spirit in the Letter to the Romans. Perhaps he revealed his true feelings in his letter to the Philippians in a passage which might say as much about his situation in Rome (assuming the letter was written in Rome) as the situation of his correspondents in Philippi:

> Beware of the dogs, beware of the evil workers, beware of the mutilation. For we are the circumcision, the worshippers of the Spirit of God and the ones who boast in Christ Jesus and do not trust in the flesh. If anyone else has reason to trust in the flesh, I have more: circumcised on the eighth day, of the people of Israel, of the tribe of Benjamin, a Hebrew of Hebrew parents; as to the Law, a Pharisee; as to zeal, a persecutor of the church; as to righteousness under the Law, blameless. (Phil. 3.2–6).

---

[153] *Adv. Haer* 3.3.2.

The stinging personal tone of the letter could easily be read as the voice of disappointment, of a man who felt slighted by Jewish Christians in Rome rejecting his authority and adopting a holier-than-thou attitude towards him. If Paul's imprisonment in Rome only worsened relations between Christians who kept the Law and those who did not, a further intervention after his death or departure, a visit from Peter, would make sense. Peter had already clashed with Paul on Jewish observance in an incident in Antioch of which we only have Paul's version of what took place (Gal. 2.11–14). Peter might have gone to Rome to mediate in a dispute that Paul's Letter to the Romans had failed to resolve and which his visit had perhaps exacerbated. It was a dispute that late-second century Christians would have found perplexing and a conflict between the apostles that they would have chosen to forget.

THE PERSECUTION OF 64 AND ITS AFTERMATH

On 19 July 64, a conflagration broke out in Rome which blazed for nine days and destroyed a quarter of the city. People at the time and historians later blamed the emperor Nero for deliberately starting the fire to clear the centre of the city for his own building projects.[154] According to Tacitus, writing in about 120, Nero alighted upon the Christians as a scapegoat:

> In order to suppress the rumour, Nero falsely blamed[155] the people, detested for their abominable crimes, who were called Christians by the populace and inflicted exquisite tortures on them. Christus, after whom they were named, suffered the extreme penalty at the hands of the procurator Pontius Pilate when Tiberius was emperor. Though repressed for a time, this pernicious superstition broke out again, not only in Judaea, the origin of its evil, but also in Rome to which very sort of crime and evil activity flows from everywhere else and is practised. Accordingly, they first arrested those who pleaded guilty; then a large number denounced by them were convicted, not so much for the crime of incendiarism than for hatred of the human race. Various kinds of mockery were added to their deaths: covered with the skins of beasts, they were executed by being ripped to death by dogs or fixed to crosses or by being set on fire so that when daylight failed they burned to serve as torches in the night. Nero offered his gardens for the spectacle and he gave circus games, mixing with the people dressed as a charioteer or standing up in a chariot. Hence, even against criminals who deserved the extreme penalty, there arose a feeling of

---

[154] Tacitus *Ann.* 15.38–44; Suetonius *Nero* 38; Dio Cassius *Rom. Hist.* 62.16–8.

[155] *subdidit reos* carries the sense in Tacitus not just of putting the blame on someone but of doing so falsely — cf. *Ann.* 1.6.3; 1.39.3.

compassion; for it was not for the public good but for one man's cruelty that they had been destroyed.[156]

This was the fate of many of those named by Paul at the end of his letter.

For Nero to have made the Christians scapegoats, they needed to be a recognisable and detestable group.[157] Though their origins in Judaea were known, they were not in any way confused with Jews; they were separate and had a distinct identity. They are simply called a *superstitio*, which really means 'alien religion', rather than being described as a Jewish sect. The same term is used in Suetonius's brief notice of the persecution, which features in a list of abuses that Nero put down between the sale of cooked food in taverns and the rowdy behaviour of charioteers. Suetonius calls them 'a race of men of a new and malevolent *superstitio*'.[158] Tacitus said that in addition to 'hatred of the human race', a charge reminiscent of his attack on Jewish insularity,[159] they were detested on account of their 'abominable crimes' (*flagitia*); they were a 'pernicious superstition' (*exitiabilis superstitio*). It is hardly likely that the Christians were known and hated across the vast city of Rome; it is more likely that, when Nero chose them as his scapegoats, their behaviour was labelled as abominable and rumours were circulated against them. Had they been regarded as a group of Jews, the rumours would either have built upon suspicions that already existed about Jewish separatism or else, to avoid the risk of a pogrom, would have emphasised how unlike their co-religionists they were. Instead, they were described as a new and dangerous religion. Furthermore, Jews themselves do not seem to have regarded them as fellow members of the people of Israel. Josephus's mission to intercede on behalf of the Jewish priests took place in the year of the fire. He successfully lobbied Nero's wife, Poppaea Sabina, who was a Godfearer, to gain their release.[160] Had she thought of the Christians as Jews, she might have sought to influence Nero on their behalf too.

To have suited Nero's purposes as scapegoats, the Christians would also have had to be numerous enough to provide a spectacle.

---

[156] *Ann.* 15.44.

[157] Mason *Josephus, Judea and Christian Origins* pp. 313–14 suggests that it was Poppaea who drew Nero's attention to the Christians; there is of course no evidence that she knew of their existence.

[158] *Nero* 16.2.

[159] *Hist.* 5.5.

[160] *Life* 16.

Their numbers, however, need not be exaggerated. Tacitus speaks of *multitudo ingens*, which might be translated as 'an immense multitude', but the phrase is a rhetorical flourish. He uses a similar expression elsewhere, *immensa strages*,[161] when he is talking of about twenty executions in one day. It therefore means no more than 'a large number', to be counted by the dozen rather than in the hundreds. This means that in 64 the Christians constituted an easily defined group, well aware of their own identity, distinct from the Jewish community, significant but not vast in numbers.

Christians were crucified. This indicates that they did not enjoy the full rights of Roman citizens. Migrants such as Aquila and Priscilla, even though comfortably bourgeois, would have been subject to that penalty, as would have slaves or perhaps informally manumitted ex-slaves. They were also burned, the penalty for arson. Tacitus's text is unclear whether they were crucified and then burned or whether these, along with being torn apart by dogs, were different kinds of death. If the latter is accepted as the more likely reading, then the persecution went beyond those convicted of arson to include other Christians whose crime was simply the fact of belonging to such an abominable new *superstitio*.

Not only is the persecution evidence of the Christians being a discrete, recognizable group in 64, its consequences must also have made them feel more self-contained and isolated. The full cruelty of the Roman state distinguished between the Jews who had accepted Christ as Messiah and the vast majority who had not. Jewish Christians were torn in a horrific and searing way from a Jewish community in Rome which prided itself on its tranquillity. The name of Christian was vilified, associated with secret abominations, and non-Christian Jews were more likely than ever to distance themselves from a hated and alien group. Gentile Christians must have had exactly the same experience of alienation from their pagan friends and neighbours. In other words, this event was a huge disruption in the development of the early Christian community, leaving a shattered remnant whose sense of self-contained identity, separate from Judaism and hated by the non-Christian world, must have been profoundly deepened.

It is impossible to estimate the damage done to the Roman church. It is possible that most of the Christians were killed — the authorities were torturing names out of the Christians whom they arrested and it is more than likely that Nero wanted as big a spectacle as his police

---

[161] *Ann.* 6.19.2 cf. *Hist.* 1.47.2.

could provide. They certainly vanished from the public view, despite the limelight shed on them by Nero's vicious smear campaign. It is hardly likely that they suddenly became the beneficiaries of a new tolerance after their terrible sufferings. When Tacitus spoke of popular sympathy for them, he was not really commenting on the public's attitude to the Christians but rather their hostile attitude to Nero. The silence of Tacitus about the Christians after Nero is significant.

Equally telling is the reticence shown by Josephus about Christianity. He moved to Rome in the aftermath of the Jewish War of 66–73 and there he published his *Jewish War* between 75 and 79 and later his *Antiquities of the Jews* in 93 or 94. A reference to Jesus as the Messiah and his resurrection in the eighteenth book of the *Antiquities* has long been recognised as, at least in part, a later Christian interpolation.[162] In the last book of the *Antiquities*, there is a brief reference to the execution of the apostle James under Agrippa I,[163] which is usually regarded as authentic, though it does presuppose that the reader has already heard of Jesus the Messiah. Otherwise, in his immensely detailed account of the religion and politics of Judaea, he makes no reference at all to Christians. Various explanations might be offered — his disdain for Christianity, the obscurity of Christianity, the gulf between Christians and Jews so that he did not really see them as a Jewish movement.[164] Given Josephus's residence in Rome, it is more than likely that Josephus's view of, or ignorance about, Christians was heavily coloured by the obscurity and isolation of the Roman Christian community.

The earliest evidence we have of the Roman Christians after Nero is two texts, the letter written from the Roman church to the Corinthian church known as *1 Clement* and a collection of strange treatises called the *Shepherd of Hermas*. They are commonly dated c 96 and c 140 respectively, but neither date is secure and either could have been written anywhere between 70 and 140.[165] The common view that *1 Clement* was written in about 96 depends on the fact that the deaths

---

[162] *AJ* 18.63–64: it is commonly called the *Testimonium Flavianum* from his name, Flavius Josephus.

[163] *AJ* 20.200.

[164] See James Carleton-Paget, 'Some Observations on Josephus and Christianity' *JTS* 52 (2001) pp. 539–624.

[165] See Andrew Gregory, 'Disturbing Trajectories: *1 Clement*, the *Shepherd of Hermas* and the Development of Early Roman Christianity' in Peter Oakes (ed), *Rome in the Bible and the Early Church* (Carlisle: Paternoster Press, 2002) pp. 142–66.

of Peter and Paul are not reported as though by eyewitnesses; but on
the other hand they are described as 'champions who lived in recent
times'.[166] Furthermore, the presbyters installed by the apostles have
died;[167] but it is perhaps idle to speculate how long presbyters might
live after their appointment. The church at Corinth is described as
ancient;[168] but 'ancient' might better be translated as going back to
the beginning, the *archē*, of Paul's preaching. The emissaries sent
from Rome to Corinth are described as living blamelessly from youth
to old age;[169] but does that mean that they lived from youth to old
age as Christians? The letter opens with an excuse for the delay in
commenting on the events in Corinth it addresses, explaining that
'sudden and repeated misfortunes and calamities' have prevented
them, which is usually taken as evidence for a date soon after 96;[170]
but the words for misfortunes (*sumphoras*) and calamities (*periptōseis*)
might also be translated 'events and happenings' and furthermore
was the execution of Flavius Clemens by Domitian in 95 an anti-
Christian or an anti-Jewish act?[171]

The dating of the *Shepherd of Hermas* depends on two pieces of
evidence, one internal and the other external. The internal evidence
is a reference to Clement, who will send a book to the cities abroad,
for that is his job.[172] The problem, of course, is determining who
Clement was — it was a very common name — and, of the various
candidates, the author of *1 Clement* is in fact anonymous.[173] The
external evidence is a document of uncertain date known as the
Muratorian Fragment which says that Hermas was the brother of Pius,
the bishop of Rome c 142–c 155.

What is clear in both works is that the church has recovered from
the trials of 64. The earlier the texts are dated, then presumably the

---

[166] *1 Clement* 5.1.

[167] *1 Clem.* 44.5.

[168] *1 Clem.* 47.6.

[169] *1 Clem.* 63.3.

[170] *1 Clem.* 1.1.

[171] Dio Cassius *Rom. Hist.* 67.14.1–2 says Clemens and his wife had drifted into Jewish
ways; Eusebius *HE* 3.17 says Domitian was a great persecutor of the Christians but
does not give any specific date or Clemens as an example. He does say that Domitilla,
Clemens's niece, was exiled for being a Christian to the island of Pontia (3.18),
whereas Dio Cassius says that Domitilla, Clemens's wife, was exiled to the neighbouring island of Pandateria for Judaising tendencies.

[172] *Visions* 2.4.3.

[173] Clement is identified as the bishop of Rome and author of the letter by Eusebius
HE 3.15–16, but the letter itself is anonymous.

less the church in Rome is thought to have suffered. The confident tone of *1 Clement* is very striking. Its purpose[174] is to address a crisis in the Corinthian church where their presbyters have been deposed.[175] Envoys have been sent from the Roman church to mediate in the dispute[176] and the letter is an attempt to persuade the Corinthians to return to harmony and peace. This is evidence both of growing institutionalisation of the Roman and Corinthian churches and, more significantly, of confidence and strength on the Roman side. Its author is clearly educated and though the letter seems shapeless on first reading it does in fact divide into parts, with sections 1–39 dealing with the general principles of reconciliation and harmony and 40–65 addressing the dispute in Corinth. It is striking that it shows no trace of internal disputes between Jewish and gentile Christians or any conflict between Judaism and Christianity. In *1 Clement*, Christianity has effectively appropriated the Jewish scriptures (about a quarter of the text is made up of quotations from the Greek translation of the Old Testament, the Septuagint) and has laid its claim to be the true heir to the covenant. The letter can, for instance, refer calmly to the example of the Temple priests without seeing a reference to the Temple as being polemically charged.[177] The examples it places before its readers are figures such as Abraham, Lot and Rahab[178] or Elijah, Elisha, Ezekiel, Job, Moses and David[179] or Daniel and the three young men in the fiery furnace.[180]

The *Shepherd of Hermas*[181] is a strangely rambling and apparently shapeless book whose oddness might best be accounted for by seeing it as a text still shaped by the demands of original oral performance.[182] It is divided up into three sections: five Visions, twelve commandments or Mandates and ten parables or Similitudes. After the first four Visions, which have an apocalyptic or revelatory character, it is

---

[174] The best commentary is Horacio E. Lona (ed), *Der erste Clemensbrief* (Göttingen: Vandenhoek & Ruprecht, 1998); see also Caragounis 'The Development of the Roman Church' in Donfried and Richardson *Judaism and Christianity* pp. 267–77.

[175] *1 Clem.* 3.3; 44.6; 47.6.

[176] *1 Clem.* 63.3; 65.1.

[177] *1 Clem.* 40.1–5.

[178] *1 Clem.* 10–12.

[179] *1 Clem.* 17–18.

[180] *1 Clem.* 45.

[181] The best commentary is Carolyn Osiek, *The Shepherd of Hermas: A Commentary* (Hermeneia; Minneapolis: Fortress, 1999).

[182] See Carolyn Osiek, 'The Oral World of Early Christianity in Rome: The Case of Hermas' in Donfried and Richardson *Judaism and Christianity* pp. 151–72.

a book of allegories, which make it an absorbing read for some and a frustrating one for others. It was enormously popular in the early centuries of Christianity. Hermas himself had been a slave, bought in Rome but then freed.[183] He became a Christian but was very unhappy with himself and his family and having bought some land he came into conflict with the social obligations involved in his business and possessions. A major theme of the work is the question of repentance (the word *metanoia* — repentance — and the verb *metanoiein* occur 156 times in the text). The text seems to contradict itself about whether Christians can be forgiven for post-baptismal sin. In one place, it says that such forgiveness can be received, but only once;[184] elsewhere, it suggests that only those newly called but not yet baptised can be forgiven and make a fresh start.[185] It might be better to translate *metanoia* in the text as 'conversion' rather than 'repentance'. Perhaps a more pressing concern to the early readers of the *Shepherd* was the problems of wealth and poverty and the co-existence of rich and poor in the one community.[186] As in *1 Clement*, the Jewish Law is not an issue in the *Shepherd of Hermas*; Jews are never mentioned. The Twelve Tribes are interpreted as twelve divisions of the human race.[187] The earlier the texts are dated, then the earlier a definitive split between Christianity and Judaism in Rome is envisaged.

What is common to both *1 Clement* and the *Shepherd of Hermas* is an interest in the church. In *1 Clement*, the Roman community is plainly one church and, in a sense, is also one church with the Corinthians. Behind the immediate concern with the questions about institutional authority raised by the deposition of the presbyters in Corinth, there is a concept of church order based on the order of the cosmos, an idea which derived more from Hellenistic Judaism than Stoicism.[188] In the *Shepherd of Hermas*, there is a sense of the church as the first of God's creatures, an old woman because she is older than the cosmos,[189] but she becomes a young woman because she is pure.[190] The church is also a tower,[191] the

---

[183] *Visions* 1.1.1.

[184] *Vis.* 2.2.4–5.

[185] *Mandates* 4.3.1–7.

[186] Carolyn Osiek, *Rich and Poor in the Shepherd of Hermas: An Exegetical-Social Investigation* (Washington DC: Catholic Biblical Association, 1983).

[187] *Similitudes* 9.17.

[188] *1 Clem.* 20.

[189] *Vis.* 2.4.1.

[190] *Vis.* 3.10–13.

[191] *Vis.* 3.3.2–5.

building of which is a major theme of the book. It is founded on Christ but continues to be built until Christ's return and the consummation of all things.

THE PARTING OF THE WAYS

There has been an extensive debate about how and when Christians ceased to think of themselves or to be thought of by others as a Jewish sect. The old view that Judaism was moribund and easily supplanted by the new vigorous Christian church has long been displaced by the recognition of the energy and creativity and religious devotion of Judaism in the generations before and after the time of Jesus. It became possible to see the first and second centuries as an age of competition and interaction between two claimants to be the true inheritors of the covenant — Jews and Christians.[192] This gave rise to an intense investigation of the process by which Christians and Jews parted, both theologically[193] and socially and historically.[194] This has raised questions about Jewish and Christian self-definition; about the best terminology to use to describe Jews and Christians and, above all Jewish Christians or Christian Jews; about whether the split should be seen as competition or complex interaction; about whether Judaism and Christianity should be considered in a parent-child relationship or rather should be seen as siblings emerging from the aftermath of the destruction of the Temple and the political aspirations of Judaism in the great wars of 66–73 and 132–5. The debate continues and no consensus had yet emerged.[195]

[192] Marcel Simon, *Verus Israel: A Study of the Relations between Christians and Jews in the Roman Empire (135–425)* (Henry McKeating (trans); Littman Library of Jewish Civilization; Oxford: Litman Library, 1986), a work which originally appeared in French in 1948.

[193] James D. G. Dunn, *The Parting of the Ways between Christianity and Judaism and their Significance for the Character of Christianity* (London: SCM, 1991) traces the points of doctrinal disagreement and dates a final split to about 135.

[194] James D. G. Dunn, *Jews and Christians: the Parting of the Ways, 70–135 CE* (Tübingen, Mohr, 1992).

[195] From a large and growing bibliography, the following represent various trends of thought: Miriam Taylor, *Anti-Judaism and Early Christian Identity: A Critique of the Scholarly Consensus* (Leiden: Brill, 1995); William Horbury, *Jews and Christians in Conflict and Controversy* (Edinburgh: T&T Clark, 1998); Adam H. Becker and Annette Yoshiko Reed (eds), *The Ways that Never Parted: Jews and Christians in Late Antiquity and the Early Middle Ages* (Tübingen: Mohr Siebeck, 2003); Daniel Boyarin, *Border Lines: the Partition of Judaeo-Christianity* (Philadelphia: University of Pennsylvania Press, 2004); Judith Lieu, *Christian Identity in the Jewish and Graeco-Roman World* (Oxford: OUP, 2004); Dan Jaffé, *Le Judaisme et l'avènement du Christianisme: Orthodoxie et héterodoxie dans la littérature talmudique Ier — IIe siècle* (Paris: Cerf, 2005).

Rome provides an unusual example of what was clearly a complex process that happened in different ways and at different speeds across the immensity of the Roman world.[196] More is known about the Jews and early Christians there than in most places; at the same time, neither the Roman Jews nor the early Roman Christians were necessarily typical of other cities. The Jews were diverse, continually reinforced by fresh migration into the city, a large community of somewhere between twenty and forty thousand people, but at their core was a well-established and prosperous community which could even reach into the houses and palaces of the Roman upper classes. They were not politicised, either in the sense of sharing the political aspirations for Israel that disturbed and divided Jews in Judaea, Egypt and the Middle East in the first and second centuries or in the sense that they organised themselves with an overarching political structure that expressed some degree of national autonomy. They were slow to develop synagogue attendance as a characteristic feature of their identity. Instead, Judaism for them was a religion of fidelity to the covenant observed by circumcision and legal observance, prayer in the home, keeping the Sabbath and the dietary laws, and celebrating Passover and the other feasts.

The Christians were regarded as Jews in 49, when Claudius expelled those Jews who were constantly making disturbances on account of Chrestus, Christ. By 64, they were singled out as scapegoats for the fire in Rome and regarded as a new and perverse alien religion. Light is shed on the intervening fifteen years by Paul's Letter to the Romans, which addresses tensions between Christians who observe the dietary regulations of the Jewish Law and consequently have limited fellowship with those who do not. It is plausible to say that the Christians who observed the Law had already become detached from the great majority of the Jewish community after the 49 expulsion while gentile Christians had grown in numbers and confidence by the time Paul wrote in about 55 or 56. The description of Paul's arrival in Rome in the Acts of the Apostles suggests that the Jewish community knew little of Christianity and that the Jews were not likely to be the main source of new recruits to belief in Jesus as the Messiah. The

---

[196] Stephen Spence, *The Parting of the Ways: The Roman Church as a Case Study* (Leuven: Peeters, 2004) reviews all the evidence and argues that the split happened earlier in Rome than elsewhere; see also James C. Walters, 'Romans, Jews and Christians: The Impact of the Romans on Jewish/Christian Relations in First-Century Rome' in Donfried and Richardson *Judaism and Christianity* pp. 175–95.

persecution of 64 probably erased many of the people and much of the achievement of the first generation of Christians and it both revealed the degree to which Christianity was divorced from the Jewish community and completed the process of the parting of the ways.

Chapter 2

COMMUNITY

Without the Jewish Law to guide them, Roman Christians in the second and early third centuries struggled not only to work out how their community should live and worship but what they should believe. An astonishing variety of proposals for the construction and definition of Christianity could be heard in Rome in the middle decades of the second century — a sign of the vitality of Christianity in the biggest and most diverse city in the Roman world. It was a propitious time for a new religion to find its way. Gibbon famously observed that 'if a man were called to fix the period in the history of the world during which the condition of the human race was most happy and prosperous, he would, without hesitation, name that which elapsed from the death of Domitian to the accession of Commodus'. Between Domitian's death in 96 and Commodus's accession in 180, the empire was ruled by men of imperishable eminence: Trajan, Hadrian, Antoninus Pius, Marcus Aurelius. The gradual shift from Rome, the city-state governing its empire, to the empire being itself the state with Rome as its capital, was apparent in the background of the men who ruled it. The early emperors from Augustus to Nero had been members of the very grandest families of the ancient Roman nobility. The Flavians, Vespasian and his two sons Titus and Domitian, came from the Italian bourgeoisie. Now, with Trajan, Hadrian and the Antonines, the emperors were drawn from the ranks of the Italian gentry settled in Spain and southern Gaul. Between Domitian and Marcus Aurelius, none of these emperors had a son to succeed him; the practice of adopting a successor produced a line of brilliant emperors until Marcus Aurelius was succeeded by his natural son, Commodus. However exaggerated Gibbon's judgment, it was something of a golden age for both Rome and its empire and therefore too for Roman Christianity.

While the parting of the ways forced Christians to re-appraise their relationship with the heritage of Judaism and the scriptures, Christians continued to see themselves as the true Israel, the heirs of all the covenants. With the remarkable and singular exception of Marcion, they sought to define their theology and their morality within the framework they inherited from their Jewish roots. The greatest challenge was the consideration of the identity of Christ which led to a variety of attempts to lay out theologies of creation, revelation and salvation which ultimately depended on differing understandings of God himself. At the same time, they established the authoritative resources of belief, the canon of scripture and the earliest creeds, while also recognising the authority of their own leaders to arbitrate on what was authentic doctrine and what was unacceptable. The practices and worship of the Christian community took a settled and regular shape while the growth in their numbers forced them to reconsider their view of human frailty and the possibility of the church being made up of sinners as well as saints. And nowhere played a greater part in this making of Christianity than Rome.

Marcion

It seems likely that the Christian Church in Rome became divorced from the Jewish community within decades of the Gospel first being preached in the city. The question of the relationship of Christians to the Old Testament,[1] however, remained very perplexing. Jesus had been an observant Jew, but what of his followers? It was not too difficult to agree that gentile Christians were not bound by the ritual precepts of the Jewish Law; the relevance to Christianity of large parts of the Old Testament, therefore, was open to doubt. While Christians might have seen Noah, Abraham, Moses, David and a host of other figures from the Old Testament as precursors of Christ, it was less easy to evaluate the significance of the detailed legislation governing food, Temple worship or the Sabbath. Jesus himself, in the Sermon on the Mount, contrasted his teaching with that of the Old Testament Law, culminating in: 'You have heard how it was said, "Love your neighbour and hate your enemy." But I say this to you, "Love your enemies."' (Mt 5.20–48). Of course, the Old Testament never commands people to hate their enemies but many Christians

---

[1] The terms Old and New Testament are used here for convenience; they are not intended to refer to the specific collections of books now found in bibles but more generally to the Jewish tradition before Jesus and the Christian Church and its scriptures. They were not terms used in the second century.

felt bound to believe that Christ not only fulfilled but in some sense superseded the teaching of the Old Testament.

Worse than that, it is not difficult to find places in the Old Testament which seem to present God as a tribal warlord, encouraging his people to fight and destroy their enemies. There are passages where God promises to reward his people with the land of their enemies if they will follow his instructions to annihilate them and drive them out. This is a God who seems to have a vividly disagreeable personality — angry, vengeful and demanding. Though these passages could be counterbalanced by vast numbers of other places where God is seen as loving and forgiving, they were sufficiently striking to present the Christian reader with an acute problem. This warlike and vengeful God seems very different from the God of the New Testament, the God who calls on people to love their enemies and forgive even those who persecute them. The New Testament God seeks to heal and comfort all who suffer and, in Christ, himself suffers for the sins of others.

The interpretation of the Hebrew Bible was not straightforward for Jews either. After the fall of the Temple in 70 and with the end of the last realistic hope of creating a sovereign Jewish state with the failure of the Bar Kokhba revolt in 135, Judaism was forced to re-define itself. How were all the passages about the Temple and legislation concerning sacrifice and the priesthood to be interpreted? What of all the promises of the land and a kingdom? Judaism had to re-read its sacred scriptures in a new way. For Christians, the problem went even deeper. They faced a fundamental question about the relationship between the covenants of the Old Testament and the new covenant that they believed had been made in Christ.

Christians offered various strategies to cope with this tension between the Old and New Testaments but none was as radical as Marcion. A ship owner from Pontus on the shores of the Black Sea, he settled in Rome in about the year 140. He was a major donor to the Roman Church, giving them the handsome sum of 200,000 sesterces,[2] but they expelled him for heresy and gave him his money back. It is interesting that they kept a document in which he had stated his earlier orthodox beliefs.[3] His expulsion can probably be dated to the summer of 144.[4] Later stories blackened his character.

---

[2] Tertullian *De Praescriptione Haereticorum* 30.

[3] Tertullian *De Carne Christi* 2.4; *Adversus Marcionem* 1.1.6; 4.4.3.

[4] *Adv. Marc.* 1.19.2.

Writing over two centuries later, in the late 370s, the great student of all the heresies of the early Church, Epiphanius of Salamis, said that Marcion had been the son of the Bishop of Sinope in Pontus and that his father had excommunicated and expelled him from the church for seducing a virgin. He had then gone to Rome to seek restitution of his position from the presbyters there and had even been ambitious to become the bishop of the church there himself, but was rejected and so instead became a heretic.[5] This sounds like a convoluted and confused version of the earlier simpler account. It would have been very tempting for his contemporaries and early critics to have accused him of immorality but none of them did so; significantly, Tertullian made a similar allegation against Marcion's follower Apelles but not against Marcion himself.[6] But Epiphanius does give an account of Marcion debating with the presbyters and arguing about the interpretation of the Gospel which has the ring of authenticity, largely because Epiphanius could scarcely have invented a scene that fitted so well the situation of the Roman church in the 140s but not the church of his own day over two centuries later.[7]

The text which Epiphanius claims was debated by Marcion and the presbyters was the passage where Jesus says that new wine should not be put into old wineskins or a patch of new cloth onto an old garment (Mt 9.16–17). This was probably an important passage for Marcion[8] and it need cause little surprise that it should have been central to his argument with the leaders of the Roman church. It touches precisely on the relationship of old and new in Christianity, of the Old and New Testaments. What was Marcion's view of the issue?

Marcion simply dismissed the Old Testament. It had, according to him, no bearing on Christianity which was an entirely fresh revelation of the hitherto unknown God of Love[9] who, in Christ his Son, reveals the inadequacy of the Law[10] and leads people away from fear.[11] In other words, he set the Old and New Testaments against each other in the starkest possible terms. It was not that the New Testament completed

---

[5] *Panarion* 42.1.7–8.

[6] *De Praescr Haer* 30.

[7] *Pan.* 42.2.1–8; for a review of the evidence concerning Marcion's life, see Sebastian Moll 'Three against Tertullian: the Second Tradition about Marcion's Life' *JTS* 59 (2008) pp. 169–80.

[8] *Adv. Marc.* 3.15.5; 4.11.9.

[9] *Adv. Marc.* 3.20.2.

[10] *Adv. Marc.* 5.13.14.

[11] *Adv. Marc.* 1.27.3.

the Old or even supplanted the Old: the Old Testament was simply bad news. The simplest way of making this assertion would have been to set aside the Old Testament as a false record of the imagined revelations of God. Marcion could have said that, though the Jews thought they were God's chosen people and that he had revealed himself to them through the ages and that their scriptures recorded their relationship with God, they were wrong. Christians were used to saying that the Jews were wrong in their interpretation of the scriptures and their claim still to be God's people, so it would not have been too surprising to have claimed that they had been wrong in the past too, that they had never been God's people and their accounts of God's dealings with them were spurious. What is perhaps most remarkable about Marcion is that this is not the way he chose to dismiss the Old Testament.

Marcion acknowledged that the Old Testament was a true revelation. What he denied was that it was a revelation of the God of the New Testament. The God of the Jews was real but he was not the God made manifest in Christ. He was the creator of the universe, the lawgiver, the God worshipped by the Jews and revealed to the prophets, but he was not the God of love. In other words, in order to dismiss the Old Testament, Marcion created for himself a new problem which would have massive repercussions. Effectively, he posited two Gods, the God of the Old Testament and the God of the New. Why did he make such a radical proposal?

It seems that, despite the split with Judaism, belief in the veracity of the Old Testament was unchallengeable in the Roman church. It is striking that, despite condemning the Old Testament, Marcion had quite a good knowledge of the text: his own familiarity with it and respect for it are evidence of the role it played in the Christianity of the 140s. He read it in a plain, literal way — too literally for some of his critics.[12] He did not question its veracity but he did question its value. Marcion appears to have drawn the idea that the Old Testament God is not the same as the God of the New Testament from another teacher who was active in Rome in the late 130s, called Cerdo.[13] Cerdo, according to Irenaeus, had held that 'the God proclaimed by the Law and the Prophets is not the Father of Our LORD Jesus Christ, for the one is known and the other is unknown, the one is just and the other is good.'[14] Irenaeus said that

---

[12] For instance, *Adv. Marc.* 5.18.

[13] Irenaeus *Adv. Haer* 1.27.1; Tetullian *Adv. Marc* 1.2.3; 1.22.10; 4.17.11; Hippolytus *Refutatio omnium Haeresium* 7.37.

[14] *Adv. Haer* 1.27.1.

Cerdo, however, was a wavering and uncertain figure whom the Church found difficult to evaluate:

> Cerdo, the predecessor of Marcion, also lived under Hyginus who was the eighth bishop. He repeatedly came back to the church, doing public penance; now teaching in secret, then doing penance, then again convicted of error and leaving the community of the brothers.[15]

Perhaps Cerdo's vacillations reveal too some degree of uncertainty on the part of the church leadership in the 130s about how to describe the relationship of the Old and New Testaments. At first, there seems to have been similar uncertainty about Marcion's views. According to Tertullian, Marcion was also ejected from the church several times.[16] Unlike Cerdo, however, he became the object of a series of attacks from the major writers of the later second and early third centuries — Justin, Irenaeus, Tetullian and Hippolytus. He was clearly regarded as an enormous threat, perhaps the most significant danger to the church of the second century. Irenaeus recorded an encounter between the venerable Polycarp of Smyrna and Marcion in Rome, when the latter called on Polycarp to acknowledge him; Polycarp replied, 'I do acknowledge you, as the first-born of Satan.'[17] Clement of Alexandria called him 'the colossus who fights against God'.[18] This was because, unlike Cerdo, his split became decisive. He gathered followers and published his vision of Christianity in two books — an edition of the New Testament, carefully selected to omit all reference to the Old, and a volume called the *Antitheses* in which he set out texts from the New Testament alongside contrasting passages from the Old.

The real problem was that Marcion's two Gods had nothing or little to do with each other. It can be argued that what Marcion was in fact doing was dividing divine justice from divine mercy, placing them in sharp opposition, though without denying that there is goodness in the creator or justice in the redeemer. On this account, it is not so much that Marcion believed in two Gods as that he stressed the tension between two aspects of God.[19] Among his early critics, Irenaeus, in

---

[15] *Adv. Haer* 3.4.3.

[16] *De Praescr Haer* 30.

[17] *Adv. Haer* 3.3.4.

[18] *Stromata* 3.25.2.

[19] This is claimed by Barbara Aland, 'Sünde und Erlösung bei Marcion und die Konsequenz für die sog. Beiden Götter Marcions' in Gerhard May and Katharina Greschat (eds), *Marcion und Seine Kirchengeschichtliche Wirkung: Marcion and his Impact on Church History* (Texte und Untersuchungen zur Geschichte der altchristlichen Literatur, 150; Berlin: W. de Gruyter, 2002) pp. 147–57.

one passage, seems to have recognised that Marcion might have been saying something like this but he insisted that the division between justice and mercy inevitably led away from monotheism.[20] This interpretation of Marcion would claim that he saw the Old Testament as revealing a God of justice who, as the creator, was unintentionally the author of the evil found in an imperfect world.[21] He certainly taught that the Old Testament Law is just and forbids evil,[22] but deplored the way the Old Testament God commands obedience out of fear.[23] He interpreted the text of Is 45.7, 'It is I who create evil things',[24] and Jer 18.11, 'Behold I send evils against you,'[25] as referring to the vengeance of God's justice, not that he was the author of evil itself. The difficulty with the view that Marcion's God of justice and God of love are really only aspects of the one God, however, is not only that Marcion's early critics were unanimous in accusing him of believing in two Gods but that his complete repudiation of the Old Testament indicates that he went far further than presenting a tension between justice and love. He might, for instance, have envisaged two phases of divine revelation — at first God is seen as the lawgiver but then in the New Testament he is seen as the loving redeemer. Alternatively, he might have presented the Old Testament creator and lawgiver as a subordinate agent of the good and loving God of the New Testament. Instead, there is good evidence that Marcion's main concern was to contrast the anger of a demanding lawgiving God with the love of Christ. Denouncing the God of the Old Testament as 'a judge, fierce and warlike',[26] Marcion drew an antithesis not so much between justice and mercy as between anger and love.[27]

Within about fifteen years of his break with the Roman church, Marcion was accused of denying monotheism and thereby denying that the creator is the true God. Writing in Rome in the late 150s, Justin Martyr attacked Marcion in two different passages of his first

---

[20] *Adv. Haer* 3.25.3.

[21] As for example in Irenaeus *Adv. Haer* 1.27.2; Clement of Alexandria *Stromata* 2.32.1.

[22] *Adv. Marc.* 1.27.1.

[23] *Adv. Haer* 1.27.3.

[24] *Adv. Marc.* 1.2; 2.14; 2.24; 4.1.

[25] *Adv. Marc.* 2.24.

[26] *Adv. Marc.* 1.6.1.

[27] Winfrich Löhr 'Did Marcion distinguish between a just god and a good god?' in May and Greschat *Marcion* pp. 131–46 argues that it is not the justice but the vehement anger of the Old Testament God that Marcion rejects.

Apology. He probably also rebutted him at length in a lost treatise against the heretical sects[28] which was probably the work of his against Marcion referred to by Irenaeus.[29] In the first *Apology*, Justin said:

> Marcion, a man from Pontus, who is actually still alive, teaches his followers to believe in another God, greater than the creator. With the help of the demons, he has caused many people of every nation to speak blasphemies, to deny that God is the maker of the universe and to assert that some other greater God has done greater works.[30]

Though the focus and wording of this passage reflects Justin's apologetic concerns,[31] the core of his attack on Marcion is the accusation that he has repudiated monotheism and with it the doctrine of creation. This remained the primary criticism of Marcion in subsequent writers — Irenaeus, writing in the 170s, Tertullian, in the second decade of the next century, and Hippolytus, about ten years after him. Tertullian, a brilliant and prolific Latin writer in North Africa, devoted his longest work to a refutation of Marcion. It was divided into five books, the first of which argued that if there was a God, there could only be one God, while the second identified the maker of the world with the good God. Again, then, Tertullian had claimed that the rejection of monotheism and the doctrine of creation were Marcion's fundamental heresies. Written perhaps in the 220s, the *Refutation of All Heresies* dismissed Marcion as the purveyor of the unacceptable philosophical ideas of Empedocles who claimed there were two causes of all things, strife and love, and who therefore believed that there were two creative principles, two Gods.[32] Though not very illuminating about Marcion, who was not influenced by philosophical ideas, the *Refutation* once more shows that Marcion was understood to have denied monotheism.

Closely following the primary charge that Marcion believed there were two Gods was the claim that he therefore also taught that there were two Christs. Since he accepted that the Old Testament was a true revelation of the lawgiving, creator God worshipped by the Jews, he was obliged to accept that the prophecies it contained of a coming Messiah were also true. But this is not the Christ of the

---

[28] *1 Apol.* 26.7.

[29] *Adv. Haer* 4.6.2.

[30] *1 Apol.* 26.5.

[31] See Sebastian Moll, 'Justin and the Pontic Wolf' in Sara Parvis and Paul Foster (eds), *Justin Martyr and his Worlds* (Minneapolis: Fortress Press, 2007) pp. 145–51 shows how Justin's account of Marcion is slanted to suit his own apologetic concerns.

[32] *Ref.* 7.29–31.

New Testament. As Justin remarked in his second comment about Marcion in the first Apology:

> As we have already said, the demons promoted Marcion of Pontus, who is at this present time teaching people to deny that God is the maker of everything in heaven and on earth and that the Christ predicted by the prophets is his son. He preaches another God besides the creator of everything and another son. Many people have believed in this man as though he was the only one to know the truth and they laugh at us, even though they have no proof of what they say but are snatched away irrationally like lambs by a wolf, becoming the prey of atheistic teaching and of the demons.[33]

Therefore, Justin went on, Marcion held that the Christ predicted by the prophets is the son of the creator while there is another Christ who is the son of the greater God. Here, Marcion was paying due attention to the fact that a number of the Messianic prophecies pointed to a Christ who would restore the Kingdom of Israel, perhaps by force. It is clear in the Gospels that this was the expectation of some of Jesus's first followers. Marcion thus saw the Old Testament God as a warlord and the Messiah prophesied in the Old Testament as a warrior yet to come who would re-establish the kingdom of the Jews.[34] In other words, Marcion had a coherent, distinctive but not wholly indefensible interpretation of the message of the Old Testament. It was challenging enough for Tertullian to devote the third book of his treatise against Marcion to Christology, reviewing the prophecies to argue that the Christ they foretold has come and has been sent by the Creator.

Another dramatic statement that shocked his critics was his claim that the holy men and women of the Old Testament would be damned while the sinners would be saved. He pictured Christ descending to Hell after his crucifixion to rescue the souls who had gone before him. There he envisaged the holy women and men of the Old Covenant who were devoted to the creator lawgiver rejecting Christ while the unjust welcomed him.[35] The division between the saved and the damned seems to be a division between the sovereignty of the two Gods and the two Testaments: Christ does not come to judge but to forgive and thus he will hand over sinners to the Old Testament God for judgment at his second coming.[36]

Marcion, in dismissing the Old Testament (and thereby depriving himself of all its resources for developing a theology of Christ) also

---

[33] *1 Apol.* 58.1–2.
[34] *Adv. Marc.* 3.21–24.
[35] *Adv. Haer* 1.27.3; *Adv. Marc.* 4.9.13–14.
[36] *Adv. Marc.* 1.27.6–28.1; 2.11.3.

faced the task of interpreting the New Testament without recourse to the Old. This obliged him to purge the New Testament text. He produced a version of the New Testament which consisted of St Luke's Gospel and a set of Pauline epistles, all heavily edited to exclude sympathetic or respectful references to the Old Testament. Luke's Gospel was a natural choice. It contains so many of the memorable episodes which exemplify the teaching of Christ on love: the raising from the dead of the widow's son at Nain, the forgiving of the sinful woman who wept on Christ's feet and dried them with her hair, the parables of the Good Samaritan and the Prodigal Son, the forgiveness of the good thief on the Cross. These are all passages that occur only in Luke. The key to interpreting the New Testament seems to have been St Paul's strictures against the Jewish Law, especially in the letters to the Galatians and the Romans. Marcion therefore produced an abbreviated version of the New Testament before any final agreed collection of New Testament texts had been settled by the Christian church. It is not unlikely that this spurred Christian thinkers on to consider further which books and which editions of books should be included in the corpus of authoritative New Testament texts, but it would be an exaggeration to think that he precipitated the church into the formulation of a canon.[37] What is most interesting is that the church decided to recognise not one Gospel but four: where Marcion sought to simplify Christian belief, the church acknowledged complexity.

Furthermore, to point up the differences between the Old Testament Law and the Gospel of Christ, Marcion set passages from the one alongside the other in his *Antitheses*. This was at least as provocative as the publication of his restricted New Testament. From the earliest Christian writings, the letters of Paul and the Gospels, Christians had been striving to demonstrate the harmony of the Old and New Testament scriptures. Irenaeus was to produce a thoroughgoing attempt to root the Gospel in the Old Testament with his small book *The Demonstration of the Apostolic Preaching*. Marcion challenged all of this by setting out to show not the harmony but the disharmony of the two. It was taken seriously enough for Tertullian to devote the last two books of his treatise against Marcion to a full-scale rebuttal of the *Antitheses* and Marcion's edition of the Pauline letters, aiming to show that there is no contradiction between the Old and New

[37] John Barton, 'Marcion Revisited' in Lee Martin Macdonald and James A. Sanders (eds), *The Canon Debate* (Peabody, Mass: Hendrickson, 2002) pp. 341–54.

Testaments. Here Tertullian grounds the goodness of creation, the unity of revelation and salvation in the oneness of God with which he opened the work.

About fifteen years after the attack on Marcion in Justin's first *Apology*, the case against him was clear enough and laid out by Irenaeus in his great work *Against the Heresies*, written in the 170s. It probably owed a great deal to Justin and the account of Marcion focuses on his rejection of the Old Testament and its Christological implications:

> Marcion shamelessly blasphemed the God announced by the Law and the Prophets, saying he is an evil-doer, a lover of wars, inconstant in his judgments and contrary to himself. As for Jesus, he claimed that he came from that Father who is above the God who made the world into Judaea in the time of the governor Pontius Pilate, Tiberius Caesar's procurator, and was revealed in human form to the inhabitants of Judaea, abolishing the Prophets and the Law and all the works of that God who made the world, whom he also calls the Cosmocrator. Moreover, Marcion mutilates Luke's Gospel, taking away from it all that is written of the LORD's birth and much also from the teaching of the LORD's discourses, those passages where it is most plainly written that the LORD confessed the maker of this world to be his Father. Marcion persuaded his disciples that he was more trustworthy than the apostles who passed on the Gospel, passing on to them not the Gospel but a small portion of the Gospel. In the same way, he mutilated the epistles of the apostle Paul, taking out the passages where the apostle speaks plainly of the God who made the world because he is the Father of Our LORD Jesus Christ, as well as all the passages where the apostle refers to the prophecies of the coming of the LORD. And salvation, he says, will be of our souls only, those souls which have learned his doctrine; but the body, because it is taken from the earth, cannot partake of salvation. On top of his blasphemy against God, he adds this also as the spokesman of the devil and speaking wholly contrary to the truth: that Cain and those like him, the Sodomites and Egyptians and those like them, and all the peoples who walk in every kind of evil have been saved by the LORD. When he descended into hell, they ran to him and he received them into his kingdom. But Abel and Enoch and Noah and all the rest of the just and Abraham and the patriarchs descended from him and all the prophets and all who pleased God do not participate in salvation. This is what the serpent which was in Marcion announced. This is because, according to him, they knew that their God was always putting them to the test and thus, thinking that he was testing them again, they did not run to Jesus or believe in his message. Thus their souls remain in hell.[38]

This sounds, for all its hostility to Marcion, like an attempt to present a fair statement of his views but several things about it are noteworthy. Though Irenaeus suggests Marcion teaches that there are two Gods, the implications of such a denial of monotheism are

---

[38] *Adv. Haer* 1.27.2–3.

scarcely explored. He also does not develop the claim that Marcion denied the salvation of the body. He seems more concerned with the assault on the authority of the apostles, the scriptures and the church which is posed by Marcion's abandonment of the Old Testament and his truncating of the New Testament scriptures. Furthermore, it is the tension between obedience to law and faith in forgiveness which outrages Irenaeus as he relates Marcion's version of the descent into Hell and the salvation of sinners but not of the just.

Nevertheless, to assign creation to the God of justice but not the saving God of love raised major questions about the value of the material order of the universe. It could easily seem that salvation would therefore amount to deliverance from the created order and that consequently human flesh would play no part in salvation. In that case, Christ himself could not have had a true body but must only have seemed incarnate. Marcion was therefore repeatedly accused by Tertullian of docetism, the idea that Christ's body only seemed, but was not truly, real.[39] Irenaeus hints at this by saying that Marcion apparently believed that the body was not involved in salvation and Marcion had given ammunition to his critics by presenting Christ as appearing from nowhere, starting his ministry in the synagogue in Nazareth, which seemed to suggest that Christ had no ordinary human birth.[40] This, however, was probably the result of his purging Luke's Gospel of all Old Testament references; Luke's account of the conception and birth of Jesus is so profoundly immersed in quotations from and allusions to the Old Testament that it must have proved impossible for Marcion to retain it in his edition of the Gospel. In another place, Tertullian admitted that he based his accusation that Marcion denied that Christ has a fleshly body on Marcion's denial that he had a human birth,[41] but it does not seem that Marcion denied that Christ was born but rather that he omitted the story from his version of the Gospel. Tertullian also accused him of denying the death and resurrection of Christ,[42] though in fact Marcion did not remove passages from the Gospel or Paul's letters which spoke about the death and resurrection and thus stressed the physical humanity of

---

[39] *Adv. Marc.* 3.8; *De Carne Christi* 1–8.

[40] *Adv. Marc.* 1.19; 3.11; 4.7.1.

[41] *De Carne Christi* 1: 'Marcion, so that he might deny the flesh of Christ, denied also the birth, or so that he might deny the birth, denied also the flesh, because of course his birth and his flesh were each guaranteed by the other, as there is no birth without flesh and no flesh without birth.'.

[42] *Adv. Marc.* 3.8.5–7.

Christ. Tertullian admitted as much, claiming, improbably, that this was a ploy to lend greater credibility to his expurgated text and that Marcion twisted the plain meaning of the words to suggest that Christ was a disembodied spirit.[43] The evidence, however, is clear enough: that Marcion's editing of the New Testament text was intended to purge it of allusions to the Old Testament, not of the references to the physical reality of Christ's body.[44]

Further evidence that he repudiated the material order was found by opponents such as Clement of Alexandria[45] and later by Epiphanius[46] in his famed emphasis on asceticism. Marcion's followers were said, for instance, to disapprove of marriage.[47] Their rituals were regarded with suspicion: they baptised with water and anointed with oil and gave a mixture of milk and honey to the newly baptised, but they used only bread and not wine at the eucharist.[48] It is quite likely that practices that might have been acceptable in the early second century and which survived among them after the rest of the church had abandoned them came to be regarded as heretical when they might better have been considered merely outdated.[49] In other words, despite the sustained polemic from the pen of Tertullian, it is more than likely that Marcion did not dismiss the salvation of the body or the reality of Christ's flesh.

Marcion's aim, then, seems clear enough — to claim that Christianity was a wholly new revelation of the hitherto unknown God of love. He accepted the Old Testament as the authentic revelation of the God who created the world, the God of the Jews, but insisted that this was a different God with a different message. This meant that he accepted the Old Testament prophecies of the Christ but said that they did not apply to Jesus of Nazareth but rather to a warrior Messiah who

[43] *Adv. Marc.* 4.43.

[44] Markus Vinzent, 'Der Schluß des Lukasevangeliums bei Marcion' in May and Greschat, *Marcion* pp. 79–94; Eve-Marie Becker, 'Marcion und die Korintherbriefe nach Tertullian, Adversus Marcionem V' in May and Greschat *Marcion* pp. 95–109 both show that Marcion's text does not disguise the resurrection.

[45] *Str.* 3.12; 3.105.1.

[46] *Pan.* 42.3.3–6; Epiphanius is reporting Marcionite practice, and possibly belief, in his own day which might reflect older practices (e.g. women baptise and the mysteries are celebrated in the presence of catechumens, 42.4.5) from which he appears to deduce that Marcion was anti-materialist.

[47] *Adv. Marc.* 1.29.

[48] *Adv. Marc.* 1.14.

[49] See Alistair Stewart-Sykes, 'Bread and fish, water and wine. The Marcionite menu and the maintenance of purity' in May and Greschat *Marcion* pp. 207–20.

would come to liberate the Jews. He presented the religion of the Old Testament as the fearful compliance with the law of a demanding and vengeful God, whose most faithful adherents could not accept the generous forgiveness offered by Jesus Christ. He not only dismissed the Old Testament as irrelevant to Christianity but purged his edition of the New Testament of any Old Testament quotations or sympathies.

He was attacked above all for denying monotheism. This was hardly his main aim but was rather the strange consequence of his insistence on both the truth and the irrelevance of the Old Testament. This in turn opened the door to claims that he denied the value of the material order of the universe, created by the God he depicted as limited and vengeful, but these allegations were probably mistaken. Nevertheless, the radical implications of Marcion's ideas, which he had presumably failed to explore, prompted his critics to consider how monotheism underlay the unity of divine activity in creation, providence, revelation and salvation. Tertullian's largest work was his assault on Marcion which, positively, amounted to a sustained attempt to show how the one God acts in a coherent and unified way through his Word, the Christ.

It was perhaps no accident that Marcion developed his view of the status of the Old Testament in Rome. If, as seems likely, Rome was the first place where a clear divide emerged between the Christian church and the Jewish community, Rome was the most obvious place for a movement to win support which denied that Christianity had its roots in the Hebrew scriptures. Marcion can best be understood as standing for the extreme repudiation of Judaism. His Christian opponents found themselves in the difficult position of endorsing the split with Judaism while wanting to claim that Christianity was its true successor, the true Israel.

VALENTINUS

Marcion's opponents regularly linked his name with another theologian teaching in Rome in the 140s and 150s — Valentinus. Justin, in a stylised debate with a Jew called Trypho, admitted that there were people who claimed to be Christians but who in fact belonged to separate groups with their own distinct ceremonies and whose teaching blasphemed the creator of the universe and the Christ he had prophesied. Among them, he listed Marcionites, Valentinians, Basilidians and Saturnilians.[50] Irenaeus gave a similar

---

[50] *Dialogue with Trypho* 35.5–6.

list of heretics as opponents of Gospel truth: Valentinus, Marcion, Cerinthus and Basilides.[51] He reported a visit to Rome of the great bishop Polycarp of Smyrna in the time of the Roman bishop Anicetus (c 155–c166), when he drew many back to the Church of God from the heretical teachings of Valentinus and Marcion.[52] He also observed that their teachings were new — there were no Valentinians before Valentinus or Marcionites before Marcion — and that Valentinus had come to Rome under Hyginus, grew in importance under Pius and continued under Anicetus. Tertullian, writing perhaps in about 206, also said that Marcion and Valentinus had been in Rome at the same time, under the emperor Antoninus Pius (138–61), and had both been members of the church but were repeatedly ejected for heresy.[53] Elsewhere, he presented Valentinus and Marcion not as having been ejected but as having abandoned the church. He described him as a 'fellow disciple and fellow deserter' with Marcion[54] and, in his treatise against Valentinus, he related another story: that he had hoped for an episcopal position in the church, which his intellectual gifts and eloquence seemed to deserve, but another obtained the place on account of having witnessed to the Faith; hurt, he broke with the church.[55]

Though some of the detail must therefore remain foggy and there is room to argue about whether Valentinus was expelled from the church for heresy or left it of his own accord through disappointed ambition, it is clear that in the 140s and 150s Valentinus, as well as Marcion, was a prominent figure in Roman Christianity and that he led a group that had become separate from the main body of the church. The repeated bracketing of their names suggests that their opponents saw deeper similarities between them. In fact, they were very different indeed. Marcion read the scriptures with a flat literalism which made many Old Testament passages very difficult to accept; Valentinus read the scriptures with the eyes of a poet and a mystic, finding in them profound truths hidden below the surface — meaning which he translated into myth. While Marcion abandoned the Old Testament, Valentinus mined it as a rich source for his theology. Whereas there was nothing secretive about Marcion and his

---

[51] *Adv. Haer* 3.2.1.

[52] *Adv. Haer* 3.3.4.

[53] *De Praescr Haer* 30.

[54] *De Carne Christi* 1.

[55] *Adversus Valentinianos* 4.1; Epiphanius later claimed he originated in Egypt, went to Rome but subsequently 'made shipwreck' of his faith in Cyprus *Panarion* 31.2.

teaching and he claimed that only faith was required to accept the truth, Valentinus held that only those born with the right spiritual insight could perceive the meaning of the mysteries veiled in the scriptures and then only after a long process of initiation. Though Marcion attributed the creation of the world to the God of the Old Testament, he seems not to have been interested in the origin of evil. Valentinus taught a doctrine which had the struggle between good and evil at its very heart.

In the late 170s, Irenaeus opened his great treatise *Against the Heresies* with a lengthy attack on Valentinus's ideas.[56] In fact, he was really reporting the ideas of Valentinus's followers, especially Ptolemy and Heracleon.[57] They were his successors in the West; others developed his ideas in the East. There was, therefore, a considerable variety of interpretations of Valentinus within a generation of his death, couched in the form of complex and highly imaginative myths. The knowledge and understanding of Valentinianism was greatly increased by the discovery in 1945 at Nag Hammadi in the Egyptian desert of a remarkable collection of over forty early Christian texts which had been buried at some point in the fifth century. Most of them were judged to be 'gnostic' in character — dualist, regarding the physical world as evil and salvation as deliverance from the material realm through spiritual knowledge, attributing creation to an ignorant or evil agent, conveying occult truths in the form of myths.[58] Several texts in particular, such as the *Gospel of Truth*, the *Authoritative Teaching*, the *Valentinian Exposition*, the *Gospel of Philip* and the *Tripartite Tractate* are believed to be expositions of Valentinian teaching, though almost certainly not written by Valentinus himself.

Lost gospels, secret teaching, hidden mysteries: these all sound intoxicating to the modern reader but when the myths are written out in cold prose they sound banal and absurd. That is precisely the technique used by Irenaeus to ridicule them. He expounds them at sufficient length that they sound wearisome or comic, though to many contemporaries they were enticing and challenging. They depict the transcendent realm of the *plērōma*, the divine fullness or perfection, as consisting of the divine Father and the aeons which

---

[56] *Adv. Haer* 1.1–9.

[57] *Adv. Haer* 6.35.6.

[58] For the texts, see James M. Robinson (ed), *The Nag Hammadi Library in English* (Leiden: Brill, 3rd ed, 1988); for gnostic teaching, see Christoph Markschies, *Gnosis: an Introduction* (John Bowden (trans.); London: T & T Clark, 2003).

emanate from him. These are arranged in pairs, such as Reason and Truth or Word and Life. Versions of the myth differ as to whether the ultimate source of the aeons is the Father alone or the Father paired with Silence. The western account envisages thirty aeons which are effectively aspects of the divine, the last of which is Wisdom (*Sophia*). The aeons do not know the depth of the Father but Wisdom ardently longs to do so and from this vaunting ambition for unattainable knowledge there arises the material from which the universe is made by her offspring, an inferior creator (the demiurge). The illegitimate yearning for knowledge (*gnōsis*) is thus depicted as an imperfection, found even within the divine realm, which leads to the existence both of the demiurge who creates and of the matter from which the universe is made. There is therefore a story of the Fall located before time began, within the *plērōma*, and the world is its result. The western tradition goes further, depicting humanity as divided into three categories: the spiritual, the psychic and the physical. Salvation is deliverance from the material imprisonment of bodily life and reintegration into the *plērōma* by means of the illumination of true revelation. In such a scheme, Christ is understood to be an aeon who has come to liberate the spiritual, the pneumatics, those who can grasp the *gnōsis*. The psychics will receive a partial and inferior salvation. The physical people are wholly material and can look forward to no life after death.

Several things are worth noting about this myth. There is no idea of creation as a willed, rational act. The aeons emanate from the Father and Silence, pouring out naturally, while the material universe is the expression of the passion of Wisdom striving for knowledge of the Father. Apart from Reason, the aeons are ignorant of the ultimate depth of the Father — imperfection is intrinsic even within the divine fullness. There is an archetypal Fall when Wisdom embarks on her self-seeking search for knowledge which is mirrored in the very existence of the material world. In other words, the problem of evil is pushed back to the realm of the divine, as is salvation, for Wisdom too needs to be saved. The possibility of salvation is determined by whether a person is spiritual, psychic or physical, categories which are fixed and innate.

Much doubt has been cast on whether the myth in this developed form can be attributed to Valentinus himself and in the process a considerably more subtle and sympathetic presentation of his ideas has been proposed, though how they could have been elaborated into such a complex and rigid mythological form within the space of about twenty years still needs to be explained.[59] Valentinus can be seen as tentatively attempting to expound scriptural texts by means of allegory under the influence of philosophical ideas that he owed to Neopythagoreanism and the unsystematic and eclectic reading of Plato common in his day.

At most, eleven fragments of his writings survive. In practice, only eight are fully deserving of close consideration, seven quoted in the *Stromata* of Clement of Alexandria written at the end of the second or beginning of the third century, and one hymn recorded in the early third-century *Refutation of All Heresies*.[60] This hymn might be regarded as vital to glimpsing his thought:

Summer

I see how all hangs on Spirit
I know how all is carried by Spirit
Flesh hanging from soul
Soul proceeding from air
Air hanging from ether
Fruits being brought forth from the Depth,
A child brought forth from the womb.

It is certainly esoteric but it lacks some of the hallmarks of thorough-going Valentinian myth: there is no suggestion that the material universe is evil; there is no reference to the demiurge; indeed it seems to be stressing the relatedness of the whole created universe. The meaning of the hymn has been much discussed.[61] In

---

[59] G. C. Stead, 'In Search of Valentinus' in Bentley Layton (ed), *The Rediscovery of Gnosticism: Proceedings of the International Conference on Gnosticism at Yale, New Haven, Connecticut, March 28–31, 1978* (Studies in the History of Religion, 41; 2 vols; Leiden: Brill, 1980–1) vol. 1, pp. 75–102 sees Valentinus as an educated Platonist of moderate culture, striving to interpret scripture allegorically in the light of philosophy; Christoph Markschies, *Valentinus Gnosticus? Untersuchungen zur valentinianischen Gnosis mit einem Kommentar zu den Fragmenten Valentins* (Wissenschaftliche Untersuchungen zum Neuen Testament, 65; Tübingen: Mohr, 1992) also sees him as a biblical Platonist and highlights the sharp contrast between Valentinus and the Valentinians who followed him; Einar Thomassen, *The Spiritual Seed: the Church of the 'Valentinians'* (Nag Hammadi and Manichaean Studies, 60; Leiden: Brill, 2006) explores the roots of later Valentinian myth in Valentinus's own writings and stresses in particular the soteriological dimension of his thinking and the significance of Valentinian initiation rites.

[60] *Ref. Haer* 6.37.7.

[61] See the contrasting interpretations in Markschies *Valentinus Gnosticus?* pp. 218–64 and Thomassen *Spiritual Seed* pp. 479–88.

the first five lines, there is a chain of dependency — flesh depending on soul which depends on air which depends on ether. Spirit, in the first two lines, is not part of the chain but rather the power that keeps the chain together. This might well be Wisdom. The key question is the relationship between the first five lines, with their strong emphasis on the unity of creation, and the last two lines in which the Depth, who is the ultimate God, the Father, produces fruits like a child from the womb. Later Valentinianism would offer a darkly pessimistic account of the disruption between the divine and the material creation. It is reasonable to say that while the tone of the poem and its title, 'Summer' or 'Harvest', certainly sounds warm and reassuring, it does seem that the last two lines should be seen as distinct from the first five. It is unlikely that the 'fruits' brought forth from the Depth are the material universe. They are more likely to be the aeons. Thus the last two lines could be read as suggesting a contrast between the material universe which is held together by Spirit and the aeons which emerge from the womb of the Depth like a child. On this reading, the hymn is asserting a contrast between the divine realm and the material creation, but not a pessimistic one.

In another fragment quoted by Clement,[62] Valentinus also stresses that, though the world is vastly inferior to its creator, it is nevertheless made in his image:

> To the same extent as the image is inferior to the living person, the world is inferior to the living aeon. What then is the cause of the image? It is the greatness of the person who provided the figure (*typos*) for the painter, so that he might be honoured by his name. The form was not regarded as equal to the original but the name filled out the deficiency in the moulding. The invisibility of God cooperates also towards faith in what has been fashioned.

Though once again the meaning of the passage is obscure and has been much discussed,[63] it is certainly asserting the similarity of what has been created to its creator. Valentinus appears to be saying that though an image is inferior to the person of whom it is a copy, it can nevertheless be regarded as something great because of the greatness of the person's name. In the same way, the world is great because of the greatness of its maker of whom it is a reflection and whose name will make up for its inadequacies. The first key question is: who is the creator, who is the living aeon? The fact that the word is in the

---

[62] *Str.* 4.89.6 — 90.1.

[63] For differing interpretations, see Markschies *Valentinus Gnosticus?* pp. 153–85 and Thomassen *Spiritual Seed* pp. 465–73.

singular suggests that Valentinus is talking about one of the aeons, a demiurge, but it seems more likely that here he is using it to refer to the *plērōma* and is claiming that the universe reflects the divine perfection. The last sentence of the fragment could therefore be read to mean that it is precisely because God is transcendent that people might be endowed with faith in him.

These passages suggest that Valentinus did not hold to the dualistic and pessimistic account of the origins of the material universe found in the myths constructed by his followers. On the other hand, his account of the creation of Adam[64] opened the door to that kind of reading. He attributed the making of Adam to two forces which are in opposition. The angels fashion Adam but the seed of the spiritual substance is planted in him invisibly so that the pre-existent prototype of humanity dwells in him. Adam is therefore an image of a prototype in whose name he is made. The angels are terrified when they hear Adam speak. This reveals the one who had placed the spiritual seed in him and they speedily ruin him. Although again there are differing readings of this passage,[65] it seems likely that here we can see the roots of the later Valentinian view that matter is evil, the product of a creative agent other than the ultimate and good God, and that human beings are fallen as a result of the simple fact of being made material at all. Here too we can see the idea that trapped within the material is a higher, spiritual identity deriving from the transcendent realm. In other words, as with many Platonists, there were both optimistic and pessimistic features of Valentinus's thinking which could become increasingly pessimistic as the myth became elaborated.

Was Valentinus's view of Jesus docetic, thinking that he only appeared to be human but did not truly live a material existence? If the human dilemma is enslavement within a material, mortal body, then it might have made sense to deny that Jesus was himself a victim of that trap. One passage from a letter of Valentinus preserved by Clement might suggest that that was his view of Christ:[66]

> Enduring everything, he was in control of himself. Jesus put his divinity into effect; he ate and drank in his own way, without discharging the food. His power of self-control was so great that even the food inside him was not corrupted for he had no corruption.

---

[64] *Str.* 2.36.2–4.

[65] Markschies *Valentinus Gnosticus?* pp. 11–53 and Thomassen *Spiritual Seed* pp. 430–51.

[66] *Str.* 3.59.3.

At first sight, this seems plainly docetic: Jesus's body was unreal. It might, however, be read to mean not that his body was an illusion but that it was liberated from its material limitations by his divinity. In other words, he was not something other than or less than human, he was fully human. By taking on the material condition of humanity, he overcame its weakness.

This might illuminate another opaque quotation from Valentinus. The idea that salvation consists in accepting the imperfection of human life in order to perfect it is not foreign to Christian thought. The idea that those who are saved share in this process of perfection precisely by sharing in the acceptance of imperfection is also one found throughout Christian history. These ideas underlie a passage in a homily, again recorded by Clement:[67]

> You were originally immortal and children of eternal life and you were willing to divide death among you so that you might consume and dissolve it and that death might die in you and by you. For when you dissolve the world and are not dissolved yourselves, you will rule over all creation and all corruption.

Being willing to accept death to consume it and dissolve it so that death itself might die in you and by you: this doctrine of participation and exchange was to have a long history in Christian theology, expressed succinctly by Valentinus's great opponent Irenaeus in the closing words of the preface of the last book of his *Against the Heresies*, Christ 'became what we are so that he might perfect us to be what he is himself'.[68] What is striking in this homily is that the 'you' Valentinus was addressing was not Christ but his listeners. It is they who were immortal but who were willing to share in death to overcome it.

This might suggest that Valentinus thought that his listeners were the pre-existent spiritual elite, the pneumatics, who had once enjoyed life and knowledge in the *plērōma* but now dwelt in the ignorance and sadness of the material world from which the *gnōsis* conveyed by Christ would deliver them. On the other hand, there is a passage where Valentinus spoke of the heart as being like an inn infested with demons. They could only be expelled by the Father, manifested by the Son. Then the heart would become bright with light and the person blessed with such a heart would see God.[69] This fragment, rich in New Testament allusions, offers no hint that only some hearts were capable of such cleansing.

---

[67] *Str.* 4.89.1–3.
[68] *Adv. Haer* 5 pref.
[69] *Str.* 2.114.3–6.

Any conclusions deduced from these short fragments must be highly tentative. It seems reasonable to say, however, that Valentinus made the first notable attempt to work out a theology drawn from scripture which could appeal to the philosophical climate of the age and which used scripture not as a text to be read literally but rather one to be read figuratively and poetically. He thought of the Father as bringing forth the aeons from within his own Depth, as from a womb, as expressions of his own fullness and that the universe was fashioned in the image of that divine realm. But he also believed that the mortality and material limitations of the human condition can be ascribed to a double agency in creating humanity — angels making the body into which a divine seed was sown. Thus, for Valentinus, salvation is liberation from the constraints of the material, achieved by union in Christ's own acceptance of death in order to overcome it. It is possible that he believed that salvation was restoration to the *plērōma* of those who had lived there before their human birth, though that is uncertain. He led a body of followers to whom he preached and for whom he composed hymns and who quite probably observed the liturgical practices which were to become distinctive of the Valentinian groups in the future. Though his ideas do not seem to have been as systematized or developed as those of his followers, he did lay down several leading ideas which were to be elaborated in their myths.

JUSTIN MARTYR

Most people would say that Christianity is the new religion, Judaism the older. The reality is more complex. Christianity's most startling innovation seems to have been the claim that, alongside God the Father, there was also God the Son, the divine Word. It could be argued, however, that this core feature of Christianity was part of the mental furniture of Judaism at the time of Christ and St Paul and that it is left as an unexpected survival in Christianity of Jewish thought which Judaism eventually erased from its belief and memory.[70] It might be better to see Christianity and rabbinic Judaism as siblings, two children who retained different aspects of the faith of Second

---

[70] Alan F. Segal, *Two Powers in Heaven: Early Rabbinic Reports about Christianity and Gnosticism* (Leiden: Brill, 1977); Daniel Boyarin, *Border Lines: the Partition of Judaeo-Christianity* (Philadelphia: University of Pennsylvania Press, 2004).

Temple Judaism. In that sense, Justin Martyr could be regarded not so much as an innovator but a traditionalist in his theology.

To begin with the Old Testament: there are many passages, especially in the wisdom books, where the Word or Wisdom of God, which might usually be thought of as aspects of God or metaphors for divine action, are personified, as God's agents distinct from him. The Word, for instance, is depicted in the silence of the night leaping down from the royal throne of heaven like a fierce warrior, wielding the sword of God's commandment (Wis 18.14–6). Wisdom is the worker of all things, the breath of the power of God, the brightness of everlasting light and the image of God's goodness who, 'being but one, can do all things' (Wis 7.22–8.1). She cries out in the streets and offers to pour out her spirit and make her words known (Prov 1.20–33). She was set up[71] before the works of God and at the creation of the world she was alongside him, rejoicing with him (Prov. 8.22–31). Wisdom has built her house and set up her seven pillars and furnished her table to which she invites all who are willing to go in the way of understanding (Prov. 9.1–6).

These passages might easily be read as ways of speaking about God indirectly in much the same way as the government of the Turkish sultan used to be referred to as the Sublime Porte or the person of the Queen might be referred to as Her Majesty. There is strong evidence, however, that they were not read as merely circumlocutions to safeguard the otherness of God. Philo of Alexandria, the brilliant contemporary of St Paul, is the most famous Jewish writer of antiquity who apparently spoke of a personified divine Wisdom or Word[72] but he was not the only one.[73] Rabbinic Judaism later condemned this, calling it the doctrine of 'Two Powers in Heaven', as it was seen to imperil monotheism.[74] Christianity retained this idea of the Word as a personified, distinct divine agent acting as God's intermediary with the created universe and made it even more wholly personal by identifying it with Jesus Christ. Rabbinic Judaism increasingly identified this Wisdom or Word with the written Law, at once both heightening the sense of Law as God's agent but also de-personalising the Word. From one common inheritance, Christianity and Judaism

---

[71] The word in the Greek version of the Old Testament of Prov. 8.22 is 'created' (*ektisen*), which was long to cause much debate about the status of Wisdom.

[72] Segal *Two Powers* pp. 159–81; Boyarin *Border Lines* pp. 112–16.

[73] Boyarin *Border Lines* pp. 116–27.

[74] Ibid., 128–47.

moved in different directions but the emergence in Christianity of trinitarian doctrine bore witness to its ancient inheritance.[75]

The term in Greek which is translated 'Word' is Logos. Beyond its primary meaning of written word or account or narrative, Logos conveyed too the idea of reason and rationality and, with that, a whole set of implications: order, structure, meaning, intelligibility, communication. To speak of God's Logos was to speak not only of his own act of self-communication but of his purpose, his mind and ultimately his nature. Logos and Wisdom were often equated — the biblical texts referring to Wisdom being simply applied to the Logos — and sometimes they were kept distinct so that God was depicted as having two agents with the texts distributed between them. But Logos seemed to be a theological concept with far more flexibility and range. Wisdom sounded like a quality of the few, a personal characteristic which could be acquired. The universe might be made with Wisdom but it would seem odd to say that the world was imbued with Wisdom. Logos by contrast could be attributed to the laws of physics or mathematics as much as to the human mind, the rational patterning and purpose which was displayed in the regular rhythms of life as much as in the intelligence and speech of everyone.

This concept of the divine Logos was put to remarkable use by Justin Martyr in Rome in the 150s.[76] He reached out to a non-Christian readership, confident that the reasonableness of the human mind reflected the rationality of God whether in Christian preacher or pagan reader. He wrote two apologies, defences or explanations of Christianity for a pagan audience. Though various ingenious theories have been proposed about the relationship between them,[77] there is no doubt about the overall coherence of his thought. It is quite possible that he invented the genre; in other words, he was the first

[75] Ibid., 129: 'The finally definitive move for the Rabbis was to transfer all Logos and Sophia talk to the Torah alone, thus effectively accomplishing two powerful discursive moves at once: consolidating their own power as the sole religious virtuosi and leaders of "the Jews," and protecting one version of monotheistic thinking from the problematic of division within the godhead. For the Rabbis, Torah supersedes Logos, just as for John, Logos supersedes Torah.'

[76] For Justin's thought, see Erwin R. Goodenough, *The Theology of Justin Martyr* (Jena: Frommann, 1923); Leslie W. Barnard, *Justin Martyr: His Life and Thought* (Cambridge: CUP, 1967); Eric Osborn, *Justin Martyr* (Tübingen: Mohr, 1973).

[77] E.g. Paul Parvis, 'Justin, Philosopher and Martyr: the Posthumous Creation of the *Second Apology*' in in Sara Parvis and Paul Foster (eds) *Justin Martyr and his Worlds* (Minneapolis: Fortress, 2007) pp. 22–37.

Christian ever to write for a non-Christian readership.[78] The scriptures and all the earliest Christian writings were written for believers. An outsider would have not have found it easy to discern the underlying assumptions behind their unfamiliar imagery and alien terminology. Some of the literature was deliberately obscure; much could only be understood with specialised knowledge. Justin's was therefore a bold undertaking.

In addition to the two apologies to the pagans, he also wrote one addressed to a Jewish readership, cast in the form of a stylised debate, the *Dialogue with Trypho*. Here there was a common language, agreed authorities and a recognised field of debate — effectively, the interpretation of the Old Testament. An apology for a pagan audience, however, could only be written on the basis that there was some level at which Christians and non-Christians could also understand each other, that there was some underlying platform of shared language and rationality on which they all stood. This was the opposite assumption to that which made gnostic texts so inward-looking and secretive. One of the common denominators of the writings usually labelled 'gnostic' is that they expressed in enigmatic utterances profound mysteries that could be known only to the initiated, quite possibly only to those innately qualified to be the recipients of the revelation, and inaccessible to the ordinary rational world of outsiders. Justin built his work on the opposite assumption: that Christianity could be expressed in terms that made sense to any rational person and indeed was the most reasonable of all faiths.

Justin's confidence owed much to his education. He was probably the first Christian theologian to have had a solid education in philosophy. Born in Neapolis (Nablus) in Palestine,[79] he described himself as a Samaritan[80] but was not circumcised.[81] He was therefore of gentile background. As a philosopher, he moved through the Stoic, peripatetic, Pythagorean and Platonic schools[82] before finally embracing Christianity. He described this as being the result of a long conversation with an old man on the seashore.[83] Justin's philosophical background has led many commentators to attribute his leading ideas to Stoic or Platonist

---

[78] This is argued by Sara Parvis, 'Justin Martyr and the Apologetic Tradition' in Parvis and Foster *Justin Martyr* pp. 115–27.

[79] *1 Apol.* 1.

[80] *Dial.* 120.

[81] *Dial.* 28.

[82] *Dial.* 2.

[83] *Dial.* 3–8.

influences but one of the striking features of the discussion with the old man was the demolition of the belief, which he might have held as a Platonist, that people have an innate intuition of sacred truth because of the natural affinity of the mind with God. The old man forced Justin to reject this idea along with the natural immortality of the soul and to abandon Platonism. Despite the views of modern interpreters, Justin did not see himself as a Platonist in Christian clothes. He claimed that Plato was a plagiarist who took all his best ideas from Moses.[84] Instead, he looked to a different source for his ideas, the scriptures, and offered a different explanation for the convergence in understanding between Christians and philosophers, the encounter with the divine Word in scripture which they then tacitly plagiarised.[85] Nevertheless, he allowed a close affinity between human rationality and the divine Word:

> We have learned that Christ is the first born of God and we have indicated earlier that he is the Logos in whom the whole human race shares. Those who have lived rationally (*meta logou*) belong to Christ even though they have been thought atheists, such as, in Greece, Socrates, Heraclitus and those like them and, among the barbarians, Abraham, Ananias, Azarias, Misael, Elias and many others whose names and actions we know it would take too long to list. Thus those who lived before Christ irrationally (*aneu logou*) were evil, enemies of Christ, murderers of those who lived rationally, while those who lived or are actually living rationally are Christians and endure without fear or anxiety.[86]

All rational people are Christians, in the sense that rationality is itself a sharing in the Logos. This is stated again in the Second Apology, in which a more careful statement of the relationship between rationality and incarnation is offered:

> Ours is evidently greater than all human teaching because that which is in the domain of reason (*to logikon*) has come from Christ, who has appeared for us body, reason and soul. Everything which has been found and said by philosophers and lawgivers, they achieved by finding and contemplating a share in the Logos. But since they did not know the whole of the Logos, who is Christ, they often contradicted themselves.[87]

The idea is re-stated and the relationship of the Logos which inspires human reason at its best — the *spermatikos Logos* — and the Logos in itself, in its entirety, is considered more fully:

---

[84] *1 Apol.* 44; 59–60; this is a commonplace but Justin is less dismissive than Clement of Alexandria's 'What is Plato but Moses in Attic Greek?' *Str.* 1.150.4.

[85] This is argued in M.J. Edwards, 'Justin's Logos and the Word of God' *JECS* 3 (1995) pp. 261–80.

[86] *1 Apol.* 46.2–4.

[87] *2 Apol.* 10.1–3.

I admit that I am a Christian and I hope and strive to be found as one, not because the teachings of Plato are different from those of Christ but because they not are similar in every way; nor are those of the others, the Stoics and poets and prose-writers. Each of them spoke well in proportion as he had a share in the divine *spermatikos Logos*. But those who contradicted themselves on the most important points showed that they did not possess infallible and irrefutable knowledge. Whatever they taught that was good is the property of Christians for, next to God, we love and adore the Logos born of the unbegotten and ineffable God, since he even became man for us so as to share in our sufferings to heal us of them. All the writers were able to see reality in an indistinct way thanks to the seed of the Logos implanted in them. But the seed and resemblance bestowed on people according to their faculties is one thing, quite another is the thing itself of which the participation and imitation are given according to the grace of which he is the source.[88]

This is the opposite of the assimilation of Christianity to philosophy. Laying claim to the best in pagan thought allows Justin to play the part of its judge. He dismissed Epicureanism as morally vacuous.[89] The Stoics were good on ethics but wrong on materialism, pantheism and fatalism.[90] The Platonists are those nearest to Christianity. The persecution and death of Socrates is a topic he often returned to, treating it is evidence of the excellence of his teaching.[91] The Platonists were right that God is transcendent, immutable, impassive, incorporeal[92] and nameless.[93] He approves of the creation myth in the *Timaeus* — the world is created,[94] though he is unclear whether out of nothing.[95] Platonists are also right about the natural affinity of the soul with God,[96] free will[97] and punishment after death.[98] They were wrong, however, about the natural immortality of the soul and its innate intuition of divine truth.[99]

Why then is there error and immorality in the world? Justin is clearly less preoccupied with this question than Valentinus or, arguably, Marcion. While the presence of the Logos in people's minds promotes wisdom and reason, the demonic provokes people

---

[88] *2 Apol.* 13.2–6.
[89] *2 Apol.* 7; 12; 15.
[90] *1 Apol.* 43; *2 Apol.* 7.
[91] *1 Apol.* 5; *2 Apol.* 7; 10.
[92] *1 Apol.* 25; 49; 53; *2 Apol.* 12; *Dial.* 5.4.
[93] *1 Apol.* 61; 63; *2 Apol.* 6.
[94] *1 Apol.* 20; *Dial.* 5.
[95] *1 Apol.* 10; 59; *2 Apol.* 6.
[96] *Dial.* 4.
[97] *2 Apol.* 7; *Dial.* 88; 102; 140; 141.
[98] *1 Apol.* 44.
[99] *Dial.* 4–6.

into false, irrational and immoral beliefs and practices. The demons are fallen angels.[100] Their power is only tolerated by God until the work of salvation is complete.[101] They lead people into idolatry, which is a fraudulent substitute for the worship of the true God.[102] Where pagan cults resemble Christian ones, as for example in the rituals of Mithraism, this too is a diabolical deceit.[103] They stimulate pagans and Jews to persecute Christians[104] and Socrates was killed by the demons before he could expose their lies.[105] Error among Christians is also a sign of diabolical influence.[106] In other words, Justin seems to feel that he needs to attribute irrationality to a rival influence to that of the Logos. It is not his sole explanation of sin in the world — he also has a doctrine of humanity's sin in solidarity with the sin of Adam, which he depicts as falling under the power of death and the serpent[107] — but, as he does not have a fully developed account of the Fall or the fallen condition of humanity, it is convenient for him to regard irrationality and the demonic as parasitic upon the good, of which is it always a counterfeit copy.

According to Justin, where philosophy can only glimpse aspects of the truth, Christianity can be certain.[108] Christ is the Logos, teaching divine virtue,[109] teaching the way to happiness.[110] The Sermon on the Mount is the universal law stripped of the national particularity of Judaism.[111] This is a message not just for the learned but also for illiterates.[112] Christ offers such illumination because he is the Logos; he is God,[113] and it is reasonable to worship him, holding him in second place as the Son of the true God.[114] It is on this basis that Justin dismisses criticisms of Christianity: that Christians are

---

[100] *2 Apol.* 5; *Dial.* 79.
[101] *1 Apol.* 28; 45.
[102] *1 Apol.* 5; 25; 54; *2 Apol.* 5; *Dial.* 55; 59.
[103] *1 Apoli.* 62; 64.
[104] *1 Apol.* 10; 57; *2 Apol.* 1; *Dial.* 131.
[105] *1 Apol.* 5; *2 Apol.* 8.
[106] *1 Apol.* 26.
[107] *1 Apol.* 61; *Dial.* 88; 94; 95; 100; 124.
[108] *Dial.* 7; 48.
[109] *1 Apol.* 12; *2 Apol.* 2; 9.
[110] *Dial.* 142.
[111] *Dial.* 93.
[112] *2 Apol.* 10.
[113] *Dial.* 125.
[114] *1 Apol.* 63.

atheists,[115] who do not offer material sacrifices to the gods,[116] and who are enemies of society.[117] The Christian virtues such as chastity[118] and humility[119] are eminently reasonable and admirable and go well with respect for the authority of government.[120] Justin also goes to the trouble of describing Christian practices such as baptism[121] and the eucharist.[122]

For Justin, then, God is present in the world as the Logos, whether the *spermatikos Logos* in the minds of rational people or the Logos revealing himself more directly in scripture or fully in the Incarnation as Jesus Christ. This is a more developed version of the kind of doctrine found earlier in the pages of Philo and other Jewish writers. God acts through the Logos because in himself he is utterly transcendent, yet it is God who acts and is revealed. The Logos is the one revealed in the Old Testament and the Logos is the author of revelation. In this, the Logos safeguards the otherness of God while making God known in himself. For instance, Justin points out that when Moses meets the God of Abraham, Isaac and Jacob in the burning bush (Exod. 3) it is indeed God who speaks to him, not an angel, but no one could say that the Creator of the universe, the Father, has left all that he is above the heavens to appear in this little corner of the world. In other words, when God speaks to Moses, it is the Logos who speaks.[123] God is beyond all names, for there is no one to name him; rather the titles used of him such as Father, Creator, LORD and Master are not names but appellations derived from his good deeds and activities.[124] He clearly regards the claim — made commonly by Jews — that it is God the Father himself who is encountered in the Old Testament theophanies as a threat to divine transcendence.[125] Justin states the idea of the Logos as the intermediary more fully:

> The ineffable Father and LORD of all does not go anywhere, does not walk or sleep or get up, but remains in his own place wherever it is. His vision and hearing are sharp, not with the eyes or ears but by a power that cannot be

---

[115] *1 Apol.* 6.
[116] *1 Apol.* 9–10.
[117] *1 Apol.* 11–12.
[118] *1 Apol.* 15.
[119] *1 Apol.* 16.
[120] *1 Apol.* 17.
[121] *1 Apol.* 61.
[122] *1 Apol.* 65–67.
[123] *Dial.* 60.
[124] *2 Apol.* 6.
[125] *1 Apol.* 63.

expressed. He surveys all, knows all and nothing about us escapes him. He, whom no place can contain, not even the whole world, does not move. He was even before the world existed. How then can he speak to someone, show himself to someone or appear in the tiniest place in the world when the people on Sinai were not strong enough to endure the sight of the glory of his envoy, when Moses himself was not strong enough to enter the tent he had made at least while it was filled with the glory that had come from God, when moreover the priest could not remain standing facing the sanctuary while Solomon brought in the ark into the house in Jerusalem which Solomon had himself had built? Thus neither Abraham, nor Isaac, nor Jacob nor anyone else has seen the Father, the ineffable LORD of everything, and Father of Christ himself. But this one who, according to the will of the Father, is at the same time God, his Son, and angel [has seen him] because he serves his plan.[126]

Speaking of the Logos as Son is an important move. It allows Justin to speak of the Logos in more thoroughly personal terms, making the identification with Christ easier. It also establishes the relationship of Father and Logos as one of sonship in which the Son is begotten, not created. The Son is begotten before all created things[127] and is with the Father before all the creatures.[128] 'The Father of the universe has a Son who, being the Logos and the first-born of God, is also God.'[129] The Logos is therefore not merely a divine characteristic or a way of describing divine activity; it is not simply distinguished from the Father by name, like the light from the Sun, but is numerically distinct[130] and is in second place to the Father.[131]

By presenting the Logos as the Father's agent, Justin can present an over-arching unity to all divine activity — creation,[132] revelation[133] and salvation. Christ is 'the whole of the Logos'.[134]

Jesus Christ is the Son and apostle of God, because he is first his Logos, and he was revealed sometimes under the appearance of fire, sometimes in an incorporeal image; finally he became man to save the human race and he suffered everything that the demons inspired in the madness of the Jews.[135]

Justin therefore sees himself as asserting monotheism against paganism and defending divine transcendence against Jews, such as

[126] *Dial.* 127: 2–4.
[127] *Dial.* 129.
[128] *Dial.* 62.
[129] *1 Apol.* 63.
[130] *Dial.* 128.
[131] *1 Apol.* 13.
[132] *1 Apol.* 59.
[133] *1 Apol.* 63; *Dial.* 55–62.
[134] *2 Apol.* 10.3.
[135] *1 Apol.* 63.

Trypho, who do not have a Logos doctrine.[136] He is able to describe the unity of all divine activity as the work of a single divine agent, so that revelation and Incarnation are not at odds with creation and human rationality but their completion. This allows him to extend a cautious hand of friendship to the pagan world around him while at the same time offering a clear solution to the relationship between Old and New Testaments or scripture and Christ. He aims at a coherent reading of all biblical passages so that the Son is glory, wisdom, angel, Lord and Logos:[137] in other words, against Marcion, the Logos is both the author and subject of all scripture and all scripture can be read Christologically.

Like Philo and the Jewish tradition which, it seems, Justin is upholding against the Jewish interlocutors of his own day, Justin is binitarian. Though he staunchly insists that he is a monotheist,[138] he also says that there are two numerically distinct divine beings, the Father and his Son.[139] He even describes him as 'another God and Lord below the Creator of everything'.[140] Saying this, he rejected what he regarded as a common teaching among the Jews, that it was the Father who spoke to Moses and was encountered in all the Old Testament theophanies:

> The Jews always think that the Father of the universe spoke to Moses when in reality it was the Son of God, who is also called his Angel and his Apostle. Thus, through the prophetic Spirit and through Christ himself, they are rightly said to have known neither the Father nor the Son. For to say that the Son is the Father is to prove that one does not know the Father and that one does not know that the Father of the universe has a Son who, being the Logos and the first-born of God, is also God.[141]

The argument that the Jews cannot know the Father if they do not acknowledge the Son must be based, in Justin's estimation, on their failure to recognise the Father's transcendence, which makes him inaccessible in the universe limited by space and time. In another passage, he addresses a different account of the Father and his Logos:

> They say that this power [the Logos] remains indivisible and inseparable from the Father in the same way that the light of the Sun is, on earth, indivisible and

---

[136] Boyarin argues that the debate with Trypho is intended to strip from Judaism its traditional Logos doctrine: *Border Lines* pp. 37–73.

[137] *Dial.* 61.

[138] *1 Apol.* 14; *Dial.* 11; 126.

[139] *Dial.* 56; 62; 128; 129.

[140] *Dial.* 56.4.

[141] *1 Apol.* 63.14–15.

inseparable from the Sun in the sky; when it goes down, the light disappears with it. Thus, they say, the Father, whenever he wanted to, could project his power and, whenever he wanted to, draw it back into himself.[142]

Justin does not say who advocates this idea that the Logos, having been projected for the purposes of divine activity, could be drawn back into the Father. Given that the *Dialogue with Trypho* is a dispute between Christian and Jewish thinking about God and his Logos, it is most likely that he is referring to Jewish thinkers. In other words, in both the first Apology and the *Dialogue*, Justin indicates signs that Judaism was abandoning belief in a distinct, personified Logos. A few decades later, Christian teachers were to show a similar unwillingness to imperil the assertion of divine unity and simplicity for the sake of divine transcendence.

Justin's account of the Logos left little room for the Holy Spirit as a distinct agent. While Justin repeatedly says that it is the Holy Spirit who inspires the prophets,[143] he also says that it is the Logos who puts them in motion.[144] In other words, there is no very clear distinction between the Son and the Spirit. On the other hand, Justin quotes the trinitarian baptismal formula derived from Mt 28.19[145] and, in denying the charge against the Christians that they are atheists for not venerating the Roman gods, he insists that they adore the Father and along with him his Son and also the Holy Spirit.[146] Even more tellingly, in a passage where he says that Plato had anticipated Christ's cross in a passage in the *Timaeus*, he says that Plato had given second place to the Logos and the third to the Spirit. In other words, while Justin might have little room in his theology for another divine person along with Father and Son, he is obliged to abide by the as yet inchoate doctrine of the Spirit.

More fundamental as a weakness in Justin's whole enterprise is the ambiguous status of the Logos. The Son is God because he is the Son; thus all the activities of the Logos are the acts of God. But the Logos only acts or even exists because of the Father's immobilising transcendence. While 'logos' is eternally the character of the mind of God, the Logos is numerically distinct, a subsistent being, generated apparently in order to create the world.[147] This was an idea that would

---

[142] *Dial.* 128.3.
[143] *1 Apol.* 33; 35; 41; 44; *Dial.* 32; 38; 43.
[144] *1 Apol.* 36.
[145] *1 Apol.* 61.
[146] *1 Apol.* 6.
[147] *2 Apol.* 6.

receive clearer articulation from a later apologist, Theophilus, who distinguished between the Logos present in the mind of God and the Logos expressed as an active agent, the *Logos endiathetos* and the *Logos prophorikos*.[148] While Justin and Theophilus after him insist that the Logos who acts as God's intermediary is the full expression of the mind of God, they raise the question of the status of a divine agent who exists for a purpose. God has no purpose; he just is. The Logos, however, does not have the transcendent condition of the Father and has been brought into distinct existence for a reason. Justin clearly felt no embarrassment about envisaging a hierarchy within God. Others did.

LEADERSHIP

Separation from the Jewish community forced the early Christians in Rome to develop their own structures of leadership. The early evidence is so imprecise and fragmentary that readers can impose upon it whatever they expect to find. Many people think of the Roman Christians as a loose federation of independent groups which gradually came together in the late second century to form a united church under one leader; in other words, a bishop emerged in Rome at a fairly late stage to hold these separate communities together. The principal argument in favour of this view is a debatable reading of the final chapter of Paul's letter to the Romans; even if several house churches could be detected in the list of names Paul supplies at the end of the letter, there would still be no reason to think that those churches survived Nero's persecution of 64. By contrast, the letter from the Roman to the Corinthian church commonly called *1 Clement* is clear evidence that the Roman Christians thought of themselves as one church in the closing years of the first or early years of the second century.

Though the Roman Christians must have had multiple assemblies at quite an early stage on account of their own numbers and the physical size of the city, there is no strong reason to think of the Roman church as a federation of independent groups.[149] But did it have one leader?[150] The author of *1 Clement* writes on behalf of the

[148] *Ad Autolycum* 2.10; 2.22.

[149] The fullest statement of the view that the church was 'fractionated' until the end of the second century is Lampe *From Paul to Valentinus* pp. 359–408.

[150] For a full review of the evidence, see Eric G. Jay, 'From Presbyter-Bishops to Bishops and Presbyters: Christian Ministry in the Second Century: A Survey' *The Second Century* 1 (1981) pp. 125–62.

church rather than in his own name. This had led people to doubt that he could have been a bishop in the later sense of the word. The main purpose of the letter is to challenge the Corinthians who have deposed some of their presbyters (chs 44; 47).[151] It uses a variety of terms to describe leaders in the church which seem to be interchangeable with presbyters — *hēgoumenoi* (ch 1), *archēgoi* (ch 14), *proēgoumenoi* (ch 21), *episkopoi* (ch 42). In a rather obscure passage (ch 44), he indicates that the apostles laid down some provision for a succession in ministry which has been disrupted in Corinth. It certainly looks as though the Roman church was led by a team of presbyters but it is also clear that there was one church and, in the author of the letter, one spokesman. The *Shepherd of Hermas* reinforces the impression formed from *1 Clement*: that the Roman church was led by a group of officials with fluid and interchangeable titles — presbyters who preside,[152] *episkopoi*,[153] *proēgoumenoi* who occupy the chief seats.[154] He refers too to deacons who exercise their office badly and exploit widows.[155] There is no reference to one leading bishop apart from an enigmatic reference to a man seated on a chair who, unlike those seated on the bench, is a false prophet,[156] who sounds like some kind of president in the assembly of leaders; but the passage is too obscure to bear much weight of interpretation.

Was the single author of *1 Clement* or the man seated on a chair in *The Shepherd* a bishop? Much is made of the silence of the letter of Ignatius of Antioch to the Roman church about their bishop. Ignatius was being taken from Antioch to Rome for execution and during the journey sent five letters to churches in Asia, a letter to Polycarp the bishop of Smyrna and a letter to the Romans. In all the letters apart from the one to the Romans he speaks of fidelity to the bishop along with his presbyters and deacons. This has led people to believe that Rome did not have a bishop. But he does not refer to the presbyters in Rome either, yet from *1 Clement* it is clear that the Roman church was led by presbyters. The whole purpose of the letter to the Romans is in fact different from the other letters and does not provide any useful information about the leadership of the Roman church. The letters to the Asian churches offer pastoral encouragement from

[151] *1 Clement* 44; 47.
[152] *Visions* 2.4.3; 3.1.8.
[153] *Vis.* 3.5.1.
[154] *Vis.* 2.2.6; 3.9.7.
[155] *Similitudes* 9.26.
[156] *Mandates* 11.1.

a bishop who knows them; the letter to the Romans asks them to understand his desire for martyrdom and not to attempt to intervene to save his life. It is of course strange to see the encounter of what seem to be two different ways of organising the church — a team of presbyters in Rome and a bishop aided by presbyters and deacons in Asia Minor; all the more so since Ignatius indicated in his letter to the Trallians (3.1) that no group without a bishop, presbyters and deacons could be called a church. A natural conclusion would be that he believed the Roman church to have a bishop.

These fragments of evidence must be treated with due caution; they are too elusive to provide any definite picture of church organisation. Though there were leaders, it is unclear how they functioned or what their responsibilities were. Two pieces of evidence suggest that they combined pastoral, teaching and sacramental roles in a way that fitted the ideal of ministry repeatedly voiced by Ignatius in his letters. When Marcion debated with the presbyters in Rome, they spoke as though they were the mouthpiece of an authoritative interpretation of the scriptures. The account comes from the late-fourth century source of Epiphanius's *Panarion*[157] but it matches the early-third century description of Noetus being judged by the presbyters in Smyrna.[158] Since Smyrna certainly had a bishop (Polycarp of Smyrna being one of the recipients of Ignatius's letters), the meeting of a presbyteral council does not preclude the existence of a bishop; but it does suggest that the presbyters had an authoritative teaching role. The other piece of evidence is Justin Martyr's account of the eucharist in *1 Apology*,[159] where he describes the president (*proestōs*) as preaching, offering the eucharistic prayer over the bread and wine and also taking up the collection to look after the needy. The combination of sacramental and teaching functions with pastoral responsibility again fits with the understanding of ministry found in Ignatius's letters.

It is clear that by the middle of the second century there were extensive contacts between churches in which mutual recognition of leadership was essential. For instance, there are two separate accounts from the pen of Irenaeus describing a visit by Polycarp of Smyrna to Rome in the time of Anicetus, which must have taken place in about 155. The veteran bishop of Smyrna was received by Anicetus and

[157] *Pan.* 42.2.1–8.
[158] *Contra Noetum* 1.4–8.
[159] *1 Apol.* 67.

preached strongly against Marcion and Valentinus.[160] Though they disagreed about the calculation of the date of Easter, they had warmly amicable relations and Anicetus made way for Polycarp to preside at the eucharist.[161] Eusebius collected[162] a dossier of letters sent out by Dionysius of Corinth to various churches touching on issues of correct doctrine and moral practice; among them was a letter to Soter of Rome, successor of Anicetus, thanking him for the aid sent to the needy in many churches and revealing that Soter's letter and the letter of Clement to the Corinthians were both read aloud in the church.[163] When Dionysius refers to Soter as a bishop, *episkopos*, the term now seems to have a clearer meaning: sole authoritative representative of the church in dealings with other churches and organiser of aid.

For the church leaders of the middle of the second century, orthodoxy was pitted against heresy. Mutual recognition of church leadership and participation in eucharistic communion were ways of aligning the orthodox against the heretics. It comes as no surprise therefore that at about the same time the succession of orthodox leaders in a church, going back to the apostles, began to be used as an argument against heretics. The earliest list of Roman bishops seems to have been compiled by an anti-gnostic polemicist called Hegesippus, who visited Rome towards the end of Anicetus's time, about a decade after Polycarp. His writings, which provided the church historian Eusebius with a good deal of his information about the early church, were intended to refute gnostic claims by pointing to the historical succession of orthodox teaching. Eusebius quoted him as saying that he drew up a succession list down to the time of Anicetus, who was succeeded by Soter, who was in turn succeeded by Anicetus's deacon, Eleutherus.[164] Irenaeus used exactly the same arguments, appealing to the figure of Polycarp as the living embodiment of tradition stretching back to the apostles and producing a succession list from Eleutherus back to Linus, who was commissioned by Peter.[165]

These anti-gnostic arguments would have been exploded embarrassingly easily had they not been based on a common opinion that there was a recognised tradition of leadership going back a long way

---

[160] *Adv. Haer* 3.3.4.
[161] Eusebius *HE* 5.24.16–17.
[162] *HE* 4.23.
[163] *HE* 4.23.9–11.
[164] *HE* 4.22.3.
[165] *Adv. Haer* 3.3.3.

behind Anicetus. Any attempt to reconcile this observation with the picture apparently found in *1 Clement* and *The Shepherd* must be wholly speculative but it might plausibly be suggested that the presbyters who led the church at the end of the first and beginning of the second centuries always needed some kind of president for them to act coherently as the leaders of one church; that the authority of this senior presbyter was most evident when the Roman church communicated with another, as in *1 Clement*, but grew in significance in the wake of the challenges to the unity of the church presented by Marcion and Valentinus. In other words, the primary function of this president of the presbyters was to be the voice of traditional discipline and orthodoxy in the community. He was readily identified as the equivalent of the bishops who led the city churches of Asia Minor, who had a clearer role as the sole centre and source of the sacramental life of their communities,[166] as for instance during the visit of Polycarp to Anicetus. The list of the senior presbyters, now recognised as specially entitled to be called bishops (*episkopoi*), eventually became a vital plank in the anti-gnostic polemic of the 160s and 170s.

It is impossible to tell what kind of authority these early bishops exercised. It is striking, however, that information survives suggesting their authority was growing and was provoking dissent on matters of discipline and even of doctrine by the end of the second century and the beginning of the third. A major row blew up over the calculation of the date of Easter in the time of Victor, in the 190s. Victor, the successor of Eleutherus, was a figure of considerable stature.[167] He used contacts at the court of Commodus to arrange the release of Christian prisoners working in the mines in Sardinia[168] and he excommunicated Theodotus the Tanner for heretical teaching about Christ.[169] According to Eusebius,[170] the churches in Asia were celebrating Easter on the 14th day of Nisan in the Jewish calendar, the date of the Passover; elsewhere, and especially in Rome, it had been decided that Easter should always be celebrated on a Sunday.

---

[166] For instance, Ignatius to the Smyrnaeans 8: 'Let that be held a valid eucharist which is under the bishop or anyone to whom he entrusts it. It is not possible apart from the bishop either to baptize or to hold a love feast.'

[167] Sufficiently so for Lampe to depict him as the first true bishop of Rome: *From Paul to Valentinus* p. 403.

[168] *Refutation of All Heresies* 9.12.10–13.

[169] Eusebius *HE* 5.28.6.

[170] *HE* 5.23–24.

Eusebius reports a major dispute between Victor of Rome and the churches of Asia Minor, which he excommunicated for refusing to comply with the Roman date of Easter, leading to an intervention from Irenaeus of Lyons criticising Victor for his intransigence. It has been plausibly suggested[171] that Eusebius had misunderstood the documents in front of him and read into the past the concepts and practice of his own time. On this account, Victor was requiring communities in Rome of immigrants from Asia to conform to Roman practice and excommunicated them for refusing; he circulated other churches with news of his decision which met with criticism from the churches of Asia and Lyons for his intolerance.

Another dispute in Rome seems also to reveal tensions about growing claims to authority by the bishop over the other presbyters. A work discovered in 1841 and first published in 1851, the *Refutation of All Heresies* or *Elenchus*, is a lengthy repudiation of a range of heresies. The first book had long been known and attributed to Origen under the title *Philosophumena* but the discovery of most of the rest of the treatise showed that it came from the pen of a Roman presbyter who had entered into a heated dispute with Callistus, who is commonly regarded as having been bishop of Rome in the years 217 to 222. The anonymous author has usually been identified as Hippolytus, a Roman presbyter deported to Sardinia with bishop Pontian in 235, whose body was brought back to Rome after his death and buried in a catacomb on the Via Tiburtina.[172] Hippolytus appears to have been leading a dissident group and was reconciled with Pontian in exile.[173] A statue found near his catacomb in 1551, bearing a list of works and a computation table for the date of Easter starting in the year 222 has also been taken as a statue of Hippolytus; though the list does not correspond closely to the works attributed by Eusebius to someone called Hippolytus,[174] it can be observed that books seldom had a universally acknowledged title in the second century and so perhaps all these point to one Hippolytus, a Roman theologian and presbyter who was transported to Sardinia and there was reconciled with the bishop with whom he was locked in a dispute.

There is no consensus about this reconstruction. The Hippolytus referred to by Eusebius might not have been the Roman Hippolytus.

---

[171] Trevor Jalland *The Church and the Papacy* (London: SPCK, 1944) pp. 115–22.

[172] *LP* 1.145.

[173] As can be seen from a monumental inscription of Damasus from the second half of the fourth century: Antonio Ferrua *Epigrammata Damasiana* (Vatican City: Pontificio Istituto di Archeologia Cristiana, 1942) 37.

[174] *HE* 6.22.

The statue has been shown to be a female figure onto which a male head was fixed in the sixteenth century; the books on the statue might not be the work of one author. In particular, two theological treatises, the *Refutation* and the *Contra Noetum*, might be regarded as having inconsistent views of the relationship of God and the Logos. The most thorough recent examination of the evidence[175] proposes plausibly that the statue does not depict a writer but rather symbolises the ethos of a school and lists the writings of its members. The author of the *Refutation* led the school into a dispute with Callistus on grounds of doctrine and church discipline. Hippolytus was his successor as leader of the school and he wrote the *Contra Noetum*, a rapprochement with the theological ideas associated with Callistus, and was reconciled with Pontian.

Less plausibly, this reconstruction goes on to suggest that the Roman Christians in this period belonged to largely autonomous communities presided over by presbyters with independent authority. Callistus and his predecessor Zephyrinus were making claims for their authority which undercut that of others. The argument between the author of the *Refutation* and Callistus was therefore not only about doctrine and discipline but also about the increasing claims to domination of one of the presbyters over the rest. The reconciliation of Hippolytus with Pontian marked the triumph of those claims: Pontian and his great successor Fabian were therefore the first bishops of Rome in the full sense. This is implausible because of the events of the 250s, when the Roman church was subject to the severe challenge of persecution: Fabian died as a martyr in 250; the presbyters governed the church but insisted that they acted provisionally until a new bishop could be elected; when a new bishop was elected, he faced a schism as a rival presbyter arranged to be ordained as a bishop; successive bishops of Rome struggled to lead the church in the face of internal division and renewed persecution, allying themselves with and quarrelling with other bishops around the world. Everything was shaped by the undisputed belief in the authority of bishops. If the position of bishop of Rome was of such recent invention, events in Rome would have been very different.

The *Refutation* did tell a remarkable tale about Callistus.[176] He was the slave of a Christian freedman called Carpophorus and ran his

---

[175] Allen Brent *Hippolytus and the Roman Church in the Third Century* (Supplements to *Vigiliae Christianae*, 31; Leiden: Brill, 1995).

[176] *Ref.* 9.11–13.

master's bank. It failed and he ran away but was recaptured and put on a treadmill. He was released but then got involved in a brawl in a synagogue, for which he was sent to work in the mines in Sardinia. Bishop Victor negotiated the release of the Christians in the Sardinian mines through Marcia, the mistress of the emperor Commodus, who was a Christian. Callistus's name was not included on the list but he managed to persuade the officials to set him free and let him return to Rome. Victor sent him to live at Antium (Anzio) on a pension. Victor's successor, Zephyrinus, brought him back to Rome, made him his deacon and put him in charge of the cemetery, the catacomb that bears his name, St Callistus. After Zephyrinus's death, he was elected bishop in his place.

The *Refutation* is undeniably a difficult text. Its accusations of venality, ignorance and theological error against Zephyrinus and Callistus are clearly not impartial. Its attack on Callistus's laxity — allowing a bishop guilty of grave offences to remain in office, ordaining men who had been married, permitting clergy who got married to remain in office, allowing women to take slaves as husbands — probably reveals a realistic adaptation to changing circumstances which would meet a far more fiery test in the persecution of the 250s.

WORSHIP

In the 150s, Justin's willingness to explain Christianity to a non-Christian readership led to his describing the two central acts of the community's life: baptism and the eucharist. He describes baptism[177] as illumination and forgiveness of sins for those who have come to believe in the truth of the Christian teaching. Having joined with the community in prayer and fasting, they are taken to a place where there is water and there they receive the 'washing with water' in the name of the Father, the Son and the Holy Spirit. Then,[178] they are taken to where the community is assembled to join together in the prayers and the kiss of peace and the celebration of the eucharist. Bread and a cup of wine mixed with water is brought to the president of the brethren who then offers praise and glory and thanks to the Father through the Son and the Holy Spirit for a considerable time; the people answer to his prayer with 'Amen', which he explains is the

[177] *1 Apol.* 61.
[178] *1 Apol.* 65.

Hebrew for 'so be it'. The deacons then give bread and wine over which thanksgiving was pronounced to those present and take it away to those who were absent.

He gives a longer account of the Sunday morning eucharist,[179] in which he explains that Sunday is the Christian holy day because it was the first day of creation and the day of the Resurrection of Christ. He says that the people assemble to listen to the memoirs of the apostles and the writings of the prophets for as long as time permits, then the president preaches, encouraging everyone to imitate what they have heard. They all stand to pray and the eucharist proceeds as he has already described it. There is then a collection to which those who can give freely; the money is given to the president who looks after the needs of widows and orphans, the sick and those in need, those who are in prison and strangers. Justin explains[180] that the eucharist is not mere bread and wine. Rather the food which is blessed by the prayer of his word is the flesh and blood of that Jesus who was made flesh and he quotes the words of Jesus from the Last Supper, 'This is my body' and 'This is my blood'.

Of course, the passage is written for a non-Christian reader. He uses the word 'eucharist' but avoids the word 'baptism'. He refers to the 'president' and the 'memoirs' of the apostles. He does not want to burden the reader with the terms the Christians used for these things among themselves. For all its bareness, his account does nevertheless reveal a great deal: that the eucharist was the chief act of the weekly assembly; that the eucharist took place in the morning and was divorced from any kind of meal; that it was not possible for all the Christians to be present (in addition to the elderly and infirm, there must have been others unable to attend as Sunday was not a holiday for anyone who was not self-employed); that baptism and eucharist constituted the twin means of becoming a member of the community; that the assembly reached out in their celebration of the eucharist both to the needy and to the absent. But it remains a bare account, conveying nothing of the emotion or colour of the occasion; it seems likely, for instance, that though Justin makes no reference to it the Christians sang at their assemblies.[181]

Since Justin says that the president offers the prayer of thanksgiving 'according to his ability',[182] it is often thought that the prayer must

---

[179] *1 Apol.* 67.

[180] *1 Apol.* 66.

[181] Pliny *Ep.* 10.96 reports that the Christians 'sang a hymn alternately to each other to Christ as to a god'.

[182] *1 Apol.* 67.

have been extemporary, though that is clearly uncertain. By the early third century, about sixty years later, Christians were putting their formulas for the different acts of worship and sacraments in writing. A much-debated document called the *Apostolic Tradition*[183] is probably a Roman text that emanated from the school of Hippolytus. It has been argued[184] that the document reveals a development in the understanding of the office of bishop, establishing the bishop as the centre of sacramental life in the church, finally conforming Roman practice to the understanding of the role of a bishop already found in the writings of Ignatius of Antioch. The text is undeniably enormously complex and seems to preserve layers of liturgical practice, with material which probably dates from the late second-century overlain with revisions from the early and mid-third. It is unlikely that the finished product was in any simple sense a liturgical book for practical use. Nevertheless, it contains the oldest version of a eucharistic prayer to have been recorded,[185] which had enormous influence on the revision of eucharistic rites in the second half of the twentieth century.

The overall impression given by the final version of the *Apostolic Tradition* is of a church with a very highly developed series of ministries and conditions of life — in addition to bishops, presbyters and deacons, there are subdeacons, confessors, widows, readers and virgins. A period of preparation and training for baptism, the catechumenate, has been instituted. Cemeteries have been established for Christian use. The regulations about and the prayers recited at the sacraments reveal a complex theology of baptism and the eucharist. Above all, the text speaks about community, a community of prayer and worship and service in which there are different ways of being a Christian but all in union with each other.

VARIETIES OF MONOTHEISM

With the strange exception of Marcion, no Jew or Christian in the ancient world wanted to be anything other than a monotheist. But

---

[183] There are two full commentaries: Alistair Stewart-Sykes, *Hippolytus: On the Apostolic Tradition* (Popular Patristics Series; Crestwood NY: St Vladimir's Seminary Press, 2001); Paul F. Bradshaw, Maxwell E. Johnson and L. Edward Phillips *The Apostolic Tradition* (Harold W. Attridge (ed); Hermeneia; Minneapolis: Fortress Press, 2002).

[184] By Stewart-Sykes in *Hippolytus*, following Brent's view in *Hippolytus and the Roman Church* of the development of the school of Hippolytus and the emergence of a single bishop in the 230s.

[185] *Apostolic Tradition* 4.

reconciling God's transcendence with his engagement in the limited and changing universe of time and space was problematic. An answer commonly embraced by both Jews and Christians was to distinguish God in himself from his creative Logos or Wisdom; but this only raised a fresh problem, the danger of talking about plurality in God. It seems that Jewish thinkers retreated from the Logos doctrine in the second and early third centuries, helped on their way perhaps by the enthusiasm with which Christians claimed the Logos doctrine uniquely as their own.[186] Jews, however, were not the only ones who feared that the Logos doctrine compromised the oneness of God. At about the same time as Jewish thinkers were condemning the idea of 'Two Powers in Heaven', some Christian teachers were equally resolute in their claims that the Logos doctrine taught the existence of two Gods (ditheism) and equally determined to find a Christian alternative.

These Christian thinkers, called at the time Monarchians,[187] were to be known to their critics in the West as Patripassians (meaning, people who say that the Father suffers) and in the East as Sabellians, followers of Sabellius. Modern commentators frequently label them Modalists. Though they caused a good deal of controversy in the third century, they did not form a single coherent group with acknowledged structures and leadership or literature. To that extent, they were different from the Marcionites and the various groups who looked back to Valentinus as their inspiration. In other words, though a few Monarchians such as Noetus or Sabellius were expelled from the main body of the church, their ideas were too unfocused and too appealing to monotheist orthodoxy to be readily distinguished as heresy. They might best be understood not so much as a movement which positively sought to assert the identity of the Father and the Son but rather as the people who resisted the Logos doctrine taught by Justin and later by the school of Hippolytus. What is probably most striking is that these ideas flourished in Rome secure from any accusation that they led to Judaism. The Roman Church did not fear the spread of ideas in their ranks which could be construed as Jewish simply because Judaism had not been seen as posing an internal ideological challenge for nearly a century and a half.

---

[186] Boyarin *Border Lines* pp. 37–73 reads Justin as constructing a distinction between Christianity and Judaism in this debate, denying Judaism its Logos doctrine.
[187] Tertullian *Adversus Praxean* 10.

The Monarchians left no writings;[188] indeed there is little sign at all that they put their ideas down on paper. They offered no fully developed alternative to the Logos doctrine and to that extent were not significant theologians. Our sources come from the pens of their opponents. The first two probably belong to the school of Hippolytus: the *Refutation of All Heresies* and the *Contra Noetum*. It has been argued that they were by different writers, perhaps successive leaders of the school of Hippolytus.[189] The third is the brilliant, funny and theologically highly sophisticated treatise by Tertullian, the *Adversus Praxean*, written in Latin in North Africa but addressing the situation in Rome. All three of these works come from the first decades of the third century. The fourth was written in Rome about fifteen or twenty years later by Novatian, the *De Trinitate*, and can claim to be the earliest treatise explicitly on the Trinity written in Latin.

Monarchianism seems to have emerged in Asia Minor in the closing decades of the second century. Irenaeus, writing in the 170s, unlike the writers of the early third century, makes no mention of it The first Monarchian to attract attention was Noetus in Smyrna. He is a shadowy figure and an attempt has been made[190] to rescue him as a bishop in succession to Polycarp of Smyrna and as a significant theologian in his own right, associated with and influencing writers such as Melito of Sardis and Ignatius of Antioch, whose project was to refute gnostic ideas stemming from Valentinus or Ptolemy. This depends on too many fragile hypotheses such as positing a very late date for Ignatius and envisaging gnosticism as Noetus's target. The attempt to reconstruct Noetus's creed from passages in the *Refutation*[191] is fraught with difficulties. It might be safer to read Monarchianism not as a movement distinguished by significant theological thought but as a resistance movement against the Logos doctrine and a reaffirmation of simple monotheism.

Noetus accused his opponents of asserting that there are two Gods.[192] Instead, he claimed that it was the Father who was born, suffered and died:

[188] A possible exception is the *On Pascha* of Melito of Sardis, written in the second half of the second century, which says of Christ with no embarrassment 'God is murdered' (96) and 'inasmuch as he begets, Father; inasmuch as he is begotten, Son' (9); but, though the text makes no careful distinction between Father and Son, it makes no attempt to elaborate their equivalence.

[189] See Brent *Hippolytus and the Roman Church* pp. 115–367.

[190] Reinhard M. Hübner *Der Paradox Eine: antignostischer Monarchismus im zweiten Jahrhundert* (Supplements to *Vigiliae Christianae*, 50; Leiden: Brill, 1999).

[191] *Ref* 9.10.10–12; 10.27.

[192] *Contra Noetum* 11.1; 14.2; *Ref* 9.10.

If I maintain that Christ is God then he is the Father, if he is God. Christ
himself, who is God, suffered. Did the Father therefore suffer? He was, indeed,
the Father.[193]

Here at its baldest, but defended by a battery of texts from Exodus,
Isaiah, Baruch and Romans, is the simple equation of Christ with the
Father on the basis that Christ is God.[194] Noetus insists that the Father
suffered since Christ suffered, as they are both one and the same. To
accept, in defence of monotheism, that God could suffer was not a
constructive step to take. Unsurprisingly, Noetus was condemned in
Smyrna by a meeting of a council of presbyters.[195]

According to the *Refutation*, Noetus's ideas were brought to Rome
by his disciple Epigonus, who found a follower in Cleomenes. There,
they were tolerated and their views met a sympathetic reception from
bishop Zephyrinus, 'an ignorant and greedy man who thought he
ruled the Church'.[196] The author of the *Refutation* claims that the
disputes over personalities and doctrine in the Roman Church grew
worse with the advent on the scene of Zephyrinus's protégé, Callistus,
whom he made a deacon, and another Monarchian theologian,
Sabellius.[197] When Zephyrinus died in about 217, he was succeeded
by Callistus. The *Refutation* accused Callistus of having thwarted
an attempt to persuade Sabellius to accept the Logos doctrine,
dismissing it as ditheism, and of having seduced him into endorsing
the beliefs of Cleomenes, Noetus's disciple.[198] Yet later, apparently out
of fear of the supporters of the Logos doctrine, Callistus condemned
Sabellius while still teaching doctrines which they regarded as plainly
Monarchian. The *Refutation* spoke bitterly of how Callistus opposed
his group, accusing them of ditheism, and set up his own school.[199]

The author of the *Contra Noetum* offered no such complex account.
He was content to say that there were certain foreigners, disciples of
Noetus of Smyrna, who were introducing his teaching and whom he

---

[193] *C. Noet.* 2.3.

[194] *C. Noet.* 1.6 ('What wrong am I doing by giving glory to Christ?').

[195] *C. Noet.* 1.4–8.

[196] *Ref.* 9.7; Zephyrinus is usually regarded as being Bishop of Rome 202–18.

[197] The *Refutation* does not supply an account of his thinking; Novatian in the middle
of the third century presented him as the principal author of Modalist Monarchianism
(*De Trinitate* 12; 18; 21–22); later writers regarded his name as synonymous with
Modalism — Eusebius *HE* 7.6; 26; Athanasius *De Sententia* 26; *C. Arianos* 3.23.4; Basil
Ep. 210; Epiphanius *Pan.* 62.

[198] *Ref.* 9.11.

[199] *Ref.* 9.12.

set out to refute.[200] Tertullian, however, named a different apostle of Monarchianism in Rome. He said that Praxeas, a man inflated with pride because he had endured a short period of imprisonment for being a Christian, was the first to import Monarchianism to Rome from Asia.[201] The identity of Praxeas remains obscure as he was nowhere mentioned in the *Refutation* or any other early source but there is no strong reason to doubt he was a real person.[202] According to Tertullian, Praxeas taught that 'the Father himself came down into the Virgin and was himself born of her, suffered and was in fact himself Jesus Christ'.[203] The Father became the Son.[204] The Father suffered and died and rose from the dead.[205] The Father and Son are one thing (*unum*).[206] Tertullian thus presented Praxeas as teaching the same crude Patripassianism as Noetus. Was this a plausible interpretation of his views?

Sacrificing divine transcendence and immutability for the sake of monotheism was a price that Christians were unwilling to pay. It is not unlikely that Tertullian's account of Praxeas's ideas about the relationship of Father and Son was a caricature, as becomes apparent when his view of Christ is compared with that of Cleomenes. According to the *Refutation,* Cleomenes was the disciple of Epigonus who was the disciple of Noetus, but the version of his theology it reported was very different from the unconsidered Patripassianism of the teacher in Smyrna. Cleomenes, as reported in the *Refutation,* seems to have attempted to preserve both the changelessness and the oneness of God by considering the tension between them not in terms of the relationship of God and the Logos but rather the relationship between the divine and human in Christ. Thus he did not speak of Father and Son as titles describing God in himself but used them rather to draw the contrast between God in himself and Christ:

> No one is ignorant that he says that the Son and the Father are the same. He speaks in this way: when the Father had not been born, he was rightly

---

[200] *C. Noet.* 1.

[201] *Adv. Prax.* 1.

[202] It is often claimed that Praxeas means 'busybody' and was therefore a sobriquet disguising the identity of Tertullian's true opponent. But why should Tertullian have wanted to shield his enemy? Furthermore, the word does not feature in even the largest Greek dictionaries.

[203] *Adv. Prax.* 1.

[204] *Adv. Prax.* 10.

[205] *Adv. Prax.* 1–2.

[206] *Adv. Prax.* 5.

proclaimed Father. When it pleased him to undergo birth, having been begotten, he became his own Son, not that of anyone else. In this way, he thinks he establishes the Monarchy, saying that the Father and so-called Son are one and the same, not another from another, but himself from himself. Named Father or so-called Son according to the change of times, it was that same one who appeared and underwent birth from the Virgin and lived as a man among men. Acknowledging himself to be Son to those who saw him on account of the birth that had taken place, he did not hide from those who could receive it that he was Father. He suffered, was nailed to the tree and gave up the Spirit to himself, dying and not dying, and raising himself on the third day having been buried in a tomb and pierced with a spear and nailed with nails. Cleomenes and his group say that this one is the God and Father of all things, drawing a Heraclitan darkness over many people.[207]

While, it is not easy to know how far this account in the *Refutation* can be taken to be accurate, it clearly marks a significant advance on the ideas of Noetus as recorded in the *Contra Noetum*. By distinguishing between God in himself, the Father, and God incarnate, the Son, Cleomenes could avoid having to admit that the Father suffered while still confessing the divinity of Christ. Son is only the name to be used to describe the incarnate Father. Thus the Son is Christ and Cleomenes could say that it was the Son, not the Father, who died ('dying and not dying'). This, however, only re-located the problem of how divine immutability could be reconciled with suffering into the composition of Christ himself. How could Christ be both divine (the incarnate Father) and yet also suffer?

Praxeas, according to Tertullian, addressed this problem. He and his allies said:

that the Son is the flesh, that is the man, that is Jesus; the Father however is Spirit, that is God, that is Christ. Those who contend that the Father and the Son are the same now begin to divide them rather than unite them, for if one is Jesus and another Christ, one will be the Son and another the Father, because the Son is Jesus and the Father is Christ.[208]

Praxeas therefore reserved the title Son for the human being with whom God, the Father, was united in Christ. To call Christ's humanity the Son was not unusual at the beginning of the third century. In a series of passages, the author of the *Contra Noetum*, an ardent advocate of the Logos doctrine, described Christ's humanity as the

---

[207] *Ref.* 9.10 The author alleges that these ideas are drawn from the philosophical ideas of Heraclitus of Ephesus which he has already reviewed in *Ref.* 1.4 and again in 9.9.

[208] *Adv. Prax.* 27.

Son;[209] when the Logos became incarnate he became the Son of Man, a title that could be ascribed to him in advance in anticipation of the incarnation (as in Dan 7.13).[210] Where Praxeas disagreed with the author of the *Contra Noetum* was in denying that there was also a distinct personified divine Son, the Logos. For him, Logos (*Sermo* in Latin) was merely a name, not a person.[211] Praxeas therefore was proposing that Christ should be seen as two distinct yet united elements, the divine and the human, Christ and Jesus, and envisaged the human as being able to act in ways that the divine could not. In other words, according to Tertullian, he reconciled divine immutability with the sufferings of Christ by allowing for a distinct realm of activity for the human.

As Tertullian observed, the corollary of insisting that there can be no distinction within God between Father and Son was to insist that there must be a clear distinction in Christ between God and man. In fact, he accused Praxeas and his friends of inconsistency. He said that they did not preserve the distinction sharply enough. They admitted that the Father suffered with the Son, which Tertullian dismissed as just as much an infringement of divine impassibility as simply saying that the Father suffers.[212]

If Praxeas held to the Monarchian view of the Trinity ascribed to him by Tertullian, that the one God is the Father and the title Son only applies to the Father incarnate, then he faced major difficulties in his account of the relationship of divine and human in Christ. The only way to escape a very confused account of the relationship of Father and Son would be to depict it as the relationship of divine and human in Christ. In other words, when Jesus addressed the Father, it would have to be explained as the human Jesus speaking to the divine Father incarnate within him. Clearly, there was further work to be done on both the Trinity and Christology.

The *Refutation* gives us an account, at first rather puzzling, of the ideas of Callistus, successor of Zephyrinus, which appear on closer inspection to be a refined version of the ideas explored by Cleomenes and Praxeas. The *Refutation* presents two statements of those ideas. The first is innocuous enough:

---

[209] *C. Noet.* 4.8; 4.10; 14.3.

[210] *C. Noet.* 4.12–13; 15.6–7.

[211] *Adv. Prax.* 7: 'For what, you ask, is a Word but a spoken utterance or sound (*vox et sonus oris*)?'

[212] *Adv. Prax.* 29.

Callistus, bringing Zephyrinus himself forward in public, persuaded him to say, 'I know one God, Christ Jesus, and beside him no other, begotten and suffering.' On one occasion, he said, 'The Father did not die, but rather the Son did.' He thus maintained the continuous faction among the people. We knew his thinking and we did not give way to him but refuted and withstood him for the sake of the truth. He drew near to insanity on account of everyone hypocritically agreeing with him, though we did not, and he called us ditheists, thus spitting out violently the venom concealed within him.[213]

There is little in this passage to justify its allegation that Callistus's ideas were poisonous, apart from perhaps a clumsy profession of faith from the mouth of Zephyrinus and Callistus's own attack on the apparent ditheism of the supporters of the Logos doctrine. His teaching that it was the Son, not the Father, who died is significant. A later passage is more substantial:

He was a sorcerer and a villain and in time he carried many away. Harbouring venom in his heart and devising nothing straight, as well as being ashamed of speaking the truth since he had reproached us in public, saying, 'You are ditheists,' but also because he had often been accused by Sabellius of having strayed from the original faith, he invented some such heresy as this: he says that the Logos himself is the Son and that he is called by name 'the Father', being one undivided Spirit. Not that one is the Father and the other the Son, but they exist as one and the same. All things, above and below, are filled with the divine Spirit and the Spirit which was incarnate in the Virgin was not other than the Father, but one and the same. This is the saying, 'Do you not believe that I am in the Father and the Father is in me?' (Jn 14.11) The one who is seen is a man, he is the Son; but the Spirit contained in the Son, he is the Father. 'For I do not,' he says, say that there are two Gods, Father and Son, but one. For the Father who existed (or: 'was born' — *genomenos*) in him took on flesh and divinized it, having united it with himself and made it one, so that he is called Father and Son, one God. And he, being one person (*prosōpon*), cannot be two. And in this way the Father suffered with the Son.' He did not want to say that the Father suffered and was one person, to avoid blasphemy against the Father. This foolish and changeable man, scattering blasphemies high and low, so that he might only seem to speak according to the truth was not ashamed to lean at one time towards the doctrine of Sabellius and at another towards that of Theodotus.[214]

This is a difficult passage. While it is clearly a polemical response to Callistus's accusation that the Logos doctrine is ditheist, its lack of clarity does suggest that it is a sincere attempt to describe a perplexing theological view. It concedes that Callistus was attempting to avoid saying that the Father suffered while he also strenuously defended monotheism. Callistus was thus attempting to produce

[213] *Ref.* 9.11.
[214] *Ref.* 9.12.

both a theology of the Trinity and a Christology. The clue to this passage is that it accuses Callistus of the errors of both Sabellius and Theodotus. Sabellius's errors were deemed to be trinitarian. As a Monarchian, he denied the distinct identity of the Logos. The errors of Theodotus of Byzantium, also called Theodotus the Tanner, were Christological. He had been condemned by bishop Victor in the 190s for teaching a version of Adoptionism in which Christ was a man adopted by God at his baptism and anointed by the Spirit, thereby becoming the Christ.[215] He too formed a separate group which was later led by the confessor Natalis.[216] His ideas were linked with those of another Theodotus, the Banker, who said that the Christ who came down upon Jesus was a copy of the heavenly Melchizedek.[217] Effectively, Sabellius identified Christ with the Father, Theodotus identified him as a man adopted by God. How could these views be confused or conjoined?

First, Callistus had a doctrine of the Trinity in which Father and Son were distinguished only by name: 'he says that the Logos himself is the Son and that he is called by name "the Father", being one undivided Spirit'. Arguably, this was claiming that there was one divine Spirit which could be called Father or Son. Instead of defining the one God as the Father and then pondering the relationship of the Father and the Logos or Son, it might seem as though Callistus defined the oneness of God as Spirit, which could be named as Father or Son. This would, of course, have dethroned the Father from his monarchical position within the Trinity and this accusation is not levelled against him. Thus a better reading might be that Callistus was identifying the Father with the Spirit and depicting the Son as another name for him.

According to John's Gospel, Christ himself had said, 'God is Spirit' (Jn 4.3). If 'Spirit' is what God was, then speaking of a distinct, personified Holy Spirit was far from straightforward[218] and it was easy, for instance, to describe the Son as Spirit.[219] It is noteworthy that this is precisely what Tertullian does. By describing the divine substance

---

[215] *Ref.* 7.35; 10.23.

[216] Eusebius *HE* 5.28.

[217] *Ref.* 7.36.

[218] Thus, the Spirit could not be called a person; e.g. *C. Noet.* 14.2: 'I will say there are two *prosōpa* and that the grace of the Holy Spirit is a third economy.'

[219] E.g. *C. Noet.* 4.11: 'he was Logos, he was Spirit, he was power'; 16.2: 'What is it that has been born from the Father if not Spirit, that is the Word?'

as 'Spirit', he can name any of the three persons as Spirit.[220] Callistus might therefore have been venturing into a trinitarian theology not wholly unlike that of Tertullian but, where Tertullian envisaged the Father as the whole substance and the Son as a derivation and portion of the whole substance,[221] Callistus prefers to describe the Son as another name for the Father or a mode of the Father's action. Tertullian safeguards divine unity and the transcendence of the Father by envisaging the Son as a distribution of the Father, distinct but not separate, like the light from the Sun.[222] In doing so, he makes a distinction between Father and Spirit and it is by sharing in the Spirit that the Son is one with the Father. Callistus attempts to achieve the same aims by envisaging the Son as a mode of the Father's activity. He too distinguished between Father and Spirit and seems to regard the Son as another manifestation of the Spirit.

Secondly, Callistus wanted to say that Christ was truly God — that the divine Spirit was incarnate in the Virgin. The account in the *Refutation* goes on, presumably tendentiously, to say that it was the Father who was incarnate because the Spirit is the Father. It is more likely that Callistus would have said that it was the divine Son, the Logos, who became incarnate. The *Refutation* is touching here on the central weakness of Callistus's theology. If he denied that the Son was a distinct divine person and said that Father and Son are only different names for the one divine Spirit, he would be open to the question of how he could deny that when the Son acts it is the Father who acts.

Thirdly, as well as insisting on the divinity of Christ, Callistus wanted to say that he was truly human and truly suffered. The humanity was also called the Son: 'The one who is seen is a man, he is the Son; but the Spirit contained in the Son, he is the Father.' This is something found in both Praxeas and the anti-Monarchian treatise *Contra Noetum*. Where this differs from Praxeas is in not referring to the human as Jesus and the divine as Christ. It seems that Callistus spoke of two Sons, the divine and the human, but it is likely from the above account that the author of the *Refutation* failed to see the point. He called the union of God and man in Christ a *prosōpon*, a person, in whom the flesh was divinized and in whom God could be said to have suffered along with the man. This too seems to have distressed the

---

[220] *Adv. Prax.* 26.
[221] *Adv. Prax.* 9.
[222] *Adv. Prax.* 8–9.

author of the *Refutation*, who read this as a mixture of adoptionism and patripassianism.

The author of the *Refutation* clearly misunderstood Callistus and he might well have misrepresented him but there are sufficient signs in the text to indicate an interesting attempt to distinguish and coordinate the divine and human in Christ which anticipated later Christian thought. Callistus's trinitarian theology looks like an attempt not so much to equate Father and Son, as Praxeas had done, as to distinguish between the divine nature, Spirit, which can be identified with the Father, and its expression as Son. His chief problem would therefore appear to have been to explain how the Father's Spirit was expressed in a Son distinguished from the Father only by name.

The resistance to the Logos doctrine and the school of Hippolytus in particular which contemporaries labelled Monarchianism provoked some important developments in trinitarian thought. From within the school of Hippolytus there emerged the *Contra Noetum* which took an attack on the simple identification of Father and Son made by Noetus as its starting point but then ventured on to a fuller defence of the Logos doctrine and its Christological implications. God, though single, was always manifold. He was never without reason or wisdom but he manifested his Logos or Wisdom for the purposes of creation so that now there was another beside himself. These are not two Gods but rather, though distinct, they are ineradicably united, like the ray and the Sun.[223] More daringly, he considers the perfect Logos becoming perfect Son at the Incarnation.[224]

The situation in Rome also provoked a far more brilliant work, Tertullian's treatise *Against Praxeas*. Creative, funny and devastating, it exposed Praxeas as ignorant and confused while laying out a strong case for the full personal identity of the Logos.[225] It can be seen as the first Latin work to address the Trinity — indeed he is the first to use the word *trinitas*.[226] He was the first to use the word *persona* to describe Father, Son and Holy Spirit.[227] He is unequivocal in his belief in plurality in the Trinity while insisting on the oneness of God, for there is one *substantia* in three united together[228] and the

---

[223] *C. Noet.* 10–11.

[224] *C. Noet.* 15.

[225] E.g. by an appeal to scripture *Adv. Prax.* 12 or by observing that a father must have a son, they are relational terms *Adv. Prax.* 10.

[226] *Adv. Prax.* 2.

[227] *Adv. Prax.* 7.

[228] *Adv. Prax.* 12.

Son is of the substance of the Father,[229] while the Spirit is 'from the Father, through the Son',[230] and is the third *persona* of the Trinity.[231] Much of his terminology anticipates later doctrinal definitions, but nevertheless he still held to the distinction between the Wisdom of God, eternally in God's mind, and that Wisdom brought forth and personified as the Son for the purpose of creation.[232]

Tertullian's achievement inspired Novatian, a Roman presbyter, to produce the first notable theological work to have been written in Latin in Rome, the *De Trinitate*. Almost certainly written in the 240s and heavily dependent on Tertullian, it is not only a refutation of docetism, Modalism and Adoptionism but also an attempt to lay out a considered account of trinitarian belief. Novatian follows the tradition in asserting that the Father is transcendent and unknowable[233] but is nevertheless the God of providence.[234] The Son is God precisely because he is the Son,[235] receiving sanctification from the Father,[236] always with the Father but subordinate to him.[237] Thus while softening the confident assertions in Tertullian that the Son had a beginning, generated for the purpose of creation, and apparently regarding the Father's precedence as logical rather than temporal, Novatian heightened the insistence on the Son's subordinate rank, observing that if the Son had the same transcendent qualities as the Father such as being unbegotten, invisible or incomprehensible, then he would be a second God. It is because he is the Son, born of the Father and not an independent and self-sufficient being, that the oneness of God can be asserted against critics who warn against believers in two Gods.[238] In avoiding ditheism, Novatian has consciously chosen to present the divine Word as subordinate to the Father, divine but not as fully divine as the Father.

Two other things are striking about the *De Trinitate*. The first is the way the Holy Spirit is dealt with as dependent on the Son in the same way as the Son is dependent on the Father. This is taken as evidence

---

[229] *Adv. Prax.* 4.
[230] *Adv. Prax.* 4.
[231] *Adv. Prax.* 11.
[232] *Adv. Prax.* 7.
[233] *De Trin.* 7.
[234] *De Trin.* 7–8.
[235] *De Trin.* 27.
[236] *De Trin.* 27.
[237] *De Trin.* 16; 31.
[238] *De Trin.* 31.

of the Son's divinity.[239] Though the Father and Son are depicted as two persons,[240] the Holy Spirit is not called a person. Nevertheless, the Holy Spirit is given a clearer role. The divine Word is the one revealed in all the Old Testament theophanies[241] but the Spirit derives from Christ and is revealed partially in the prophets and fully in the apostles and makes the Church pure and perfect.[242] In other words, the Holy Spirit is the continuation of Christ's activity.

Secondly, in his determination to reject docetism where he insists that Christ is truly human[243] and Adoptionism where he insists that Christ is God as well as man,[244] Novatian begins to develop some description of the divine and human in Christ, employing terms which stressed the conjunction and binding together of two mutually dependent realities (such as *concordia; concretus; confoederatum, coniunctum, connexum; contextum; permixtum*). He was apparently the first to use the word 'incarnate'.[245] The maintenance of the Logos doctrine and the clash with Adoptionism was leading to a fuller articulation of a Christology which recognised duality and oneness in Christ.

What is remarkable is that the first work of Latin theology produced in Rome should address so acutely the profound puzzles at the heart of Christianity, the doctrine of the Trinity and the acknowledgment that Christ is both God and man. Novatian was deeply indebted to his North African predecessor, Tertullian, but he also spoke from a distinctively Roman theological tradition that went back through the school of Hippolytus to Justin Martyr and the rich complexities of theological debate in the middle years of the previous century.

A MIXED CHURCH

The list of names to whom Paul's letter to the Romans was addressed looks like a very diverse group of people. It is more than likely that in the great and varied city of Rome the Christian community was always made up of a great assortment of people. As the church grew in size in the second century, and despite its increasing clarification

239 *De Trin.* 18.
240 *De Trin.* 10; 27; 28.
241 *De Trin.* 18–20.
242 *De Trin.* 29.
243 *De Trin.* 10.
244 *De Trin.* 11.
245 *De Trin.* 24.

of doctrinal unity, it became ever more diverse socially and culturally. It probably took a long time to get beyond the Greek-speaking immigrant communities in which it found its origin: Latin probably only started to be used by Christian writers in Rome in the 240s.[246] Its appeal must always have been strongest among the ranks of the poor, slaves and immigrants (the many catacomb burials with no inscription are mute testimony to the illiteracy of the overwhelming majority) but there are clear signs in the second century that there were educated Christians and that Christianity was beginning to penetrate the social and political elites of the city. As the church grew in size and attracted an ever greater variety of people, so it also had to show more flexibility in its standards of behaviour and moral attitudes.

There was a close correlation between education and class in the ancient world. The poor had no opportunity to go to school; illiteracy, or very limited literacy, was common. Educated slaves were therefore very valuable and, on being given their freedom, could hope to make a good living. The literary evidence of the second and early third centuries points to a sprinkling of educated people among the Christians. The author of *1 Clement* was well educated, though not to a highly refined level.[247] Hermas tells us himself that he was a freedman who had run a successful business which failed and finally had a small farm; his Greek is serviceable and clear but unpolished.[248] Marcion was a prosperous ship-owner. Justin was well educated and functioned as a professional philosopher, though it would be a mistake to overstate either his abilities or the sophistication of his education.[249] Valentinus was plainly influenced by his reading of Plato and it is arguable that his appeal was directed particularly at better-educated Christians.[250] There was a hint of snobbery in the attacks on Zephyrinus and Callistus made by the author of the *Refutation*. It is likely that he belonged to a group of writers with some philosophical knowledge and interests. Novatian, writing in Latin in the 240s, commanded a style that indicates a good education and which marked him out from his fellow presbyters.

Though none of these could be compared advantageously with the great Christian intellectuals of Alexandria in the late second or early

---

[246] The possible exception is Minucius Felix, of whose origins and date there is room for dispute.

[247] Lampe *From Paul to Valentinus* pp. 207–17.

[248] Ibid., pp. 218–36.

[249] Ibid., pp. 257–84.

[250] Ibid., pp. 292–313.

third centuries, Clement and Origen, they do indicate the existence of a Christian middle class in Rome who read their books and absorbed their ideas. There are signs of people of even higher social station. Justin referred[251] to a wealthy woman who tried to divorce her licentious pagan husband and who was denounced by him as a Christian, which precipitated the martyrdom of a number of Christians. About twenty years later, a man of distinguished background and education called Apollonius was executed in Rome for being a Christian.[252] Marcia, the mistress of Commodus, was at least a sympathiser with the Christians or a Christian herself. At the same time, a number of Christians in middle-ranking positions in the imperial service began to show enough confidence to declare their faith on their grave stones,[253] the most distinguished of whom was Prosenes, a freedman of Marcus Aurelius who rose in the service of Commodus and Caracalla from being responsible for the supply of wine to the palace, to being director of the gladiatorial games, then to being steward of imperial assets and finally to becoming chief chamberlain, at the top of the palace administration. He died in 217. Prosenes had a brilliant career and, at some point (presumably after he gave up responsibility for the gladiatorial games), became a Christian. He died while accompanying Caracalla on an campaign against the Parthians; his freedmen went to the great trouble and expense of bringing his body back to Rome for burial. His fine sarcophagus chronicles his career; on the side is a discreet, private inscription recording his Christian faith.[254]

In the second and third centuries, the Christian community, while predominantly made up of the poor and slaves, included rich and educated people who owned slaves themselves. This clearly posed problems. Despite the idealised portrait of the early Christian community in the Acts of the Apostles, the Christians had never attempted to emulate its complete sharing of possessions. Of wealth, they were duly cautious, for they knew from scripture and experience that it had its dangers as well as its benefits. Hermas, for instance, offered in his third Vision a picture of the Church as a tower built from stones assembled by the angels. Some stones are used at once to build the tower — the apostles, bishops, teachers and deacons

---

[251] *2 Apol.* 2.

[252] Eusebius *HE* 5.21; see Lampe *From Paul to Valentinus* pp. 321–29.

[253] See Paul McKechnie 'Christian Grave-Inscriptions from the *Familia Caesaris*' *JEH* 30 (1999) pp. 427–41.

[254] Lampe *From Paul to Valentinus* pp. 330–34.

who have walked according to God's holiness and ministered to the elect, the ones who have suffered for the LORD's name, those who have walked in righteousness and kept the LORD's commandments. Others are thrown away, but not far away — the sinners who wish to repent who might yet be used in the tower's construction. Others are smashed up into pieces and thrown far away, or are cracked, or are too short — the wicked hypocrites who have attracted the LORD's anger, or the ones who do not have true peace in their hearts, or those who have a measure of lawlessness along with righteousness. Then there are the round stones. These are the people of faith who are also rich, who will deny the LORD in persecution because of their riches and their business affairs; but if their riches are trimmed and they become square stones, then they will be useful for the building.[255] The theme of the tower and the suitable stones is picked up in his ninth Similitude, where the trimming of the stones is explained: the round stones are round because their wealth hid them a little from the truth but the LORD commanded that their wealth be cut away, 'but not completely so that they could achieve some good with what they had left.' Thus trimmed, they can become part of the tower.[256]

These passages in the *Shepherd of Hermas* reflect the common attitude of Christians towards property in the early Church. It has its dangers: where your treasure is, there will your heart be also. Too much wealth makes a believer vulnerable in time of persecution. On the other hand, wealth can be used generously, for the good. No one need give up all their possessions, but they should not have too much and should use what they have for the benefit of others. So, Hermas urged his readers to give indiscriminately to all in need: 'give to everyone, for God wants his own gifts to be given to everyone.'[257] Almsgiving was linked particularly to fasting; Hermas advised his readers to use the money they have saved on a fast day and give it to the widow, the orphan or the needy person.[258] Hermas even goes so far as to depict the poor and the rich in a relationship of mutual dependence. The prayers of the rich are weak. They need the prayers of the poor, which are so much more powerful before God, and their almsgiving makes up for the inadequacy of their prayers. The poor, meanwhile, need the rich to support them in their need and they

---

[255] *Visions* 3.14.5–7.
[256] *Similitudes* 9.30.4–5.
[257] *Mandates* 2.4–5.
[258] *Sims* 5.7.

pray for the rich in thanksgiving. He concludes, startlingly enough: 'Blessed are those who have possessions and recognise that their wealth is from the LORD; for the one who realises this will be able to do some good work.'[259]

This outlook was shared seventy-five or a hundred years later by the North African Latin writers of the first half of the third century. Like Hermas, Tertullian and Cyprian did not regard the loss of possessions as a disaster, but rather something to be borne with patience.[260] Riches, especially when pursued at the cost of the poor, brought unbearable worry and entanglements that distracted the mind and heart from God.[261] The love of money, the root of all evil, opened the believer to temptations,[262] and was judged by Cyprian to be a major cause of the apostasy of so many in the persecution of Decius.[263] Cyprian devoted an entire treatise to almsgiving. Towards the end, Cyprian put a remarkable speech to Christ into the mouth of the Devil: those who misuse wealth are the Devil's servants and destined for Hell, those who use wealth well are feeding and clothing Christ himself.[264]

This attitude towards the dangers and responsibilities of wealth owed far more to the Old Testament and early Christian heritage than Roman attitudes towards philanthropy. Christianity drew from the Jewish tradition of almsgiving in which generosity was a sign of stewardship — sharing with the needy was a recognition that God the Creator was the giver of all good things and lover of the poor as well as the rich. Romans could not have agreed about the dangers of wealth; Romans would have expected a reward for their generosity and good citizenship, at the very least recognition for their good deeds. Christians were not conforming to the standards of society around them in not applying universally the command of Christ to sell everything and give the money to the poor.[265] Instead, they were taking a broader, less radical but wholly traditional older view of the right use of wealth. This might have been less radical but it nevertheless represented a sharp break in attitudes to almsgiving for

---

[259] *Sims* 2.5–10.

[260] Tertullian *De Patientia* 7; Cyprian *De Patientia* 17–18.

[261] Cyprian *Ep.* 1.12; *De Oratione Domini* 19–20.

[262] Cyprian *De Oratione Domini* 19–20.

[263] *De Lapsis* 6; 11.

[264] *De Opere et Eleemosyne* 22.

[265] The most extreme 'spiritualisation' of Mt. 19.21 is the early third-century *The Rich Man's Salvation* by Clement of Alexandria.

those who converted to Christianity. For one thing, almsgiving was to a considerable degree channelled through the leadership of the church. Instead of the indigent being directly dependent on the benevolence of the donor, they depended on the church administration, which passed on the funds received from all benefactors, whether affluent or not.

If the clergy emerged as the managers of relations between rich and poor, they also asserted themselves as the arbitrators between saints and sinners. The accusations of the author of the *Refutation* against Callistus, that he was a laxist who exceeded his authority in reconciling and tolerating sinners, reveal not only the range of moral probity among the Christians but also the burgeoning claims of the higher clergy to determine what behaviour was consonant with the Christian Gospel. These disputes were to be repeated bitterly in the context of the persecutions of the 250s when rigorism, represented by Novatian, could not accept the reconciliation of those who had collapsed under the threats of government officials. As the Christian church became more permissive, so the clergy became more powerful. At the same time, persecution brought into sharper relief the problem of Christian engagement with pagan society, the daily compromises every Christian had to make in business or private life or even in the realm of literature and the imagination with the sheer density of pagan religious myth and practice. This was the arena where the clergy had greatest difficulty gaining control of the outlook and behaviour of their people for it was the most complex and least susceptible to clear guidance.

CONCLUSIONS

A century after Paul wrote the letter to the Romans, major questions could not be ignored by reflective Christians. The answers they gave could have taken Christianity along very different paths. Christians had parted company with Judaism long before, but they needed to consider the relevance and authority of the Old Testament to their own faith; in other words, was Christianity the fulfilment of what had gone before, was it an ancient faith, or was it something radically new. That in turn raised questions about how the scriptures should be read, literally or figuratively. Could Christians devise ways of interpreting the text so that it had a different meaning from, or as they would claim a deeper and truer meaning than, what it plainly originally meant? Could Christians legitimately find in the pages of pagan philosophers ways of thought and concrete ideas that could shed light on their own faith and the interpretation of the sacred texts? Were the texts so impenetrable that their meaning could only be fathomed by those specially graced, perhaps predestined to be specially graced, to know the hidden truth? How could Christians reconcile belief in an unchanging, infinite and eternal God with the creation of a changing, limited universe in time? Did the envisaging of the transcendent Father working through his personified Word, the Logos, raise more problems than it solved, undermining monotheism? How could Christ be described as God if he suffered and died?

As Christians felt their ways towards answers to these questions, they also began to develop a view of orthodoxy and heresy which led to division and fragmentation. While Jews had some very sharp theological arguments, divisions among them had historically revolved around the interpretation of the Law and attitudes to the Temple or the political aspirations of Israel. Christians found new reasons for division: they divided over doctrine. Marcion and Valentinus both led groups that were clearly separate from the church which counted Justin as a member. Sabellius was condemned by Callistus. Theodotus of Byzantium was condemned by Victor. Major and permanent features of Christianity — creeds, a canon of New Testament scripture, bishops as authoritative judges of doctrine — all emerged as part of this process of the Christian search for the foundations of its belief. At the same time, the exploration of the contours of Christian community — how they worshipped, how they were led and how they understood their own imperfections — gave them the power to withstand the trials ahead.

Chapter 3

PERSECUTION

The one thing everybody thinks they know about the early Christians is that they were persecuted. Images of arenas and lions spring to mind the moment that the words Christians and ancient Rome occur in the same sentence. If asked why the Romans persecuted the Christians, most people would be inclined to suspect that it was simply the result of the bloodthirsty cruelty of the most ruthless society in the ancient world. If asked why, in that case, the Romans did not persecute the Christians a great deal more and a great deal more effectively, the position of Christians within the Roman state begins to look a great deal more interesting.

Though there is no evidence of any legislation declaring Christianity illegal, it was universally recognised in the empire that it was. Christians were persecuted because they could not be fully assimilated into ancient society, which was shaped and expressed at every level by religion. They were perceived as enemies of the human race because they refused to participate in many aspects of civic life which were regarded as essential to civilised living. Of course, Christians had to feel their way about which aspects of life around them they would take part in and which they would avoid, but broadly speaking they found it very difficult to substantiate their claim to be good citizens. They were always subject to oppression and risked open persecution. That did not mean that they were persecuted everywhere, all the time. In fact, it is more accurate to say that they were persecuted intermittenly in particular places until the middle years of the second century, when at last the imperial government made an attempt to suppress a religion that was beginning to present an unacceptable challenge.

WHY WERE THE CHRISTIANS PERSECUTED?

In about 110, Pliny the Younger was sent to be governor of Bithynia and Pontus on the southern shores of the Black Sea. He was in

120

his late forties and had already enjoyed a highly successful career in Rome as a barrister, politician and writer. His published letters gained him a golden reputation (the most famous of which now are his descriptions addressed to Tacitus of the eruption of Vesuvius, which he witnessed, and the death of his uncle, Pliny the Elder, who commanded the fleet at Misenum across the Bay of Naples and lost his life observing the phenomenon and attempting to rescue survivors[1]). He had been sent by the emperor Trajan as a new broom to reform the administration of the province and he set about his task with enthusiasm. Trajan had given him clear instructions before he left Rome and this led them into an extensive correspondence about their practical application. He also consulted Rome about the application of the law when its implementation looked unduly harsh, asking for remission of its full severity. One query concerned convicted criminals who had improperly been allowed to become paid public servants;[2] Trajan's response gave the hoped-for respite.[3] The other concerned the Christians whom Pliny encountered in Bithynia; this correspondence is very revealing of official attitudes to Christianity in the second century.[4]

Pliny observes in his letter[5] that he has never participated in trials against Christians. He is even unclear whether it is the mere fact of being a Christian ('the name of Christian') which merits punishment or the crimes (*flagitia*) associated with the name. It is remarkable that, though he is well aware that it is illegal to be a Christian, one of the best barristers in Rome is unsure about exactly why it is illegal and about the correct way of dealing with them. This suggests that trials of Christians were infrequent and had not been particularly newsworthy in Rome during his career in the 90s and the first decade of the second century. In Bithynia, however, he found surprisingly large numbers of Christians presented to him for prosecution. He executed some and marked down others, Roman citizens, to be brought back to Rome for trial. The result was that the pagan temples, which had been deserted for a long time, were attended again and the sacred rites were celebrated. The flesh of sacrificed animals was again on sale, whereas previously scarcely anyone could be found to buy it. Nevertheless, the numbers of

[1] Pliny *Epistles* 6.16; 6.20.
[2] *Ep.* 10.31.
[3] *Ep.* 10.32.
[4] As early as c 197, Tertullian quoted the correspondence in his *Apology* 2.6–9 to show how baseless was Roman persecution.
[5] *Ep.* 10.96.

Christians being denounced to him were growing and he could see that Christianity had penetrated beyond the towns into the countryside.

Though he summed up his judgment of them as a 'degenerate and immoderate cult' (*superstitionem pravam et immodicam*), in his investigations of Christians and ex-Christians he had formed the impression that their practices were harmless enough (meeting regularly before dawn on a fixed day to chant verses alternately among themselves to Christ as a god and binding themselves by oath not to steal or commit adultery or commit any breach of trust). He was clearly concerned about whether anonymous accusations should be pursued, about whether the law should apply to women and children as well as men and about the correct procedure concerning people who abjured Christianity by reviling Christ or venerating the emperor's statue in the court room and those who claimed that they had ceased to be Christians years before.

This is a remarkable document, indicating uncertainty at the highest level about legal procedures against Christians and especially their purpose. Were they intended to punish the crime of having been a Christian, or were a way of compelling people into conforming to the traditional cults of the city and the empire? If the former, people should be punished for having been a Christian in the past whatever their religious affiliations at present; if the latter, then they should be excused when they apostatised. Trajan's response[6] is equally fascinating. He says that Pliny has acted well, for no general rule can be laid down according to a fixed formula. He says that Christians must not be sought out but, if they are reported to the authorities, they must be punished. He avoids Pliny's question about the extent of the punishments. He makes no comment on Pliny's failure to find anything disgraceful in the behaviour of the Christians as a group. He firmly rejects anonymous delation of Christians as wholly against the spirit of the age. He agrees that anyone who denies that he is a Christian and shows it by offering prayers to the gods must be pardoned: thus he confirms that, whereas with all other crimes people are punished for what they have done in the past, Christians are punished for what they are in the present and can escape punishment by abandoning their faith.

There has been extensive discussion of the reasons why the Roman authorities prosecuted Christians,[7] yet no evidence of any

---

[6] Pliny *Ep.* 10.97.

[7] The single most important essay is G. E. M. de Ste Croix, 'Why were the Early Christians Persecuted?' *Past & Present* 26 (1963) pp. 6–38, reprinted along with his other essays on the subject in his *Christian Persecution, Martyrdom and Orthodoxy* (Michael Whitby and Joseph Streeter (eds); Oxford: OUP, 2006).

kind of general law has ever been found.[8] It seems clear, and the correspondence between Pliny and Trajan confirms it, that they were not punished for criminal acts such as incest or cannibalism, though rumours of that sort of behaviour circulated against them.[9] One unusual case where Christians were accused of these crimes and, despite abjuring Christianity, still faced punishment for them was the persecution in Lyons in 177.[10] Almost invariably, Christians were prosecuted for the simple fact of admitting the name of Christian,[11] which led to the anomaly pointed out by Tertullian that judges wanted someone to deny he was guilty so that they could render him innocent.[12]

Having noted the oddity of the legal position of Christians in his *Apology*, written in about 197, Tertullian reviewed the reasons why Christianity was illegal: sacrilege against the gods;[13] by implication, disloyalty to the empire for it was the gods who made Rome great[14] and thus insult to the emperor;[15] hostility to the empire and society;[16] causing calamities.[17] Tertullian's analysis shows how politics, public welfare and religious practice overlapped in the Roman mind. Both the state and the prosperity of society depended on winning the favour, or at least avoiding attracting the hostility, of the gods. Much ancient religion might therefore be described as a way of negotiating the great elemental forces, personified as deities: the sky, the sea, love, war, fire, the harvest. The particularity of place — the home, the street, the town — was marked too by a sense of the protection of its own tutelary gods. To survive and prosper, people needed to show the right respect and avoid disrespect to the gods with whom their endeavours led them into contact. This was more than a matter of personal piety; the welfare of each person was bound up with the good of all and so religion was a collective activity. The practice of

[8] For an excellent summary of the evidence, see T. D. Barnes 'Legislation against the Christians' *JRS* 58 (1968) pp. 32–50, reprinted in his *Early Christianity and the Roman Empire* (London: Variorum, 1984).

[9] See Tertullian *Apology* 7.1.

[10] Eusebius *HE* 5.1.14, 33–34.

[11] Tertullian *Apol.* 2.18–20.

[12] *Apol.* 2.6–7.

[13] *Apol.* 10.1; Justin Martyr also regarded the primary charge against Christians as 'atheism' *1 Apology* 4; 6; 13.

[14] Tertullian *Apol.* 25.1–2.

[15] *Apol.* 28.3.

[16] *Apol.* 37.1; Justin Martyr acknowledged the same accusation *1 Apology* 11–12.

[17] Tertullian *Apol.* 40.1–2.

civic religion was intended to promote the wellbeing of the city or the state in which all could share.[18] Conducted by the city officials, who were themselves the representatives of the economic and social as well as political elite, sacrifices were offered in public at the public expense on behalf of the welfare of all. That did not mean that these acts of public homage to the gods were attended by great crowds of worshippers, though on occasions such as the games in the amphitheatre they would have been witnessed by thousands of people. The civic officials were not leading the people in worship so much as acting on their behalf. Nevertheless, both space and time, the topography of the city and its calendar, were mapped out by its public religion, by the temples and the commemorations which made the people citizens.

Tertullian's explanation of the persecution of Christians amounts to their refusal to participate fully in the life of the city, for which the clearest evidence was their practice of an alien cult. What mattered was not that it was foreign; people well knew that foreigners worshipped the gods in different ways. A broad equivalence between the various descriptions of the gods and the ways they were worshipped was accepted. Migrants resident in a city could be regarded as doing honour to the gods by worshipping them in their own way. The problem was not even that Christianity rejected all other forms of worship and denied that the gods existed. The same was true of the Jews, yet they were allowed to reverence their own God, for he was the God of their people and their laws. The Jews did not accept that the God they worshipped was in any way equivalent to the gods of the pagan pantheon, but pagan opinion insisted that he was. Before the Temple in Jerusalem was destroyed, the Jews were known to offer sacrifice there for the well-being of the emperor. After its destruction, the Jewish God had been humbled and shown to be inferior to Jupiter. Jews worshipping God in a pagan city could therefore be understood to be doing honour to the gods. The problem with Christian monotheism was that it was not and, in the view of the authorities, had never been the religion of any city or state. It was a religion without any national identity or laws. As Christians did not adhere to the cult of any city, they had renounced the possibility of being true citizens. Theirs was a cult that subverted the Roman idea

---

[18] See James B. Rives, *Religion in the Roman Empire* (Malden, MA: Blackwell, 2007); Mary Beard, John North and Simon Price, *Religions of Rome* (2 vols; Cambridge: CUP, 1998).

of civilised society. They were atheists, enemies of the human race, disloyal to the emperor and empire and, probably, guilty of the kind of disgusting crimes that destroyed the fabric of society such as incest or cannibalism.

There is a sense in which the pagans were right. Given that every aspect of citizenship, whether political, commercial or recreational, was shaped by religious rites, it was not easy for Christians to claim to be active participants in the life of their city. Christians themselves were unsure about the scale and level of involvement that was consonant with their faith. Christian apologists such as Justin Martyr[19] or Tertullian[20] insisted on the commitment and contribution of Christians to society, that they were good citizens. The reality was not so simple. Tertullian wrote a treatise on idolatry for Christian readers mapping out where the boundaries lay. The shibboleth was the avoidance of all participation in pagan sacrifices but that was precisely also the dilemma. Unlike Jews, who had the Mosaic Law and an increasingly complex body of commentary upon it to guide them, Christians had to feel their way through uncharted waters. In the market place, in the home, in political affairs, in public entertainments, sacrifices were daily encountered. Tertullian tried to navigate a course through what was permitted and what was forbidden. The privileged child who went to school found pagan mythology on every page of the literature he studied. Tertullian said it was all right to study literature but it was unacceptable to teach it.[21] People involved in the building trade or the production of luxury goods were exhorted to avoid producing any pagan decoration.[22] Some professions were incompatible with Christianity — astrology,[23] trading in frankincense or training gladiators.[24] Since written contracts were sealed with an oath to the gods, they could not be made with pagans; Christians should try and borrow only from their fellow Christians.[25] The festivals of the pagan calendar[26] and festivities associated with emperors[27] found the Christian walking a fine line between observing

[19] *1 Apol.* 11; 12; 17.
[20] *Apol.* 30–42.
[21] *De Idolatria* 10.
[22] *De Idol.* 8.
[23] *De Idol.* 9.
[24] *De Idol.* 11.
[25] *De Idol.* 23.
[26] *De Idol.* 13.
[27] *De Idol.* 15.

the celebration and not engaging in religious acts, which were not always easy to define. It was all right to attend domestic celebrations such as weddings or the coming of age ceremony when a young man assumed the toga and to be an observer, not a participant, at sacrifices.[28] On the other hand, since offering sacrifice, presiding at the games, taking oaths or trying capital cases were unacceptable,[29] Christians could not hold public office. For all that, it was common for Christians to keep their faith secret from their neighbours.[30] The ability of these Christians to pass unnoticed indicates the degree of accommodation that they had contrived with the society around them.

Two areas of life reveal the kinds of quandaries Christians faced: the army and the games. The games affected everyone. A circus and an amphitheatre, along with a forum, baths and temples, constituted the physical shape of a Roman city. This was where the city assembled and, on occasion, made their views known to the governing classes. As with all other aspects of public life in the empire, the games were inextricably bound up with politics and religion. There was no unanimity among Christians about whether attendance at the circus games and theatrical performances was permissible or not. Though Minucius Felix's *Octavius* records as a significant criticism of Christians that they did not take part in the public games and shows[31] (which Octavius justifies on the grounds of the blood-lust, uncontrolled emotional hysteria and obscenity that characterise the games and plays[32]), it is clear that not all Christians were as rigid in their refusal to attend. Tertullian's treatise *De Spectaculis* was a learned as well as rhetorically brilliant demonstration of why it was wrong for Christians to take part — the games were consecrated to idolatry and drenched in blood lust — but the crucial point is that Tertullian is addressing his fellow Christians. At the start of the book, he reviews the Christian arguments he intends to refute which claimed that attendance was innocuous.[33] In other words, Tertullian was contributing to a common Christian debate and seeking to alter Christian attitudes. Though it was one of his most dazzling performances, it did not settle the question. About fifty years later in Rome, Novatian also wrote a

[28] *De Idol.* 14–16.
[29] *De Idol.* 17.
[30] *De Idol.* 13.
[31] Minucius Felix *Octavius* 12.
[32] *Oct.* 37.
[33] *De Spectaculis* 1–2.

treatise against the games with the same name, *De Spectaculis,* which also opens with a statement of his dismay at Christian attendance and a review of arguments in favour of participation. He admits that some people say that the holy scriptures offer no warrant for a condemnation of the spectacles; Elijah was the charioteer of Israel and David danced before the ark; scripture talks of music and dancing with approval and uses the imagery of the boxing match and the race and its prize, the garland.[34] Novatian has clearly not invented these arguments, which he then goes on to rebut. Neither Tertullian nor Novatian treats Christians who attend the amphitheatre, the circus or the theatre as simply sinners who know they are doing wrong. Both acknowledge that there are reasoned arguments for declaring the games or the theatre morally indifferent. Both set out to persuade, not simply to rebuke. In other words, there was a real debate about how far Christians could be involved with the pagan society around them which divided Christian opinion throughout the first half of the third century.

The other area of dispute among the early Christians concerned military service. In an empire of perhaps sixty million people, about one million lived in Rome. Very few of those living outside Italy held Roman citizenship before the third century but in a sense everyone owed allegiance to Rome. Even in the third century, when citizenship was extended to almost all free inhabitants of the empire, people retained a sort of dual citizenship, of the empire but also of their own town or commune with its customs and laws. The army was one of the most important expressions of what it was to be a Roman. In practice, the army was a major employer of aspiring young manpower. With the reign of Augustus had come a standing army, made up of legions composed of Roman citizens, in other words largely Italian, and auxiliary detachments which offered Roman citizenship after long service. In the third century, the army grew in size and was an even more important embodiment of the empire. Christian attitudes towards the army were complex. Tertullian declared confidently in his treatise on idolatry that no Christian could serve in the army.[35] Every aspect of army life was permeated with idolatrous religion. In another treatise, the *De Corona,*[36] he praised a soldier who refused to wear a celebratory

[34] Novatian *De Spectaculis* 1–2; he expresses disgust at Christians hurrying to the games straight from the eucharist, 5.5.

[35] *De Idol.* 19.

[36] *De Corona* 1.

garland on receiving his annual bonus and thereby annoyed his fellow Christians in the ranks who did not want the unfavourable attention it would attract; this Christian soldier faced arrest and risked martyrdom for his obduracy. But the striking point is that Tertullian describes him as 'more steadfast than the rest of his brethren, who imagined they could serve two masters'. Objections to military service had nothing to do with pacifism but everything to do with idolatry yet there were evidently significant numbers of Christians who did not think the rituals and symbols of life in the armed forces were incompatible with their faith.[37] This was in fact an issue on which Tertullian had changed his mind. When he wrote his *Apology* in about 197, he had cited the presence of Christians in the army as a sign of their loyalty to the empire and their sheer numbers.[38]

If Christians disagreed about two such fundamental features of the Roman world as the games and military service, they must have been far from clear about countless encounters with non-Christian religion in daily life. Society was pervaded by religious practice yet the Christians whose faith was unnoticed by their neighbours, the soldiers who found the religious trappings and ceremonies of army life not incompatible with their Christian faith and the Christians who found no conflict between their love of sport or the theatre and what they read in the scriptures had all found ways of compromising with it. The task of moralists such as Tertullian and Novatian was to urge an ever stronger sense of detachment from society, to persuade people to compromise less readily and hold aloof more confidently. One way of doing that was to coin a name for the non-Christian world, the society from which Christians or the faithful, the *fideles*, stood apart. In scripture, Jews were distinguished from the nations, *ta ethnē*, the earliest Latin translations of the Bible translated this as *gentes*. The Latin writers of the third century, however, began referring to non-Christians as *gentiles*.[39] This word usually meant people of the same nation as the speaker or the person being spoken

---

[37] For a full review of Christian participation in the army, see John Helgeland, 'Christians and the Roman Army from Marcus Aurelius to Constantine' *ANRW* 2.23.1 (1979) pp. 724–834.

[38] In the *Apology* in about 197 he had drawn attention to the fact that there were soldiers in the army of Marcus Aurelius, *Apol.* 5.6, and that Christians filled fortresses and the camp, *Apol.* 37.4.

[39] A selection from many possible references: Tertullian *Ad Uxorem* 1.5; 1.6; 2.2; 2.3; 2.5; 2.7; 2.8; Cyprian *De Lapsis* 3; 6; 7; *De Bono Patientiae* 21; *De Dominica Oratione* 36; *De Mortalitate* 8; 15; 20; Novatian *De Spectaculis* 2; 3.

about, 'compatriots'; it was unusual for it to mean 'foreigners'. It became a standard part of the Christian vocabulary in the fourth century so that the new Latin translation of the scriptures by Jerome, the Vulgate, rendered *ta ethnē* not as *gentes* but as *gentiles* (eventually giving the English language the word 'gentile'). For third-century writers such as Tertullian, Cyprian and Novatian to coin a word for 'non-Christian' is a clear indication of how they viewed themselves and the society around them. They were not only conscious of their own identity as the faithful, the Christians, but had an equally clear view of the non-Christians as not only distinct but alien.

What was a *gentilis* according to these Latin Christian writers? From the way they use the word, its definition seems to be entirely negative — the non-Christian. It had the connotations of the blindness, immorality and violence they attributed to the non-Christian world but they were not inventing the concept of the 'pagan'.[40] They did not coin a word *gentilitas* to mean paganism.[41] They did not think of *gentiles* as followers of another religion (paganism), for they knew that the polytheistic practices of their neighbours did not constitute a set of beliefs or a structured system of worship. It might therefore be best not to translate the word *gentilis* as 'pagan' but rather by the less precise term 'heathen'. The heart of the matter is that they did not equate being a *gentilis* with being a *Romanus*. They did have a concept of *Romanitas* (a word of Tertullian's invention[42]), the cultural and political complex of ideas and practices which described the Romans, but their own relationship with Romanitas was ambivalent. On the one hand, they could be excoriating about the absurdity of polytheistic myth and worship and the immorality of Roman religion and society; on the other hand, they claimed that they were the heirs of the best in philosophy and civilisation. They tended, therefore to see themselves as good Romans or the true Romans, refusing to accept that, in their terms, Romanitas was necessarily heathen.

---

[40] *Paganus* meant a person who lived in the countryside or a civilian as distinct from a soldier (Tertullian used it in that latter sense e.g. *De Corona* 11); it was first deployed to mean non-Christian by late-fourth century writers such as Augustine (*De Diversis Quaestionibus* 83, speaking of marriage uses both *paganum coniugium* and *paganismus*).

[41] When Minucius Felix uses this very unusual word of the Jews, *Oct.* 10, and Tertullian of various other peoples, *De Virginibus Velandis* 2.1; *De Anima* 24.9; 30.2, they mean no more than 'nationality'.

[42] *De Pallio* 4.1.

Unfortunately for them, this was a point on which they and the *gentiles* among whom they lived did not agree.

The very elegant defence of Christianity by Minucius Felix, the *Octavius*, is presented as a dialogue between a pagan and a Christian who go from Rome for a day out at the seaside at Ostia. Its date and provenance are uncertain — was it written in Rome or North Africa, was it a third-century work based on Tertullian or was it a second-century work and possibly Tertullian's source? Two points in favour of the latter view are, first, that one of the criticisms levelled against the Christians are that they eschew cremation and prefer to bury their dead,[43] a complaint that would fit the second century far better than the third, and secondly that Minucius does not use *gentilis* to refer to non-Christians.[44] The *Octavius* is an erudite work written in refined Latin. Its discourse is civilised. Its intended readership is obviously educated non-Christians and, implicitly, it suggests that Christianity is their natural religion. The force of Minucius's attack on Rome's political position in the world is all the more striking given his endorsement of its professed admiration for reason and debate. It is even cast in the guise of a conversation between lawyers taking a day off as the law courts are closed.[45]

The pagan attack presented by Minucius is subtle. It argues that the only sensible attitude to have towards the unknowable is scepticism, which should lead to compliance with the traditional cults rather than a new faith. It points out that unlike other religions, including Judaism, Christianity does not have temples and sacrifices, so it cannot be a proper religion; in fact it is a secretive and depraved cult. At the heart of the pagan critique is the argument that religion is all about achieving success; it is the mark of a good religion to promote the success of its adherents and no religion has been more successful than the Roman for no people have been more successful than the Romans — the Jews are dismissed as failures whose God proved unequal to Jupiter and the Christians are miserable, poverty-stricken and persecuted.

The debate's Christian response, put into the mouth of Octavius, goes far beyond the conventional arguments that the harmony of the universe is evidence for monotheism and divine providence; he offers

---

[43] *Oct.* 11; 34.

[44] He uses the word once, simply to mean 'nations': *Oct.* 6.

[45] According to Jerome's *De Viris Illustribus* 58, Minucius had been a distinguished barrister in Rome.

the standard rejection of slurs against the morality of Christians; he launches the expected full-scale attack on the immoral superstitions of pagan myth and worship. What is surprising is that he does not repudiate but instead agrees with his pagan interlocutor's picture of the Christian community as detached, largely poor and always threatened by the danger of persecution.[46] He embraces what has been one of the pagan's principal jibes. Christians do not really benefit from the prosperity of the Roman empire and to that extent are marginal people. Octavius is therefore refusing to accept that a criterion for a worthwhile religion is the success of its followers. Instead, he does something shocking: he attacks the Roman empire itself. Roman power, he insists, is built not on religion but on bloodshed and violence. By despoiling the temples of conquered peoples, the Romans demonstrated their taste for sacrilege, not their piety.[47] This is a breathtaking attack not just on Rome's religion but its history and its destiny. Whether written in the second or the third century, it was a frighteningly provocative assault on Romanitas.

Minucius was not alone in decrying Rome's dream of manifest destiny. Tertullian argues in his *Apology* that since the gods do not exist it is not to them that Rome should attribute its 'unlimited empire' (*imperium sine fine*) but rather to its irreligion, its overturning of the gods of the cities it sacked; every empire is established by war and conquest.[48] Cyprian of Carthage, in a treatise against idolatry, also dismisses the claim that the gods were the authors of Rome's greatness, observing that the Assyrians and the Persians, the Greeks and the Egyptians all had their day, and that the chance of history has now given dominion to the Romans, which they hold for a limited period of time.[49]

Christianity was illegal and intermittently persecuted in the empire because it was thought incompatible with good citizenship, whether of one's native city or of the empire. Good citizens not only played a full part in civic life but also showed their loyalty by taking part in or supporting the religious acts which constituted the public life of the city and guaranteed its prosperity by averting the displeasure and winning the favour of the gods. Christianity was dismissed as an anti-social cult. Its stateless monotheism and its rigid refusal to honour

---

[46] *Oct.* 8; 12; 37.
[47] *Oct.* 25.
[48] *Apol.* 25.14–16.
[49] *Quod idola non dii sint* 5.

the gods amounted to atheism. In fact, Christians did collaborate in the life of the city and the state in a variety of ways and disagreed among themselves about the compromises they had to make to live in the Roman world. But the writings of moralists such as Minucius, Tertullian, Cyprian and Novatian revealed how far the Roman authorities were right in their suspicions. There was a sense in which Christians could never be good citizens in any simple and uncomplicated way. To that extent, intermittent persecution was inevitable.

WHEN WERE THE CHRISTIANS PERSECUTED?

For the most part, Christians were accepted by their non-Christian neighbours and rulers. When things went wrong for Christians, it was the result of a local breakdown of the modus vivendi that usually pertained. They were likely to be safe in peaceful and prosperous times but they could attract punishment when something had gone wrong or it was feared that something might go wrong. Thus, the official precariousness of their position meant that Christians were vulnerable to local circumstances, to local anxieties and misfortunes, to local rivalries and disputes. Roman officials, lacking a powerful police force, waited for criminals to be reported to them to apply the law. Persecution was therefore usually initiated from below, by people bringing pressure to bear on the authorities, rather than from the top by zealous officials. The Roman authorities were not heedless of the dangers of casual or opportunistic denunciation. Trajan had directed Pliny to ignore anonymous accusations against Christians. Hadrian issued an even firmer order roughly twelve years later, in about 124, to the governor of Asia, Minicius Fundanus. He told him to ensure that Christians could only be punished after a court case in which their accusers had formally prosecuted them; anyone initiating proceedings out of the hope of financial reward should get his just deserts.[50]

Christians were vulnerable to the attitude and feelings of their neighbours. They were also subject to the attitude and feelings of magistrates — not only how zealous they were in the pursuit of their duties but their own religious mentality. The particularly brutal execution of Perpetua and Felicity in Carthage in 203 probably owed much to the preoccupation of the governor, Hilarianus, with distin-

---

[50] Eusebius *HE* 4.9.

guishing carefully between improper and proper cults.[51] In a treatise addressed to a proconsul in Africa who had started to persecute Christians, Tertullian cited contrary examples of judges, whom he named, who thwarted their prosecution: one helped Christians so that they could give the right answers in their trial and he could release them; another released a Christian on the grounds that to satisfy his fellow citizens would disturb the peace of the community; another did not demand the act of sacrifice from a man who had given way under torture; another refused to proceed with the case unless the accuser appeared in person, tearing up the document.[52] He also reported a case in Asia Minor when the governor was confronted by a group of Christians demanding to be executed; he executed some and told the rest (in Greek) to go and hang themselves or jump off a cliff.[53]

One trigger that could force people to treat Christians as enemies of humanity was natural disasters. If the gods ignored the due worship of the city and still inflicted famine or disease or floods or conflagration upon it, then it seemed more than likely that some people had alienated them. Angry crowds in the circus at a time of calamity could quickly identify scapegoats and it would be a brave magistrate who ignored them. The obvious candidates were the Christians, as Tertullian observed:

> To justify their hatred, they allege, among other empty claims, that they regard the Christians as the cause of all public disasters and the misfortunes of the people from the beginning of time. If the Tiber floods the city, if the Nile does not flood the countryside, if the sky stands still, if the earth moves, if there is famine or pestilence, at once they cry: 'Christians to the lion!' So many to one lion?[54]

Despite the rhetorical flourish with which Tertullian makes his point, this was a real danger. Accusations of responsibility for natural accidents were addressed elsewhere by both Tertullian[55] and Cyprian.[56] This view of disasters might well have been the attitude that underlay Nero's selection of the Christians as scapegoats for the fire of 64. Tacitus's account of the punishment of the Christians is preceded by the description of how the Sibylline books were consulted, in the light of which public prayers were offered to Vulcan, Ceres, Proserpine

---

[51] James Rives, 'The Piety of a Persecutor' *JECS* 4 (1996) pp. 1–25.

[52] *Ad Scapulam* 4.3.

[53] *Ad Scap.* 5.1.

[54] *Apol.* 40.1–2.

[55] *Ad Nationes* 1.9; *Ad Scap.* 3.1–3.

[56] *Ad Demetrianum.*

and Juno. Married women celebrated ritual banquets and all-night vigils. But none of this could stifle the rumour that Nero had ordered the blaze and he wanted to find plausible culprits. The persecution, however, went beyond those convicted of arson: according to Tacitus, a large number (*multitudo ingens*) 'were convicted not so much for arson as for hatred of the human race'. It looks as though Nero was accusing the Christians both of being the arsonists and also of having alienated the good will of the gods who should have protected the city.[57]

The punishments Christians faced were terrible but they were only the savage penalties of the law imposed on other criminals: they could be crucified, thrown to the wild beasts, burned to death or beheaded; they could also be sent to the mines to be worked to death or be transported to the islands.[58] Perhaps more typically, they could spend a long time in prison awaiting trial,[59] where they might be sought out by those asking them to reconcile them with God and give them peace,[60] and then eventually be released. This experience of imprisonment became sufficiently familiar to require a title for those who had endured it: confessors.[61] Imprisonment was not a punishment in itself; prisons merely held people until they could be brought to trial. But since the object of the law was to get people to conform, Christians were presumably left to languish in prison in the hope that they would. It seems likely that often enough the case against the Christians must have collapsed and they were set free.

The prosecution of Christians in Rome after 64 was as sporadic as anywhere else. The city could not have been the scene of so much intellectual vitality in the 140s and 150s had the Roman Christians been repeatedly purged and driven into the shadows by the inter-vention of the authorities. There is a good deal more evidence in the early Roman church of confessors than of martyrs. There is an enigmatic passage in *1 Clement* which refers to 'many among us who have given themselves up to prison so that others might be freed, and many who have sold themselves into slavery and given the money to

[57] An example of persecution in Cappadocia following earthquakes in 235 is provided in the letter of Firmilian of Caesarea to Cyprian: Cyprian *Epistle* 75.10.1–2.

[58] Tertullian *Apol.* 12; 39.6; 44.2; *Ad Martyras* 12.

[59] Tertullian *Apol.* 39.6; 44.2; *Ad Martyras* is a treatise to encourage those in prison; *De Ieiunio* 12 says that those in prison are in training for martyrdom.

[60] Tertullian *Ad Mart.* 1; *De Pudicitia* 22.

[61] The first use of the word (in Greek: *homologoi*) seems to be the letter of the survivors of the martyrdom at Lyons in 177, cf. Eusebius *HE* 5.2.3.

feed others.'[62] This might be some kind of reference to persecution. More clearly, the *Shepherd of Hermas* reports different categories of people entering the tower, which represents the church: those who have wrestled with the devil and overcome him, those who have been persecuted but neither suffered death nor denied the law and those who are reverent and righteous and have walked with a clean heart and kept the LORD's commandments.[63] These seem to be those who have suffered death, those who have endured imprisonment and ordinary virtuous Christians. Valentinus was said to have hoped to have been elected to episcopal authority and to have been disappointed when a confessor was chosen in his place.[64] By the beginning of the third century, confessors were recognised as having a formal status in the Roman church; a distinction could be made between those who had been put on trial or shut up in prison or been condemned with some penalty and those who had abused and endured domestic punishment (presumably slaves suffering at the hands of their masters). The *Apostolic Tradition*, in a much debated passage, says that the former were regarded as having the honour of the presbyterate on account of their confession and did not need the laying on of hands for the diaconate or presbyterate, whereas the latter did.[65]

From the fragmentary surviving evidence, examples of Roman confessors can be found. The *Refutation of All Heresies* affords one remarkable glimpse into the situation of the Roman church at the end of the second century from the perspective of the early third. Bishop Victor used the influence of Marcia, the emperor Commodus's mistress and a Christian, to secure the release of Christians working in the mines in Sardinia. It is striking both that Victor had a list of names that could be submitted to the Roman authorities and also that one noisy Christian, Callistus, was not on it as he was clearly considered a criminal and not a confessor.[66] Tertullian observed that one of the boasts of Praxeas, the Monarchian theologian in Rome at the beginning of the third century, was that he had endured a brief time in prison.[67] Tertullian was contemptuous of his boasting but being a confessor did award him significant status in the community.

[62] *1 Clement* 55.2.
[63] *Similitude* 8.3.6–7.
[64] Tertullian *Adv Valentinianos* 4.
[65] *Apostolic Tradition* 9.
[66] *Ref.* 11.10–13.
[67] *Adv. Praxean* 1.

Bishop Pontian and the presbyter Hippolytus were exiled to Sardinia in 235. Pontian resigned his office in September but did not long survive on the island. His body and that of Hippolytus were brought back to Rome by his successor, Fabian and he was interred in the new crypt in the catacomb of St Callistus[68] which was to become the burial place of the bishops of Rome.

Of direct martyrdoms in Rome from the time of Nero and Ignatius of Antioch, there is little trace. In Irenaeus's list of the early bishops of Rome, one, Telesphorus, is singled out has having been martyred.[69] While that almost certainly means that the others were not, it is also a reminder that there must have been martyrs of whom no record survives. The most famous and well attested is that of the apologist, Justin, the author of the two apologies and the *Dialogue with Trypho*. One of the differences between his first and second apologies was that, while the first spoke generally about the accusations against Christians, the second was provoked by a recent case in which a dissolute husband delated his wife as a Christian in revenge for her attempt to divorce him, which led to the execution of the man who had instructed her in Christianity, Ptolemy, and two others who implicated themselves.[70] Justin remarked that he expected to be denounced himself, perhaps by a rival philosopher, Crescens, who played to the crowd by calling Christians 'atheists'.[71]

Finally, Justin and his friends did fall victim to an accusation and the account of the ensuing trial is one of the earliest martyr stories to have survived.[72] They were summoned before the urban prefect Q. Iunius Rusticus, who was in office at some point between 162 and 168. Rusticus was an eminent Stoic philosopher, singled out by the emperor Marcus Aurelius in his *Meditations* (1.7) as the man who converted him to a philosophical way of life. Unsurprisingly therefore, he opened the proceedings by asking Justin to outline his doctrines, which provided Justin with the opportunity to lay out a brief account of Christian teaching. Rusticus moved on to ask where the Christians met. Justin was clearly unwilling to implicate others and in reply he offered an evasive answer, observing that they could

---

[68] ICUR 4, 10670; *LP* 1. 145.

[69] *Adversus Haereses* 3.3.3.

[70] Justin *2 Apology* 2.

[71] Justin *2 Apol.* 3.

[72] It exists in three recensions, the shortest of which is the most authentic; they are all published in Herbert Musurillo, *The Acts of the Christian Martyrs* (Oxford Early Christian Texts; Oxford: Clarendon Press, 1972) pp. 42–61.

not all gather in one place. Rusticus pressed the matter and Justin responded that throughout his whole time in Rome he had lodged above the baths of Myrtinus[73] and that he would 'impart the words of truth' to anyone who wanted to visit him there. When Rusticus then asked him whether he admitted he was a Christian, Justin replied directly that he was. Turning to Justin's friends, Rusticus received similarly direct admissions of Christian faith from Chariton, Charito (a woman), Evelpistus and Hierax. Someone else, Paeon, seems to have then implicated himself by standing up and saying that he also was a Christian. Rusticus began to ask how they became Christians, whether they had been instructed by Justin. Hierax said he had long been a Christian; Paeon said he learned it from his parents; Evelpistus likewise said he had learned Christianity from his parents in Cappadocia; asked where his parents were, Hierax said that he had been dragged from Phrygia a long time ago. Rusticus then secured a final admission of Christian faith from another person in the court room, Liberian.

It is possible that Rusticus was attempting to get the accused to name other Christians — those who organised meetings or had instructed them. It is also possible that he was attempting to build up a case against Justin as the main instigator of illicit meetings, responsible for perverting others to following the Christian cult. Either way, he made a final attempt to persuade Justin to recant. He asked Justin whether he believed that if he were scourged and beheaded he would go to heaven. Justin replied that he was fully convinced of it. Rusticus gave a further warning that if they did not obey, they would be punished. Justin spoke for them all, saying that they were confident that if they suffered the penalty they would be saved. Rusticus passed sentence: 'Those who have refused to offer sacrifice to the gods are to be scourged and executed in accordance with the laws.'

Eusebius records[74] another case but with just insufficient detail to make it very frustrating. A man called Apollonius, whom he describes as 'one of the faithful most distinguished for learning and philosophy', was denounced by one of his servants as a Christian. The trial was heard by Perennis, who made his views of the informer plain by having his legs broken. At Perennis's request, Apollonius defended himself before the senate with an eloquent statement of

---

[73] The text is corrupt at this point, showing that memory of this address was soon lost in the Christian community.

[74] *HE* 5.21.

Christianity which did nothing to save him from losing his head. In fact, Perennis was the praetorian prefect in Rome between 183 and 185. Eusebius said he had a copy of Apollonius's speech before the senate in his own archives but, disappointingly, did not reproduce it in his history. Unlike Justin, whose publications survive and whose trial and death were recorded by a contemporary who preserved the court records, Apollonius was ill-served by the historical memory. A strangely distorted version of his trial and execution written some centuries later, in which the whole story is transported to Asia Minor, might contain traces of the original story but is probably worthless.[75]

Until the middle years of the third century, Christians lived with the intermittent hazard of prosecution for being enemies of humanity and enemies of the state, atheists, adherents of a subversive cult. Their position depended on the attitudes of outsiders who might denounce them and on judges who might or might not regard their case severely. If arrested, they might be consigned to a long and difficult imprisonment. If condemned, they might be subject to any one of a variety of hideous deaths. For most Christians most of the time, however, the threat of prosecution seems not to have been urgent. The evidence of persecution in Rome between the time of Nero and the middle of the third century is slight and that was probably not untypical of many cities in the empire. The events of 249 were to change all that.

THE CRISIS OF THE THIRD CENTURY

In 226, the Parthian empire saw the rise to power of a new king and a new dynasty. Ardashir of the house of Sassan, having swept aside the old feudal magnates who ruled the regions of the Parthian empire and kept it in a state of permanent internal unrest, was crowned King of Kings (Shahanshah). This inaugurated four centuries of Sassanid rule. Unlike the previous rulers of the Parthian empire, Ardashir was intent on taking the reins of power firmly in his own hands by appointing provincial rulers loyal to himself in place of the old local nobility and then launching all-out war against the great neighbouring empire of Rome. Religion lay at the heart of this aggressive new Iranian empire. Ardashir's monotheist faith, Zoroastrianism, gave unity and purpose to the regime and the state. This mattered to Rome because the campaigns of Septimius Severus

---

[75] *The Martyrdom of Apollonius* in Musurillo *Acts of the Christian Martyrs* pp. 90–105.

in 197–98 had brought the two empires into collision and contiguity in Mesopotamia. Rome's eastern frontier had been the middle Euphrates; now it was the upper-middle Tigris. In advancing into Mesopotamia, Rome ceased to be a purely Mediterranean power and became a major player in the Middle East. Thus it was in the territory between the Tigris and the Euphrates, modern Iraq, that the Iranian empire of Ardashir and his son and successor Shapur I tested and eventually humiliated Roman military pride.

In 231, the emperor Severus Alexander abandoned an attempt to drive Ardashir back when one of his three armies advancing into Persian territory was defeated. Ardashir was on the offensive again in 237–38, capturing cities deep in Syria. His son, Shapur, who succeeded in 241, was forced back from these gains by the emperor Gordian III in 242. These separate campaigns were effectively one rolling war, requiring heavy investment of troops and resources to prop up threatened cities and endangered supply lines. Gordian met his end in 244. The circumstances of his death were obscure but one thing was clear — he had been beaten by the Persians. His praetorian prefect, Philip the Arab, took power and made peace with Shapur by paying a substantial sum in gold. That purchased peace in Syria and Mesopotamia for about eight years. Shapur reopened hostilities in 252 and, according to Persian reports, destroyed a Roman army of 60,000 men on the Euphrates. Antioch, the Roman capital of the east, was captured in the 250s and then again in 260. That year saw the biggest disaster for the Roman forces in the east. The emperor Valerian led another expeditionary force which was defeated near Edessa. Valerian and the general staff were taken prisoner, perhaps while negotiating with the Persians. He spent his remaining years in captivity, acting as Shapur's mounting block; after his death, his skin was hung as a trophy to decorate a room in the palace. Roman administration in the east collapsed and the Persians advanced deep into the Roman provinces of what is today Turkey.

Shapur's wars were not, in the end, wars of conquest. He pulled back and allowed the chastened Romans to resume control of their ravaged territories. But for the Romans this was not only humiliating, it was extremely expensive. The Sassanid Persians were the only rival who could field huge, highly disciplined and well-equipped forces which could defeat Roman armies in battle and capture cities with sophisticated siege equipment. Fighting these wars was enormously costly. The Persians, however, were not the only enemy. The northern frontier of the empire was marked out by the Rhine and Danube, stretching from the North Sea to the Black Sea. Protecting the border had largely been a policing operation since the time of Augustus, repelling the occasional raids of Germanic tribes intent on fame and plunder. But the frontier was also a market. The Germanic peoples on the far side of the Danube and the Rhine were inevitably affected by centuries of economic and cultural contact with the empire. Tribal leaders became richer and enhanced their status ostentatiously with the luxuries that Rome could offer. Surrounded by warrior retinues whose loyalty they rewarded with generous gifts of gold, jewellery and silver, these kings were very different from their ancestors, who could mount no more than seasonal expeditions to gather what plunder they could before returning home for the harvest. Three great tribal confederations emerged, replacing the old patchwork of small and competing tribes, presenting a vastly more formidable threat to the third-century Empire. For the first time, the names of peoples who were to change the map of Europe surface in the record — Goths, Franks and Alamanni. Their first major incursions were in the 230s across the lower Danube; they were soon threatening the coastal cities of the Black Sea and Asia Minor where they were often bought off with subsidies. Roman military efforts to deal with the pressure on the Danube frontier were considerable but were not enough to avoid a major defeat in 251 in which the emperor Decius and his son lost their lives. By the 250s, the threat on the Rhine was so great that the emperor Gallienus moved his headquarters to Cologne in 253 and stayed there for several years. The Roman authorities in Gaul made a unilateral declaration of independence, setting up a Gallic Empire which embraced Britain and Spain too: they saw no point allowing their resources to be siphoned off to support the war effort in the Balkans or Mesopotamia leaving them undefended. It survived for nearly fifteen years as a separate empire.

The military crisis was therefore also a political one. In the fifty years between the assassination of Severus Alexander while he was on campaign against German tribes on the Rhine in 235 and the accession of Diocletian in 284, there were fifteen legitimate emperors and about fifty co-emperors or usurpers. Almost all died violently — some in battle, most in military coups. Power in the Empire was passing into the hands of professional soldiers, often from obscure backgrounds, who rose to the top by drive and ability, only to be destroyed by the inherent instability of a military regime facing dire pressures. It was also an economic crisis. Military expenditure increased dramatically just as the resources of the Empire in the east were ravaged by Persian and Germanic invasions and the west were lost to the independent Gallic Empire. The coinage was repeatedly debased and finally the government had to resort to requisition of supplies in kind. Some parts of the Empire were unaffected and knew new prosperity; other parts saw an agricultural collapse and a dramatic reduction in the size of towns, while inflation drove prices inexorably up.

It was against this background that, for the first time, the Roman state decided to persecute the Christians.

THE EDICT OF DECIUS AND ITS AFTERMATH

On 21 April 248, Rome celebrated the millennium of its foundation. For a city accustomed to grand occasions and colourful spectacle, it cannot have been easy for the pageants and games provided in the Circus Maximus and the Campus Martius to have matched the solemnity of the event, but it was a splendid opportunity for the imperial government to assert its legitimacy. It was the good fortune of Philip the Arab to have been emperor in the millennial year. A man of obscure origins from a remote village in Trachonitis in southern Syria, he rose by sheer ability to be praetorian prefect under Gordian III. When Gordian was defeated by Shapur I in 244 and died in dubious circumstances, Philip succeeded him. He quickly made peace with the Persians by paying them a heavy sum in gold and then turned his attention to the northern frontier. He won some rapid victories against tribes who had trespassed across the Danube and awarded himself a triumph in Rome in 257. For all that, it was clearly in his interest to make the most of the millennial celebrations of 258 and he seems to have succeeded.

For an Arab whose claim to power lay in the military failure of his predecessor, this was an opportunity for Philip to portray himself as the heir of Rome's past and its traditions, as its champion against its enemies, as the one whom the gods' protecting mantle now enveloped. But he could claim more than that. The festivities were based on the Secular Games, traditionally celebrated in Rome every 110 years, the most recent having been in 204. These games and religious rituals, observed at fixed intervals beyond anyone's possible life span (*saeculum*), marked the beginning of a new age and sought divine blessing on the future. The millennial celebration, following the pattern of the Secular Games and timed to round off the thousandth year, did not so much look backwards as forwards.

Philip thus had his chance to be the harbinger of the next thousand years of Roman glory. Along with the gladiatorial fights and the parades, there were enormous numbers of religious sacrifices attended, unusually, by great crowds of people. Instead of the magistrates and priests offering sacrifice on behalf of a largely absent populace, these were major public events.[76] Unfortunately, the first signs of the new age were military revolt and barbarian invasions on the Danube. Philip sent an able soldier of senatorial background, Decius, to restore order and repel the invaders but Decius's success led to his being proclaimed emperor by his troops. He marched on Italy and defeated and killed Philip at Verona in the summer of 249.

Decius's position was scarcely strong. He owed his throne to a mutiny and civil war; the northern frontiers were still not pacified; the eastern frontier was quiet for the moment because Philip had made a large financial settlement with the Persians. It was in this situation, in September 249, that Decius did something unprecedented. He called on the whole empire to join in an act of worship to the gods.[77] What was unprecedented was, first that it was an empire-wide religious act ordained by imperial authority and, secondly that it required the participation of everyone, men and women and children, registered by individual certificates of compliance. In both respects, this was a very odd thing for him to have done.

Decius never revealed his motives or, if he did, they were not recorded for posterity but in attempting to interpret this unprecedented event two important points stand out. First, Decius was in Rome when he issued the decree. The millennial games of the previous year must have been in his mind as he pondered Rome's and his own future. The millennial games had been a massive, popular affirmation of confidence in the gods' protection of Rome. In the light of what had happened since, another massive manifestation of homage to the gods was called for. Secondly, in 212 Caracalla had extended the citizenship to all free inhabitants of the empire. His motives were probably financial — to exact more revenue in taxes — but it did mark the way the empire had changed. No longer was the empire the unprecedentedly vast hinterland of the most successful

---

[76] For the fullest description of the Secular Games, see Zosimus *Historia Nova* 2.5–6.

[77] See J. B. Rives, 'The Decree of Decius and the Religion of Empire' *JRS* 89 (1999) pp. 135–54; Reinhard Selinger, *The Mid-Third Century Persecutions of Decius and Valerian* (Frankfurt-am-Main: Peter Lang, 2002).

city state in history; the empire was now the state and Rome was its greatest city. The relationship between Rome and the provinces had shifted and so the new millennium was not just a turning point for the city but for the whole empire. Therefore it would make sense for Decius to engage all the people of the empire in this act of supplication of the gods by means of an edict, addressed directly to them, rather than instructions sent to officials. They were required to worship the gods as citizens, recording their sacrificial duty with certificates (*libelli*) that looked just like the certificates they received when they fulfilled their usual duty as citizens, paying their taxes.

The edict was exceptional but it was not revolutionary. The gods to whom people were required to offer sacrifice were the gods of their own city or place, not specifically the gods of Rome, still less the person of the emperor. Loyalty to the empire was still mediated through local allegiances. Perhaps the certificates were not primarily intended as a way for the bureaucracy to keep a record of who had offered sacrifice but were a token of good citizenship to be prized by those who had taken part.[78] It was not a new expression of the central-ising power of the state; the bureaucracy was clearly overstretched by the exercise. It did, however, have massive and probably unforeseen consequences for the Christians.

This unprecedented imperial act would have passed unnoticed into the oblivion which claimed so much else of the third century — one of the least well-documented periods in history — were it not for a few letters preserved by the church historian Eusebius and, vastly more importantly, the enormous file of correspondence of bishop Cyprian of Carthage. Cyprian was bishop of the leading city of Roman North Africa for the decade 248–258. One of the first 'gentlemen' to have been elected as a bishop, he stood out among his contempo-raries not only by education and personal wealth but by strength of character and political astuteness. He was a figure of great stature. His correspondence[79] was a very effective way of stamping his fellow African bishops with his outlook and ensuring agreement with his policies; it was also intended to secure agreement across the Christian world and above all with Rome on how to cope with the crisis that confronted the church throughout the decade of his episcopate. Inevitably, those years are reported from his point of view and as

[78] Remarkably, forty six survive.
[79] A translation with full commentary is provided by G. W. Clarke (ed), *The Letters of St Cyprian of Carthage* (4 vols; New York: Newman Press, 1984–9).

though he were their leading player. He does, fortunately, supply enough information for us to have some idea of what was happening across the Mediterranean in Rome.[80]

It would be inaccurate to describe Decius's call for universal sacrifice to the gods as a deliberate persecution of Christians across the empire but that is how it seemed to them. It is not impossible that some Christians were targeted at once by the local authorities. The moment the edict reached Alexandria, for example, an official was sent to arrest the bishop, Dionysius. He searched for him everywhere except his house, refusing to believe he could be so foolish as to stay there; after four days, Dionysius quietly slipped away.[81] It seems likely that the bishops of Rome, Jerusalem and Antioch were also arrested at an early stage in the process. The death of the Bishop of Rome, Fabian, on 20 January 250 shows that he fell an early victim of the edict.[82] He was buried in the catacomb of St Callistus near the tomb of his predecessor, Pontian, in a part of the catacomb later to be known as the crypt of the popes.[83]

Fabian's early arrest might be seen as evidence that the new regime in Rome felt there was a score to settle. According to Eusebius, Decius's persecution was a reaction to his predecessor Philip's toleration of the Christians.[84] That is not a sufficient explanation of Decius's edict, which was not intended to attack Christianity directly, but it might make sense of events in Rome. Eusebius reports the strange tale that Philip had wanted to attend the Easter Vigil in 249 but on Fabian's insistence took his place with the penitents.[85] Eusebius's archive certainly did contain letters — which infuriatingly he does not quote — from the incomparable theologian and biblical scholar Origen, to both Philip and his consort Severa and to bishop Fabian.[86] If there is any truth in Eusebius's information that Philip had shown interest in

---

[80] For Cyprian, see J. Patout Burns, *Cyprian the Bishop* (Routledge Early Church Monographs; London: Routledge, 2002) and Geoffrey D. Dunn, *Cyprian and the Bishops of Rome: Questions of Papal Primacy in the Early Church* (Early Christian Studies, 11; Strathfield, NSW: St Paul's Publications, 2007).

[81] Eusebius quotes a letter from Dionysius describing these events *HE* 6.40.2.

[82] Eusebius reports that the bishop of Rome died as a martyr and the bishops of Jerusalem and Antioch both died in prison: *HE* 6.39.1–4.

[83] *LP* 1.148. His grave slab, simply recording that he was bishop and martyr, was discovered in 1854: ICUR 4, 10694.

[84] *HE* 6.39.1.

[85] *HE* 6.34.

[86] *HE* 6.36.3–4.

and warmth towards the Roman Christians, a change of regime might well have marked Fabian out for special attention.

With their bishop dead, the Roman church passed under the direction of the presbyters. Early in the crisis, they wrote a remarkable letter to the clergy of Carthage, in not very good Latin (revealing the modesty of the educational attainments of most of them). It is the letter's confident tone that is most striking. Cyprian had left Carthage and gone into hiding. The Roman presbyters advise their Carthaginian counterparts to consider their responsibilities in the absence of their bishop, suggesting that they were very clear that they knew theirs.[87] It was not too hard to see in this an implication that their bishop, Fabian, had set the right example by dying as a martyr, whereas Cyprian had abandoned his people. The Roman presbyters reported that, though some of the more socially prominent members of the church had offered sacrifice, they had restrained others, maintaining discipline with firm leadership.[88] They announced that they had a workable policy concerning those who had conformed to the edict: that they should do penance but could at present only be reconciled on their deathbeds.[89] At the same time, they noted that it was dangerous to retrieve the bodies of martyrs for burial,[90] revealing that some had paid for their recusancy with their lives. The letter was sent in the name of the brethren in chains, the presbyters and the whole church.[91]

The tone of this letter suggests that Rome had suffered less than elsewhere in the Christian world. All over the empire, Christians had hurried along with everyone else to offer sacrifice. Bishop Dionysius of Alexandria described how many of the more socially eminent Christians of the Egyptian capital came forward at once, others in public positions were compelled by their business and others were dragged reluctantly by the crowd. Some were white-faced and trembling as they performed the sacrifices; others rushed forward, looking as though they had never been Christians.[92] Cyprian painted much the same picture in Carthage, of Christians making haste to offer sacrifice even before they were obliged to do so.[93] He observed

[87] Cyprian *Ep.* 8.1.2 — 8.3.2.
[88] *Ep.* 8.2.2.
[89] *Ep.* 8.2.3 — 8.3.1.
[90] *Ep.* 8.3.2.
[91] *Ep.* 8.3.3.
[92] Eusebius *HE* 6.41.11.
[93] *De Lapsis* 8–9.

that people could have evaded the persecution by leaving Carthage but did not do so for fear of losing their possessions. Worldly riches had therefore been their downfall.[94] In Smyrna in February 250, the bishop led his people to offer sacrifice decked in a garland.[95] In the same way, in Italy, Bishop Trofimus led his community to conform to the edict,[96] as did a number of other bishops such as Repostus of Saturnurca in Africa Proconsularis.[97] Some African presbyters also gave way and offered sacrifice.[98] Others withdrew. Cyprian was not the only one to seek safety outside Carthage; many of the other clergy did too. He remarked that there were scarcely enough clergy left in Carthage to perform the daily liturgies[99] and that many of the clergy were absent.[100] He observed that the majority of his flock were ravaged.[101] He finally admitted that the majority of the laity and a portion of the clergy had been overwhelmed by the pressure to conform.[102] They had a word in Latin for those who had complied with the demands of the edict: the *lapsi*, the fallen.

Those who stood out and refused to sacrifice seem to have been subjected to punishments intended to force them to conform. In Smyrna, for example, the presbyter Pionius did not follow the example of the bishop Euctemus and endured considerable moral pressure before succumbing to physical tortures. He was burned to death alongside a member of the Marcionite sect, called Metrodorus[103] — a sign that the small Christian groups were swept up into the persecution too. The full horror of imprisonment was described in a letter from Lucianus in North Africa to his fellow African, Celerinus in Rome:

> By the emperor's command, we were ordered to be killed by hunger and thirst and were gaoled in two cells so that they could weaken us by hunger and thirst.

---

[94] *De Lap.* 10–12.

[95] *The Martyrdom of Pionius* 16; 18 in Musurillo *Acts of the Christian Martyrs pp.* 157; 161.

[96] Cyprian *Ep.* 55.11.1–2.

[97] Cyprian *Ep.* 59.10.3.

[98] Cyprian *Ep.* 40.1.2.

[99] *Ep.* 29.1.1.

[100] *Ep.* 34.4.1.

[101] *Ep.* 11.1.2.

[102] *Ep.* 14.1.1.

[103] *Martyrdom of Pionius* 21 in Musurillo *Acts of the Christian Martyrs* p. 165; this must explain why, having said that they were Christians, Pionius and his fellow confessor Sabina were asked which church they belonged to, to which they answered the Catholic church *Martyrdom* 9 in Musurillo *Acts of the Christian Martyrs* pp. 147–49.

Moreover, through the searing heat our suffering was so intolerable that no one could bear it. But now we have attained the Light itself. Beloved brother, greet Numeria and Candida [to whom we grant peace] according to the instruction of [the martyr] Paulus and the rest of the martyrs whose names I add: Bassus in the mines, Mappalicus under torture, Fortunio in prison, Paulus after torture, Fortunata, Victorinus, Victor, Herennius, Credula, Hereda, Donatus, Firmus, Venustus, Fructus, Julia, Martial and Ariston who, by God's will, were starved to death in the prison. In a few days you will hear that I am their companion. It is now eight days that I have been imprisoned again to the time of writing this letter to you. For the previous five days I received only a small amount of bread and water.[104]

On the one hand, there were martyrs and confessors enduring extreme suffering; on the other hand, many Christians, especially socially prominent Christians, gave way and offered sacrifice. It was a grave crisis but the administration of the edict was so erratic that much could continue as normal. Cyprian remarked that there was no immediate danger to some presbyters and deacons who could fulfil his duties in his absence.[105] The daily liturgies in Carthage continued.[106] They were even going into the prisons to celebrate the eucharist with the confessors; Cyprian urged them to be cautious, telling the presbyters to take turns and to be accompanied by a different deacon each time.[107]

The situation in Rome was probably little different. The Roman clergy wanted to stress that in this crisis they stood firm. They commanded considerable moral authority. Though Cyprian was clearly stung by their letter to his clergy with its implicit criticism of his escape,[108] he felt he needed to justify his behaviour to them and spoke to them with marked respect.[109] He also wrote an admiring letter to the Roman presbyters Moyses and Maximus and the other confessors in gaol in Rome.[110]

In fact, the application of the edict had been inefficient and corrupt. Many of the Christians bribed the officials to supply certificates indicating that they had complied with its requirements.[111] Some received certificates from third parties, thereby not directly

---

[104] Cyprian *Ep.* 22.
[105] *Ep.* 14.2.1.
[106] *Ep.* 29.1.1.
[107] *Ep.* 5.2.1.
[108] *Ep.* 9.
[109] *Ep.* 20.
[110] *Ep.* 28.
[111] Cyprian *Epp.* 20.2.2; 21.3.2; 27.1.1–2; 30.3.1; 55.14.1.

being involved in bribery themselves.[112] As conformists by means
of obtaining a certificate, they were dubbed *libellatici*. Though the
evidence is, of course, strongest from Carthage on account of
Cyprian's extensive correspondence,[113] the same happened in Rome.
When Cyprian raised the matter with the Roman presbyters,[114]
they joined in his condemnation of the practice.[115] Cyprian later
commended the new bishop of Rome, Cornelius, as having been in
no way compromised by a certificate.[116] In fact, there was nothing
new about Christians bribing officials to escape the full force of
persecution[117] and it was clear even to Cyprian that this was honestly
regarded as a reasonable way of avoiding sacrifice[118] but, while
Cyprian acknowledged that there were grades of sin,[119] he was fully
determined to insist that acquiring these certificates, even indirectly,
should be counted as apostasy.[120]

This reveals typical confusion about acceptable behaviour on the
part of Christians towards the Roman state. This is not surprising.
The treatise in which Tertullian condemned the bribing of officials
to escape persecution, *On Flight in Persecution*, was a vigorous attack
on the course of action Cyprian himself adopted, of disappearance
to evade arrest. This was just another episode in the long-running
Christian debate about levels of engagement and compromise with
pagan society. This crisis presented the church leadership around
the world with a challenge and an opportunity to assert their own
authority in that debate. They faced the danger of being outflanked
by the moral and personal authority of confessors, whether in prison
or recently released, whose blessing could be sought by penitent
lapsi. Again, there was nothing new in this,[121] apart from the issuing

---

[112] Cyprian *Epp.* 30.3.1; 55.14.1.

[113] Cyprian *Ep.* 23 is a letter from the confessor Lucianus to Cyprian announcing that
the confessors are granting peace; *Ep.* 21.3 is a request from a Carthaginian resident
in Rome asking Lucinanus to grant peace to his sisters, one of whom sacrificed and
the other bribed the officials but who are both now ministering to Carthaginian
refugees in the city; *Ep.* 27.1–2 is a letter of Cyprian to the Roman clergy deploring
the practice.

[114] *Ep.* 27.

[115] Cyprian *Ep.* 30.3.1.

[116] *Ep.* 55.10.2.

[117] Tertullian *De Fuga* 5.3.

[118] *Ep.* 55.14.1.

[119] *Ep.* 15.3.1.

[120] *De Lap.* 27–28.

[121] Tertullian reports the practice: *Ad Mart.* 1; *De Pud.* 22.

of certificates of reconciliation, *libelli pacis*, mimicking the certificates of compliance issued by the government officials. One problem with the confessors' *libelli pacis* was also a shadow of the *libelli* issued by the government officials: it was possible to get hold of them without full repentance in the same way as it had been possible to get government *libelli* without compliance to the edict. Some were even being issued offering blanket reconciliation to the friends of the recipient.[122] This both derailed the carefully worked out and still somewhat fragile system of repentance and reconciliation cautiously accepted over the previous fifty years and also, more seriously, undercut episcopal authority, thereby gravely threatening the whole structure of the church.

The Roman clergy replied at length to Cyprian's letter to them. Their spokesman, writing in an elevated style, was the theologian Novatian,[123] by far the ablest of the Roman presbyters. Between the first and second letters of the Roman clergy, he had clearly emerged as their leader. Affirming their dedication to 'the ancient severity, the ancient faith, the ancient discipline', he stated:

> Far be it from the Roman church to lessen her old strictness with such profane ease and loosen the sinews of her severity by overthrowing the grandeur of her faith.[124]

This is the authentic tone of ancient Roman virtue, appropriated here by the clergy of the Roman church who cast themselves in the role of custodians of the stern, unbending ways of the past. They repeated the policy that they adopted towards the *lapsi*, that in danger of death they could be reconciled but otherwise they would have to await the appointment of a new bishop.[125] The letter trumps mercy, represented by Christ's parable of the unforgiving servant (Mt 18.32), with justice, 'Whoever disowns me before men, I will also disown before my Father and his angels' (Mt 10.33): 'God is compassionate, but he also demands, indeed strictly demands, obedience to his precepts'.[126] There was a ferocity here which suggested the shape of things to come.

The correspondence between Cyprian and the Roman clergy continued, ensuring that they agreed on their policy concerning the

---

[122] Cyprian *Ep*. 15.4.
[123] As Cyprian reveals in *Ep*. 55.5.
[124] Cyprian *Ep*. 30.3.3.
[125] *Ep*. 30.8.
[126] *Ep*. 30.7.1–2.

reconciliation of the lapsed.[127] Where Carthage seemed to be in crisis, Rome seemed to stand secure. The fact that Rome was receiving refugees from elsewhere — bishops from distant provinces[128] and sixty-five fugitives from Carthage[129] — shows that in the vastness of the city it was easier for Christians to escape notice. The letters from the Roman clergy and confessors, presumably all penned by Novatian, spoke with the calm, measured voice of confidence and reassurance. But their tone was deceptive.

SCHISM AND RECONCILIATION

Decius's edict had run its course by the spring of 251. In Rome, they set about electing a successor to the martyred Fabian. The presbyters had led the church for fourteen months with, apparently, great success. This must in large part have been the personal achievement of Novatian but he was not chosen. The choice, rather, fell on Cornelius, a worthy but undistinguished presbyter. Novatian refused to accept him and set himself up as a bishop against him. He claimed that he felt compelled to become bishop by the pressure of others.[130] He certainly had at least the endorsement, perhaps the positive encouragement, of a significant body of the Roman confessors,[131] which posed a huge threat to Cornelius. The presbyter Moyses had died in prison[132] leaving the leadership of the confessors to Novatian. Furthermore, a dissident presbyter from Carthage, confusingly called Novatus, had gone to Rome and he too joined Novatian.[133] Novatus was one of a group of Carthaginian clergy who had opposed Cyprian vigorously during his exile, calling for speedier reconciliation of the lapsed. His support for Novatian looks like an improbable alliance of laxist and rigorist. Mutiny acquaints a man with strange bedfellows but the underlying consistency of both Novatus and Novatian was their endorsement of confessors against their bishops. Novatus's

---

[127] Cyprian *Epp.* 35; 36.

[128] Cyprian *Ep.* 30.8.

[129] Cyprian *Ep.* 21.4.1; they were looked after by the lapsed sisters of the North African, Celerinus, who was living in Rome; one had bribed an official to say she had sacrificed, the other had offered sacrifice.

[130] Eusebius *HE* 6.45.1.

[131] Cyprian *Epp.* 46; 47; 49; 51.

[132] *LP* 1.148–9; Cyprian *Ep.* 55.5.2.

[133] Cyprian *Epp.* 47.1.1; 52.2.1–2.

intrigues in Rome probably had as their ultimate object the undermining of Cyprian.

Cornelius, in a letter to Fabius of Antioch quoted by Eusebius, related how Novatian had himself consecrated bishop:

> [Novatian] chose two accessories who had renounced their own salvation and sent them to a small and very obscure corner of Italy to entice by some trick three uneducated and simple-minded bishops of the region to come from there to Rome, insisting emphatically that they were needed as they could act as mediators along with other bishops and resolve the differences that had arisen there. As we have said, they were too simple-minded for the unscrupulous schemes of the wicked and they were shut up by some men as disorderly as himself. By the end of the afternoon they were drunk and sick with the after effects; he forcibly compelled them to make him a bishop by a false and invalid laying on of hands, an office he assumed by cunning treachery as it was not his by right. One of the bishops, not long afterwards, returned to the church, bewailing and admitting his fault, and we had communion with him as a layman, since the lay people with him pleaded for him. As for the other two, we appointed successors and sent them to their places.[134]

While Cornelius relished telling such a scurrilous tale against the sophisticated puritan Novatian, he could not dismiss him so easily. He was shocked that the African bishops were, for a time, willing to consider the validity of Novatian's election and that they insisted on making their own enquiries before they would recognise him as the legitimate bishop of Rome.[135] Much worse than that, he risked losing the moral ascendancy to Novatian who could claim the support of the confessors and to be the true voice of resistance to the evil assault that had afflicted the church.

Cornelius's principal asset was the size and unity of the church he led — as he observed to Fabius of Antioch, the Catholic church of Rome included forty-six presbyters, seven deacons, seven sub-deacons, forty-two acolytes, fifty-two exorcists, readers and doorkeepers and they provided support for fifteen hundred widows and needy people.[136] This must have made them the biggest church in the world and effortlessly dominant in Italy. Cornelius demonstrated his strength by convening a synod of bishops to address the aftermath of the devastation wrought by Decius's edict. He assembled sixty bishops and an even larger number of presbyters and deacons in Rome.[137] They endorsed unanimously the excommunication of Novatian, cutting

---

[134] *HE* 6.43.8–10.
[135] Cyprian *Epp.* 44; 45.
[136] Eusebius *HE* 6.43.11.
[137] Eusebius *HE* 6.43.2.

him off from any episcopal support in Italy. Cornelius put forward a policy of reconciliation of the lapsed which they also endorsed: the people who had bribed officials into giving them a certificate of compliance, the *libellatici*, could be reconciled at once while those who had offered sacrifice were required to continue as penitents with a promise of reconciliation in danger of death.[138] This was a decision of immense significance. Without admitting that compliance with the edict in the form of bribing officials did not constitute apostasy, it recognised that it was an offence of a wholly different order from the full compliance of those who had offered sacrifice; in practical terms, it provided a way back into the church for people who probably felt the judgment against them was unnecessarily harsh. It also ensured that the bishops remained the final arbiters in the long-running debate about acceptable and unacceptable Christian behaviour in a pagan society.

The most striking decision of the synod was to endorse the reconciliation, as a layman, of the Italian bishop Trofimus who had burnt incense in conformity with the edict of Decius. He was reconciled along with his whole community, some of whom had offered sacrifice.[139] In other words, an exception was made to the rule for the sake of the welfare of the whole group. Cornelius also welcomed back into communion, without repentance, some of the confessors who had supported Novatian.[140] However menacing Novatian's rival church had seemed at first, Cornelius had succeeded in detaching from his party some of the confessors who had supported him while moving firmly in a more laxist direction. He had won the support of the Italian bishops and asserted Roman ascendancy over them afresh. He had also gained the endorsement of the major bishops overseas — Dionysius in Alexandria, Fabius in Antioch[141] and Cyprian in Carthage.

If the challenge facing Cornelius in Rome was the rigorism of Novatian, the challenge facing Cyprian in Carthage was from the opposite direction, a desire to offer more generous and rapid reconciliation to the lapsed. While Cyprian had been in retreat from

---

[138] Cyprian says the Italian bishops agreed with the decisions reached in North Africa, *Ep.* 55.6.2, which he laid out in *Ep.* 55.17.

[139] Cyprian *Ep.* 55.11.

[140] He explained his policy, Cyprian *Ep.* 49, and was congratulated for it by Cyprian *Ep.* 51.

[141] Fabius had been somewhat inclined towards the schism but was influenced in Cornelius's favour by Dionysius; see Eusebius *HE* 6.44.1.

Carthage, five of his presbyters, led by Felicissimus, had taken the decision to reconcile the lapsed without his sanction.[142] This opened up a new challenge to his authority as bishop and to the unity of the higher church leadership in the face of the crisis. It was to force him to move in a laxist direction. Other presbyters had refused to act without him but kept him informed of the pressing need for reconciling repentant *lapsi*.[143] It is likely that the dissidents had a long-standing grudge against Cyprian. He excommunicated them and they broke away forming a separate, laxist church.[144] Cyprian claimed that they had influence over the confessors.[145] The danger now was they would attract the lapsed to join them; a danger made all the more alarming by the fact that the lapsed included many of the richer Christians of Carthage. His first reactions from exile were muddled. He produced a hard-line attack on the lapsed, the *De Lapsis*, but he also felt it wise to acknowledge that the lapsed in danger of death could be reconciled by a presbyter or even a deacon if they had a *libellus pacis*;[146] significantly but unhelpfully he decreed that those who did not have a *libellus* from the confessors would have to wait until there was a general peace,[147] a position he soon modified to allow reconciliation to all dying penitents.[148] After his return to Carthage, he moved rapidly to outflank Felicissimus and the dissident laxist clergy. He convened a council of bishops after Easter 251 who confirmed the excommunication of Felicissimus and his fellow presbyters while offering immediate reconciliation to the *libellatici*. Those who had offered sacrifice were required to continue as penitents till their death bed,[149] though even among them he acknowledged a wide range of kinds of guilt.[150] In other words, he led the African bishops in a decision that matched that of the Italian bishops led by Cornelius. On the spectrum of opinion which stretched from Novatian the rigorist to Felicissimus the laxist, both Cornelius and Cyprian had moved a long way in the direction of laxity.

[142] Cyprian *Ep.* 17.2.
[143] Cyprian *Epp.* 24; 25.
[144] *Epp.* 41; 42; 43.
[145] *Ep.* 43.2.1–2.
[146] *Ep.* 18.1.2.
[147] *Ep.* 19.2.1.
[148] *Ep.* 20.3.2.
[149] *Ep.* 55.17.
[150] *Ep.* 55.13.2.

Nevertheless, Cyprian still faced opposition from those who thought his concessions too little and too late. In the spring of 251, a laxist hierarchy was set up by Privatus, former bishop of Lambaesis along with several bishops who had offered sacrifice during the persecution. They consecrated Fortunatus, one of Cyprian's dissident presbyters, as a rival bishop of Carthage.[151] Fortunatus sent a delegation led by Felicissimus to Rome, seeking recognition. Cornelius allowed them to present their credentials before his clergy, retaliation presumably for having had the validity of his own election scrutinised by Cyprian the year before.[152] As a further disturbance to the unity of the Carthaginian church, Novatian despatched a former Roman presbyter, Maximus, as a rival to Cyprian as bishop of Carthage in 252.[153] Cyprian now had two rivals claiming to be the authentic bishop of Carthage, Fortunatus the laxist and Maximus the rigorist. Of the two, there was no doubt that it was the laxists, who had opposed him throughout his exile in 250 and continued to oppose him after his return in 251, who presented the greater challenge. Still seeking to undercut their appeal among the people, Cyprian and the African bishops decided to grant reconciliation to the penitential *sacrificati* after their synod in the early summer of 253.[154]

Compared with Carthage, the situation in Rome seemed relatively calm. Novatian's rigorist church seemed to have lost the support of some its leading figures and was not growing in strength. Nothing illustrated better the strength of the Roman church and Cornelius's own inspiring leadership in 251–52 than the way it coped with a further unexpected calamity — Cornelius's arrest in 252 and deportation to Centumcellae, modern Civitavecchia, about forty miles north of Rome.[155] Cyprian's letter to him congratulating him on his arrest and witness to the faith suggests that, as he was taken away, he was accompanied by a crowd of supporters, including many of the *lapsi*.[156] Cornelius died in exile in 253 and was succeeded by Lucius who was also promptly deported, though his exile was fairly brief.[157] The immediate banishment of Lucius suggests that they were not suffering from the hazards to which any Christian leader was then

---

[151] Cyprian *Ep.* 59.10.

[152] Cyprian *Ep.* 59.1.1– 2.5.

[153] Cyprian *Ep.* 59.9.2.

[154] *Ep.* 57.1.1.

[155] *LP* 1.150; Cyprian *Ep.* 60.

[156] *Ep.* 60.1–2.

[157] Cyprian *Ep.* 61.1.1.

subject but rather that there was some coherent policy underlying his and Cornelius's treatment. It is impossible to know what was happening, but Cyprian, writing to each of them, spotted at once how their moral authority was enhanced by the fact that the persecution was directed at them and not against Novatian.[158] Lucius died the following year and both he and Cornelius were described by Cyprian as martyrs in a letter to the next bishop of Rome, Stephen.[159] It was clearly in Cyprian's interests as well as that of the leadership of the Roman church to embellish their memory with a moral authority that could eclipse that of Novatian.

The Unity of the Church

As Stephen assumed control of the Roman church in 254, he might have surveyed Rome, Italy and the wider world with some confidence. Novatian was still a problem, but one that seemed safely contained. The Roman church had distinguished itself in preserving its unity and vigour during the previous two years even when its bishop had been in exile. The moral authority of his position was assured as his predecessors had witnessed for the faith as martyrs and confessors. The Italian bishops had demonstrated their support for Roman leadership in Cornelius's synod of 251. Though Cyprian faced two contenders for the episcopal leadership of Carthage, his position as the leader of the North African hierarchy was unassailable. The principal bishops all over the Roman world had settled on similar policies regarding the aftermath of the catastrophe caused by Decius's edict and gradually the damage it caused was being repaired — or at least, so it seemed.

The schismatics, whether laxist in union with Felicissimus or rigorist in union with Novatian, were receiving and baptising new believers. A new problem arose when these people approached the bishops of the great church, the Catholic church as they called themselves, and asked to be accepted into membership. Cyprian had a very clear view of their status. As far as he was concerned, outside the church there was no salvation. The church was the bride of Christ — anyone who did not have the church as mother could not have God as Father. The church was Noah's ark: for those inside, there was safety; for those outside, there was destruction. The church was like the

---

[158] *Ep.* 60.3; 61.3.
[159] *Ep.* 68.5.1.

seamless garment of Christ; no one could possess the robe of Christ if they tore his church in disunity. He stated this view in a brilliant short treatise on the church[160] and applied it to the status of people baptised by schismatics in several of his letters.[161] The argument was simple. The church is the Body of Christ; schismatics have left the church and so are not part of the Body of Christ; how then can they baptise people and make them part of Christ's Body? Cyprian put it succinctly: 'How can heresy, which is not the bride of Christ, give birth to children through Christ to God?'[162] Unsurprisingly, this was a theology he shared with Novatian who denied the baptism of those outside his church. Cyprian admired his logic.[163]

Stephen took a contrary view, though one that can only partly be reconstructed as his opinions are known to us only from the letters of his opponents who probably misunderstood or even misrepresented him. He received into communion people baptised by schismatics by the laying on of hands, the gesture of reconciliation of penitents.[164] He was thus accused by Cyprian of accepting the baptism performed by groups with unacceptable beliefs about Christ and the Trinity, Marcionites and Valentinians,[165] but it is more likely that he distinguished between different bodies outside the Catholic church and simply did not regard Novatian and his followers in the same light as the full-blooded heretics. Cyprian also quoted Stephen as citing the practice of heretics in not re-baptising in support of his position, deriding him as taking lessons from heresy.[166] This again was probably tendentious. Stephen claimed to be following the old custom but he was almost certainly not using the heretics as evidence of its antiquity. It is more likely that he was observing how novel but alarmingly similar were the practice of Cyprian and Novatian. He claimed Roman practice was apostolic in origin[167] and in so far as he offered any justification for it (which is unclear from Cyprian's account) he seemed to say that what effected baptism was 'the power of the name'[168] which might be taken to mean the formula and rite

---

[160] *De Unitate Ecclesiae* 6–9.
[161] *Epp.* 69; 70; 71; 72; 73.
[162] *Ep.* 74.6.2.
[163] *Ep.* 73.2.1–3.
[164] Cyprian *Ep.* 74.1–2.
[165] *Ep.* 74.7.3.
[166] *Ep.* 74.4.1.
[167] Cyprian *Ep.* 74.2.2–3.
[168] *Ep.* 74.5.1.

rather than the standing of the baptiser. As far as he was concerned, Cyprian and Novatian were therefore practising re-baptism.

Cyprian was unusually violent in his reaction to the letter he had received from Stephen which he dismissed as 'arrogant, irrelevant, self-contradictory, ignorant and imprudent'.[169] The axis so tenaciously maintained between Rome and Carthage throughout the crisis and its aftermath had been abandoned. Stephen clearly lacked any of the political or diplomatic finesse of Cornelius. He refused to accept the delegation of bishops which Cyprian sent to Rome or even allow them to be given hospitality.[170] Both Stephen and Cyprian sent off letters to bishops around the Mediterranean stating their arguments. Dionysius of Alexandria was alarmed by their tone. Writing some years later to Stephen's successor, Sixtus, he reported how Stephen had written to the bishops of Asia Minor saying he could no longer be in communion with them since they re-baptised heretics.[171] Firmilian of Caesarea in Cappadocia replied to Cyprian, expressing outrage that Stephen had broken peace with Cyprian and was effectively excommunicating himself by excommunicating everyone else.[172] He dismissed as patently absurd the claim that all Roman customs are apostolic in origin, quoting the well-known innovation in the dating of Easter.[173] What riled him most was Stephen's claims to some kind of petrine primacy: 'he boasts of the place of which he is bishop and claims that he holds the succession from Peter on whom the foundations of the church were laid'.[174]

In fact, Stephen did have a case for saying that he was observing the more ancient practice. Eusebius, reporting the dispute, admitted as much.[175] It had been the old practice in North Africa, contested by Tertullian,[176] but changed in the 230s by a synod of the African bishops. Cyprian acknowledged that his practice followed their decision;[177] it had long been decreed by his predecessors.[178] Firmilian acknowl-

---

[169] *Ep.* 74.1.2.

[170] *Ep.* 75.25.1.

[171] Eusebius *HE* 7.5.4.

[172] Cyprian *Ep.* 75.24.2.

[173] *Ep.* 75.6.1.

[174] *Ep.* 75.17.1; Firmilian also discusses the meaning of Mt. 16.18, suggesting that the text was used by Stephen to support his position.

[175] *HE* 7.2.

[176] *De Baptismo* 15.

[177] *Epp.* 71.4.1; 73.3.1.

[178] *Ep.* 70.1.2.

edged that the issue had been a disputed one in Asia Minor, settled by a council at Iconium,[179] an event referred to also by Dionysius of Alexandria.[180] In other words, one dimension of the dispute was Roman practice ranged against provincial conciliar decisions. Significantly, this is not the way that Cyprian took the argument. He presented the dispute instead as one between old custom and good theology: that the Roman practice must give way to the coherence of his ecclesiology.[181] It seems likely that Stephen took it the other way, insisting on the authority of Roman practice as apostolic, established by Peter and Paul, which seemed to his correspondents to be a claim for the superior authority of his see.

The interpretation of these events to some extent governs also the interpretation of one of Cyprian's most significant treatises, on the unity of the Catholic Church, *De Ecclesiae Catholicae Unitate*. It is a powerful statement, initially written after the African synod of 251 and sent to the Roman confessors supporting Novatian,[182] of his view of the oneness of the church and that outside it there is no salvation. One section of the book survives in two versions, which has been the cause of much controversy. The fourth chapter, according to one version commonly called the primacy text, says that though all the apostles received similar power there is one chair and the primacy is given to Peter; though there are many shepherds, there is only one flock led by all the apostles, so that anyone who does not hold fast to the oneness of Peter or deserts the chair of Peter is not a member of the church. The other version, which is longer and has an additional paragraph at the start of the next chapter, is commonly called the received text. That says that the other apostles were all that Peter was, endowed with equal dignity and power, though the start comes from him alone; it is the oneness of the church — rather than the oneness of Peter — to which the faithful must hold fast and bishops are to demonstrate that the episcopal power is also one by united action.

A superficial reading would suggest that the primacy text claims that the church's unity depends upon Peter, and therefore the bishop of Rome, whereas the received text insists that the unity derives from all the apostles and is now expressed collegially by the bishops. In other words, Cyprian appears to have changed his mind about

---

[179] Cyprian *Ep.* 75.19.4.
[180] Eusebius *HE* 7.7.5.
[181] *Epp.* 71.3.1; 73.13.1.
[182] Cyprian *Ep.* 54.3.4.

what unites the church and the role of the bishop of Rome between writing one version and the other. The dispute with Stephen could easily be the occasion on which Cyprian abandoned a pro-Roman view of church unity. A better informed reading, which has won wide assent,[183] suggests that this view of papal primacy would be anachronistic. When Cyprian speaks of Peter, he is not referring specifically to the bishop of Rome as his successor but rather speaking of all the bishops, each of whom occupies Peter's chair among his own people.[184] In other words, Cyprian is saying the same thing in both texts: that the unity of the church depends upon the exercise of apostolic, petrine, authority by each bishop and all the bishops. The reason why Cyprian produced two different versions would again be the dispute with Stephen. The primacy text was initially written in 251 to address both the laxist dissidents in North Africa and the Novatianist dissidents in Rome, stressing the urgent need to be united with their bishops. Stephen's assertion of his prerogatives as bishop of Rome led to a re-drafting, not because Cyprian had changed his mind but because talking of Peter as the source of episcopal authority could easily be misread to refer to the Roman claims. The immediate problem with this proposal is that, if Cyprian re-issued the *De Unitate* as a contribution to the debate about the admission to the church of those who had received schismatic baptism, he should have seized the opportunity of making a fuller revision of the text than a modest restructuring of chapters 4 and 5; then the book would have addressed the new issues more directly. A more fundamental problem is that it is based on the assumption that Stephen was proposing a version of Roman primacy which the slender evidence cannot endorse. It would be highly anachronistic to imagine that Stephen had devised a view of his authority which would anticipate later developments by well over a century.

A third interpretation of the text suggests that it was even further removed from any consideration of Roman claims and had nothing to do with the baptismal controversy or Stephen. This reading agrees that the two versions are both about episcopal (and not specifically Roman) authority, with the primacy text pointing to Peter as its source and model whereas the received text speaks of the oneness of

---

[183] Stated for instance in his edition of the text by Maurice Bévenot, *Cyprian:* De Lapsis *and* De Ecclesiae Catholicae Unitate (Oxford Early Christian Texts; Oxford: OUP, 1971).

[184] See for instance *Ep.* 33.1.1.

the church and the concerted exercise of authority by the bishops. The primacy text was written in the light of the North African synod of 251; it was a severe warning to the laxists that they needed to stand in the unity of the church by communion with their bishops. The received text, which more overtly stresses the need for bishops to express the church's oneness, was then written the following year after Novatian's intervention in North Africa threatened to set schismatic bishops against Catholic bishops. The redrafting therefore had nothing to do with anxieties about how Stephen or his allies might have used the text to defend their position.[185] A further suggestion has been made[186] to explain the received text. Instead of being a response to the threat of a Novatianist schism in Africa, it was written after Cornelius had received Felicissimus as the envoy of the newly consecrated laxist bishop Fortunatus and allowed him to present his credentials before the Roman clergy. Cyprian's *Epistle* 59 was written in response to that; the revised version of the *De Unitate*, with its stress on the need for unity among the bishops, could well have been written at the same time.

The dispute about baptism petered out with Stephen's death in 257, though a rather more irenic correspondence continued afterwards between his successor Sixtus and Dionysius of Alexandria.[187] The idea that Stephen was making a bid to place his authority as bishop of Rome above that of all other bishops can be safely put to one side. He was animated more by opposition to what he regarded as a wholly unacceptable practice, rebaptism. If baptism could be performed again, then the whole sacramental system would be dissolved and the status of the individual Christian undermined. He simply refused to accept the claim of Cyprian and the bishops of Asia Minor that they were not baptising for a second time. The fact that they shared a view of baptism and the church with Novatian was damning enough and against them and Novatian he appealed to the long-standing (as far as he was concerned, apostolic) practice of the Roman church as evidence of the validity of baptism performed by schismatics. There is no reason to suppose that he could offer any theological understanding of the church to justify his position or any more elevated view of his office than that he was the spokesman of

---

[185] Stuart G. Hall, 'The versions of Cyprian, *De unitate*, 4–5. Bévenot's dating revisited' *JTS* 55 (2004) pp. 138–46.

[186] Dunn *Cyprian and the Bishops of Rome* pp. 99–102.

[187] As recorded by Eusebius *HE* 7.5.3 — 9.6.

apostolic custom. He was just another conservative Roman, though an unusually belligerent one.

THE PERSECUTION OF VALERIAN

The emperor Decius died fighting Gothic invaders in early June 251. He had left Rome in the spring of the previous year, as his edict demanding universal sacrifice across the Empire was coming into effect in the provinces, and spent a year campaigning south of the Danube, fighting to repel the Goths. His call for a grand act of supplication to the gods did not do him any good: he and his son were killed in the battle of Abrittus where they were out-generalled by the enemy. The surviving commander, Gallus, was proclaimed emperor by the troops, bought the Goths off with a heavy bribe and made his way to Rome to secure his position. While he was in Rome, the fragile peace in Mesopotamia purchased by Philip the Arab eight years before finally collapsed. In 252, Shapur led his Persian armies again deep into Roman territory and captured Antioch. The following year, the Roman governor in the lower Danube region, Aemilian, attacked the Goths and was proclaimed emperor by his army. He marched on Rome. Gallus summoned troops from the north to join him, commanded by an elderly senator, Valerian. He headed north himself but was murdered by his own troops at the end of July 253, along with his son, before they joined battle with Aemilian. Valerian now advanced towards Aemilian's army and, once again, a mutiny in the camp forestalled a battle; Aemilian and his son were murdered by their own troops and Valerian emerged as the universally acknowledged emperor.

Valerian was in his sixties, a man of great distinction, a member of the old aristocracy; he faced enormous challenges both in the east from the Persians and on the Danube from the Goths. He made his son, Gallienus, co-emperor and entrusted to him the task of defending the Danubian provinces. He took control of the east and set about attempting to repair the damage of the recent Persian invasion. Once again, military, political and economic problems intertwined and exacerbated each other.

It was against this backdrop that Valerian launched a direct persecution against the Christians.[188] He issued letters to his officials across

---

[188] See Christopher J. Haas, 'Imperial Religious Policy and Valerian's Persecution of the Church, AD 257–260' *Church History* 52 (1983) pp. 133–44.

the empire ordering them to act against bishops and presbyters. Official court records have been preserved of the appearances of Dionysius of Alexandria[189] and Cyprian of Carthage[190] which reveal that the letters decreed that those who did not practise the Roman religion had to observe Roman rites; that Christian meetings were banned; that no one was allowed to enter the Christian cemeteries. These instructions were binding on pain of death. Both Dionysius and Cyprian were sent into exile having had perfectly civilised conversations with the provincial governors. People of lower social standing were not treated with such courtesy. Cyprian recorded that nine bishops in Numidia, along with presbyters and deacons and lay people, including women and children, were sentenced to the mines.[191] It is not easy to make sense of this persecution — either Valerian's motives or the way his orders were put into effect — but it was the first direct attack on Christians initiated by imperial authority in Roman history since Nero. Hitherto, Trajan's policy as laid down in his letter to Pliny had been followed, that the Christians were not to be actively pursued. The prosecution of Christians had remained local and sporadic until the edict of Decius, which was plainly not aimed at persecuting Christians whatever its unintended consequences. For the first time, an imperial directive sought to forbid Christian worship and burials and required officials to seek out the Christian leadership and demand their conformity to Roman worship.

Far more significant was a rescript issued a year later. Valerian was in the east, preparing for war with Shapur, when he sent a rescript to the senate in Rome. Its contents were reported to Cyprian within days of its arrival in the capital:

> Valerian, in a rescript to the senate, had ordered that bishops, presbyters and deacons should be executed at once; that senators, men of rank and Roman knights should be deprived of their status and goods and that if they continued, despite this, to say they were Christians, that they should be put to death; that matrons should be deprived of their goods and sent into exile; that members of the imperial household who had confessed Christ previously or confessed Christ now should have their goods confiscated and should themselves be put in irons and assigned to the imperial estates. The emperor Valerian had added to his rescript a copy of the letter that he addressed concerning us to the provincial governors. We hope daily to see this letter arrive, standing in the firmness of our faith and ready to suffer, awaiting from the wealth and mercy

---

[189] Eusebius *HE* 7.11.6–11.

[190] *The Acts of St Cyprian* 1 in Musurillo *Acts of the Christian Martyrs* pp. 169–71.

[191] Cyprian *Ep.* 76.6.2. He wrote to them *Ep.* 76 and sent them aid for which they thanked him, *Epp.* 77; 78; 79.

of the LORD the crown of eternal life. Know that Sixtus was executed in the cemetery on the 6 August with four deacons. The prefects in the city press this persecution more actively each day, executing those who are handed over to them and confiscating their goods into the treasury.[192]

Rescripts did not enact new laws but rather were expositions of existing legislation. They were intended to clarify what the law was. This rescript was therefore intended to resolve uncertainty about the meaning of the previous year's decree. The fact that it was addressed to the senate reveals who had asked for the clarification and, to that extent, indicates that the primary target of the fresh enforcement of the decree of 257 was the city of Rome.

There is no sign that the bishop of Rome, Sixtus, or his clergy had been troubled by the 257 decree. The cemeteries had clearly not been closed, for it was in the catacomb of St Callistus that he was arrested along with four of his deacons. The rescript was intended to remedy that negligence. It was also intended to purge the social and administrative elite — the upper and middling nobility, rich widows and the imperial household. In other words, as Valerian gathered his forces for war with Persia, the Roman senate sought to crush the Christian church in the capital by eliminating its leadership and to sweep Christians out of positions of power and influence. Valerian heeded their request with a rescript which applied primarily to Rome but also required a more vigorous application of the decree of the previous year.

The immediate trigger of the senate's action in calling on Valerian to issue the rescript might have been an event that took place on 29 June 258. It is possible that as a response to the threat of fresh persecution, Sixtus instituted a feast to celebrate the apostles Peter and Paul in three places, at the sites of the martyrdoms of Peter on the Vatican and Paul on the road to Ostia and at the catacomb of St Sebastian where they had long been venerated.[193] This might

---

[192] Cyprian *Ep.* 80.1.1–4.

[193] The earliest Roman calendar, dated to 354, records a feast on 29 June for Peter 'in catacumbas' and Paul on the Ostian road, when Tuscus and Bassus were consuls (258), MGH Chron. Min. 71; this is found in expanded form in the early fifth-century *Martyrologium* of the Ps-Jerome, to say the feast was of Peter at the Via Aurelia on the Vatican hill, Paul on the Via Ostia, and both 'in catacumbas', when Tuscus and Bassus were consuls, which is interpreted by the editor to mean that the commemoration was instituted in that year in all three places, see Henri Quentin (ed) *Commentarius Perpetuus in Martyrologium Hieronymianum* in *Acta Sanctorum Novembris* 2.2 (Brussels, 1931) pp. 342–43.

have been part of a wider policy of veneration of the apostles in a time of persecution. There is abundant archaeological evidence of a cult of Peter and Paul at the catacomb of St Sebastian. According to the *Liber Pontificalis*, the shrines on the Vatican and the Ostian way were developed by Cornelius in 251 when he moved relics from the catacomb to the sites of the martyrdoms.[194] Sixtus's institution of a celebration at all three sites on 29 June was probably therefore a continuity of the same policy, and a daring one in 258. Less than six weeks later, the imperial rescript reached Rome and Sixtus and the central leadership of the community were liquidated.

According to Cyprian, Sixtus and four of his deacons were arrested and executed at the catacomb of St Callistus on 6 August 258. The *Liber Pontificalis*[195] gives a somewhat different account, saying that on his arrest Sixtus was asked to offer sacrifice and executed when he refused, and that six deacons were executed on that day. The two accounts could be reconciled by envisaging the remaining two deacons, Felicissimus and Agapitus, as being apprehended in a separate raid. They were buried in the catacomb of Praetextatus whereas Sixtus, with Januarius, Magnus, Vincent and Stephen were buried in St Callistus.[196] Cyprian's informant, writing at once, had presumably not heard of the deaths of Felicissimus and Agapitus.

Four days later, on 10 August 258, the surviving deacon, Laurence, was executed along with Claudius the subdeacon, Severus the presbyter, Crescentius the reader and Romanus the doorkeeper and buried in the catacomb of Cyriaces on the Ager Veranus on the Via Tiburtina. The cult of Laurence was to eclipse all other Roman martyrs with the exception of St Agnes; stories were told about his having distributed the church's property among the poor and his gruesome death on a gridiron.[197] According to the *Liber Pontificalis*,[198] in the early fourth century, Constantine built a basilica[199] adjacent

---

[194] *LP* 1. 151.

[195] *LP* 1.155.

[196] See G. W. Clarke 'Prosopographical Notes on the Epistles of Cyprian — III Rome in August, 258' *Latomus* 34 (1975) pp. 437–48.

[197] See Anna Benvenuti Papi *Il Diacono Lorenzo tra Storia e Leggenda* (Florence: Edizioni della Meridiana, 1998).

[198] *LP* 1.181.

[199] The fullest account of the history of the site and its buildings is by Richard Krautheimer and Wolfgang Frankl in Richard Krautheimer, Wolfgang Frankl and Spencer Corbett (eds), *Corpus Basilicarum Christianarum Romae* (5 vols; Città del Vaticano: Pontificio Istituto di Archeologia Cristiana, 1937–77) vol. 2, pp. 1–144.

to the catacomb and constructed stairs going down and back up for pilgrims to visit the tomb of Laurence, where he constructed a richly decorated chapel. It is clear enough that Constantine was responding to, rather than creating, a cult of Laurence which the distribution of the church's funds could explain. The arrests of 6 August were evidently carefully planned; the authorities intended to destroy the central administration of the Roman church, the bishop and his seven deacons, at a stroke. Laurence escaped and, as the sole survivor of the Sixtus's senior staff, presumably found the episcopal resources at his disposal which he handed over to the poor, presumably aided by the church officials who died with him. His death on the gridiron was either exemplary punishment for his contumacy or a tardy attempt to discover the whereabouts of the funds by torture.

One other notable victim of the persecution in Rome might well have been Novatian. It is possible that he had already endured the same penalty as Cyprian in Carthage and Dionysius in Alexandria in 257 by being exiled from Rome: three of his treatises, in one of which he describes himself as a bishop, were addressed to his community from exile.[200] The fifth-century historian Socrates said that he died as a martyr under Valerian[201] and a grave has been found in a catacomb on the Via Tiburtina, not far from the catacomb where Laurence was buried, with an inscription 'to the blessed martyr Novatian'.[202] If this was indeed Novatian's fate, he received from the imperial authorities a recognition of episcopal authority that was denied him by most of his fellow Christians.

At this point, the failure of the Roman authorities to act more decisively is very revealing. The move against Sixtus and his deacons had shown planning and determination; they clearly had good intelligence about the leadership of the Roman church. They had launched a very successful operation against the bishop and his central staff and, most likely, had also attempted unsuccessfully to seize the church's central funds. Their attempt to close the cemeteries was less evidently successful as the burial of the martyred bishop and his deacons in Rome attests. Threats against the senatorial and equestrian nobility and the imperial household had presumably been effective; though there is no record of any penalties being exacted

---

[200] *De Spectaculis* 1.1; *De Cibis Judaicis* 1.1–4; *De Bono Pudicitiae* 1.1–2 (he calls himself a bishop in *De Bon. Pud.* 1.2).

[201] *Historia Ecclesiastica* 4.28.

[202] ICUR VII, 20334.

from these categories of Christian, it is likely that the senate merely wanted to force them into a more subdued and compliant temper. But they did not go any further. They failed to pursue the presbyters (apart from Severus who died with Laurence) which allowed them to resume control of the church as they had done in 250 when Fabian died. Various reasons for this lack of vigour could be proposed but the most likely is that they had never intended to try and crush the church. Their aim was to purge, not destroy. The senate had a very limited purpose which the rescript endorsed and they achieved it quickly in the August of 258: to topple a church leadership that mirrored their own leadership in Rome and to warn Christians in the social and political elites to be very discreet. Of course, the real effect of the persecution was to reinforce the moral stature of its leadership and probably to deepen its popular support among the poor.

All over the Roman world, church leaders and more humble Christians met their deaths as a result of the rescript and letters of Valerian. Cyprian's execution on 14 September 258 was almost liturgical as he seemed wholly in control of the choreography of his death, flanked by his deacons, attended by a chanting crowd of the faithful, with handkerchiefs and towels placed in front of him to soak up the blood as relics for his people.[203] The cheering crowds accompanying him to his place of execution and the presence of his deacons at his death indicate again the limited intentions of the authorities in enacting Valerian's orders. In some places, the hands of the authorities were forced to act more energetically. Christians astonished the magistrates by coming forward and volunteering to be martyred — as for instance in Caesarea in Palestine where three men made their way into the city from the countryside and presented themselves before the court; they were thrown to the wild beasts, along with a woman who belonged to the Marcionite church.[204]

As for Valerian, his campaign against Shapur ended with unmatched catastrophe. In the summer of 260, along with most of the general staff, he was taken prisoner in obscure circumstances and spent the rest of his life in captivity. He was made to act as Shapur's mounting stool and, after his death, his skin was hung as a trophy in the Shah's palace. It has been argued that he bravely refused any attempt to negotiate his release so as not to force the Romans into a disadvan-

---

[203] *Acts of St Cyprian* 5 in Musurillo *Acts of the Christian Martyrs* pp. 173–75.
[204] Eusebius *HE* 7.12.

tageous peace.[205] If that is so, he transformed the ignominy of his captivity by a sort of martyrdom of his own.

ARMISTICE

It might not seem surprising that the persecution ended after the death of Valerian. If to the religious mind the point of harrying the Christians had been to win the favour of the gods, it had proved spectacularly unsuccessful. Valerian's son and successor inherited control only of the central core of the empire — Italy, North Africa, Egypt, the Danubian provinces and Greece. The East was in turmoil and the western provinces, the Gallic empire, broke away. Surprisingly, Gallienus did not simply allow the persecution to lapse but formally rescinded it. He was petitioned by Dionysius of Alexandria, the veteran of both the persecutions of Decius and Valerian, and responded to it in these words:

> The emperor Caesar Publius Licinius Gallienus Pius Felix Augustus to Dionysius, Pinnas, Demetrius and the other bishops. I have ordered that the benefit of my munificence should be proclaimed throughout all the world so that all places of worship will be restored and so that you may use the decree of this rescript so that no one may harm you. This power to act has long since been conceded by me and therefore Aurelius Quirinius, who is in charge of the treasury, will observe this my ordinance.[206]

Eusebius said he had a copy of another decree from Gallienus restoring the cemeteries. In other words, Gallienus handed back the church's property and effectively declared a large measure of official toleration.[207] This held in effect for decades. Despite rumours that Aurelian planned a persecution in the 270s, the Christians were little further troubled until 303.[208] It was not a final peace; perhaps it was an extended armistice, but those forty years were a time of great growth and consolidation, the years when the Christians laid down

---

[205] J. F. Drinkwater, 'The "catastrophe" of 260: towards a more favourable assessment of the emperor Valerian I' *Rivista Storica dell'Antichità* 19 (1989) pp. 123–35.

[206] Eusebius *HE* 7.13.

[207] His motives were probably a mixture of seeking Christian support against the eastern usurper Macrianus and to avoid Christians in the east being seduced by Persian toleration; see Lukas de Blois, *The Policy of the Emperor Gallienus* (Leiden: Brill, 1976) pp. 177–85.

[208] Christians were still subject to the risk of persecution as in the case of Marinus, to be promoted centurion but exposed as a Christian — a story vividly told by Eusebius *HE* 7.15.

the solid foundation on which they were to construct their bid to become the major religion of the empire in the fourth century.

After Sixtus's death, the Roman church was again governed by its presbyters for two years until, in the summer of 260, a new bishop, Dionysius, was elected. Given all that the Roman church had endured in the previous decade, he proved a remarkably successful bishop. According to a somewhat garbled memory in the *Liber Pontificalis*,[209] he seems to have set up the system of parishes in Rome and placed the cemeteries under the control of the priests and to have organised the dioceses in the vicinity of Rome under his metropolitan control. Whatever these structural and administrative changes were, they probably counterbalanced and completed the changes made under Fabian fifteen years before when he divided the city between the seven deacons. He demonstrated how far the Roman church had recovered from the depredations it had undergone by sending major financial relief to the churches of Cappadocia and providing funds for the ransoming of Christians taken prisoner in barbarian raids,[210] presumably restoring good relations with Firmilian of Caesarea in the process. These administrative and financial achievements were typically Roman; what was even more remarkable was his participation in a brisk debate with his namesake at Alexandria about the correct formulation of the doctrine of the Trinity. More remarkable still, his letter was still being quoted as an authoritative text nearly a century later. Dionysius of Alexandria was accused of believing that the Son was a creature and not of the same substance (*homoousios*) as the Father.[211] Dionysius of Rome feared that Alexandria was teaching a doctrine which both undermined monotheism and denied the full divinity of Christ. He convened a synod to reject these unacceptable teachings and despatched a formal statement of trinitarian belief which anticipated the debates of the next century in which he would be quoted.[212]

Persecution said as much about the Christians and their ability to be good citizens in a pagan world as the attitudes and powers of the Roman state. It had a profound effect on Christianity and the way it understood itself and the world of which it was part. There

---

[209] *LP* 1.157: 'Hic presbiteris ecclesias dedit et cymiteria et parrocias diocesis constituit'; Duchesne takes 'ecclesias' and 'cymiteria' as the objects of 'dedit', translates 'parrocias' as rural dioceses and 'diocesis' as the diocese of Rome.

[210] Remembered a century later by Basil of Caesarea *Ep.* 70.

[211] Athanasius *De Synodis* 43.

[212] Athanasius *De Decretis* 26.

was a balance sheet to be drawn up of loss and gain. As the Roman church looked back and counted its dead, they venerated well over two hundred martyrs. A very large proportion of these probably died in the 250s; others, including soldier saints, died in the 290s when Diocletian attempted to purge the army of Christians; some might have died in the persecution of 303–306. The catacombs allowed their memory to be preserved.[213] The cult of martyrs eventually more than outweighed the effects of the lapsation and divisions in the church. The principal beneficiaries of the persecution, however, were the higher clergy. In the second and third centuries, Christians had argued and disagreed about where they stood in dealing with the pagan society around them. Those disagreements fed into the different reactions to persecution in 250 and the demands for conformity of the Roman state. They led to formal division and schism whether in the direction of laxity or rigorism in the 250s and a huge struggle by the bishops to keep control of their people and to act in concord. The Roman authorities had recognised the senior clergy's importance by singling them out as their target in 258 and, in doing so, gave them the definitive moral authority to be the unchallenged arbitrators of Christian discipline.

[213] Agostino Amore *I Martiri di Roma* (Rome: Antonianum, 1975) lists over 260 martyrs, their names preserved in a variety of documents such as early calendars, catacomb inscriptions, Pope Damasus's monuments and guides for visitors to Rome written in the seventh and eighth centuries.

Chapter 4

THE CATACOMBS

Until the closing decades of the second century, Christians appear to have been buried alongside their non-Christian neighbours. This was the period when Roman funeral customs changed and cremation was replaced by inhumation, the burial of the body. As inhumation demanded far more space, even the wealthy began to excavate underground to find more room for burials. This was easy in Rome as the local rock is a soft volcanic stone called tufa. The earliest Jewish and Christian burials were in these kinds of private subterranean burial chambers called *hypogea*, which gradually developed into vast systems of tunnels. By the middle of the third century, catacombs could be found along all the major arterial roads leading out of Rome. They were called cemeteries, a distinctive word meaning sleeping chamber, reflecting the Christian faith in the resurrection. The term catacomb was a place name, applied originally to the cemetery of St Sebastian and in modern times to all these underground burial chambers. About sixty Roman catacombs and *hypogea* have been found, fanning out from the city along all the major roads. Perhaps three quarters of a million people were buried in them from the start of the third century till the second half of the fourth when they were gradually superseded by graveyards within the city.

They provide powerful evidence of the desire of Christians to be buried together, mirroring the belief in the community's solidarity in Christ. They demonstrate the growing power of the central administration of the church. Their decoration saw the beginning of Christian art. The grave inscriptions, of which 40,000 survive, reveal the faith and the life of prayer of the community as well as giving a good deal of evidence about its social composition. They stand, above all, as remarkable evidence of the size and vitality of the Roman Church in the century between 250 and 350 and of its appeal to people who found Christian belief in resurrection probably the single greatest attraction of this new faith.

ROMAN GRAVES

One of the oddest books to survive from ancient Rome is the *Satyricon.* Its author, Petronius, was an aristocrat who became the central cultural figure at Nero's court in the mid-60s. It is a kind of novel but, as it only survives in several large fragments, much of Petronius's overall meaning remains elusive. A mixture of satire, burlesque and parody, it casts a sardonic and darkly cynical eye on life and attitudes in imperial Rome. It was, no doubt, hilariously funny when written. The longest section which survives complete is a description of a banquet in the house of a freedman called Trimalchio, a self-made millionaire, who stands out as the only coherently portrayed, rounded character in the book. Trimalchio is a grotesque figure, in turns morbid, vulgar, boorish, ostentatious, capricious, ignorant and arrogant; ultimately, he is rather sad. But there is just enough realism to the portrait to make him one of the great creations of satire.

At the climax of the banquet,[1] Trimalchio's thoughts turn to death. To elicit from his guests and slaves affirmations of admiration and gratitude, he calls for the reading of his will and talks of the enormously elaborate tomb that he wants built, set in a garden and surrounded by fruit trees and vines, so that he will continue to live after he is dead; but he will arrange for one of his freedmen to protect the tomb, to ensure no one defecates on it. He describes in some detail its decoration and the statue of himself with an inscription outlining his career and virtues, ending like so many other epitaphs with the boast that he had never succumbed to some common fault, in his case that he had never studied Philosophy. Finally, he becomes maudlin, self-pityingly calling for his friends to play out a mock funeral in which they can say nice things about him.[2] The trumpeters play a dead march, which wakes up the neighbourhood causing the fire brigade to be summoned, who break into the house with water and axes, ending the party.

The fact was, of course, that any traveller approaching Rome would find tombs not unlike Trimalchio's, competing with each other to attract notice and admiration, with splendid inscriptions recording the glory and virtues of the deceased.[3] People were not

[1] *Cena Trimalchionis* 71.

[2] *Cena* 78.

[3] For a well-illustrated introduction to Roman tombs and burial customs, see Susan Walker, *Memorials to the Roman Dead* (London: British Museum, 1985). Stephen L. Dyson, *Community and Society in Roman Italy* (Baltimore: Johns Hopkins University Press, 1992) pp. 147–53 describes and explains the graveyards surrounding a Roman town.

allowed to be buried within the sacred boundary of the city, the *pomerium,* and consequently vast cemeteries lay outside the walls. The main arterial roads were lined with sepulchres. The rich, like Trimalchio, put up splendid edifices to house their ashes. Some very strange ones survive: the pyramid of Gaius Cestius near the Porta Ostiensis, built in the Augustan era, is still a significant landmark in Rome today and the tomb of Marceius Virgilius Eurysaces, a master baker and contractor, was built near the Porta Maggiore at the end of the Republican period to look like a huge bread oven.[4] Families would construct mausolea, effectively small houses, with niches inside for the urns containing the cremated remains of the dead. During the second century, cremation gradually gave way to inhumation, the burial of the body, which gave the rich even wider scope for ostentatious display with magnificent, beautifully decorated sarcophagi to house their corpses. Mausolea of the second and third century often reveal the transition from one burial custom to another, containing both funeral urns and sarcophagi.[5] People of the more middling sort banded together in funerary associations, *collegia funeraticia,* which guaranteed a good funeral and a resting place in the common mausoleum of the *collegium.* Service in a great household could also bring the privilege of a proper burial. Several immensely impressive, partly subterranean, mausolea have been found with semi-circular or rectangular niches for hundreds of urns (hence their common name *columbaria,* dovecots), which from the inscriptions are known to have been the burial places of connections or freedmen of the imperial family.[6]

One of the largest graveyards was on the Vatican hill, stretching up from the Tiber. Excavations under St Peter's basilica in the 1940s and 1950s revealed a remarkable complex of mausolea lining a narrow street parallel to the Via Cornelia which ran west out of Rome and adjacent to Nero's circus. These were the dignified tombs of prosperous families, well decorated inside and out. Walking along

[4] See J.M.C. Toynbee, *Death and Burial in the Roman World* (London: Thames and Hudson, 1971) pp. 127–28.

[5] Ibid., pp. 39–42. The replacement of cremation by inhumation appears to have begun with the Roman upper classes in the years 140–80, perhaps influenced by Greek practice, and then spread unevenly but surprisingly rapidly down the social scale and throughout the Empire: see Ian Morris, *Death-Ritual and Social Structure in Classical Antiquity* (Cambridge: CUP, 1992) pp. 52–62.

[6] Toynbee *Death and Burial* pp. 113–16; see also Keith Hopkins, *Death and Renewal* (Cambridge: CUP, 1983) pp. 211–17.

the street of tombs, modern visitors to the excavation, the *Scavi*, can easily appreciate why these graveyards were called *necropoleis*, cities of the dead. They look exactly like a street of houses. More recent excavations to the north of the basilica, further along the Vatican hill, have revealed further stretches of what must have been a massive cemetery. The *Autoparco* excavation of the late 1950s discovered tombs dating from the time of Nero down to the early third century at a place where the hill was very steep, so that it was much affected by landslides. Many of these were the modest *columbaria* of funerary associations or of imperial freedmen and slaves. Interestingly, they show the shift to inhumation with graves as well as niches for urns, several bodies being buried in the same grave. The tombs found at the nearby *Santa Rosa* excavation, undertaken in 2003–2006, ranged from the mausolea of the wealthy, close to the Via Triumphalis which ran north-south, to the *columbaria* of freedmen and funerary associations further up the hill. This was a graveyard throughout the whole period from the end of the reign of Augustus to the early fourth century. The status of the dead was shown by the splendour of the mausoleum, its proximity to the road and by its structural durability. The *columbaria*, by contrast, were built into each other, depending on each other for support on the landslide-prone hillside. Here were also found the simplest graves, holes in the ground for pottery urns or shallow trenches for bodies.

Inhumation requires a great deal more space than cremation. Since it was difficult to find land on the surface for extensive graveyards, the inevitable result was to excavate underground. Rome is surrounded by a soft volcanic rock called tufa which can be easily quarried. Family mausolea designed originally for urns were extended underground to provide burial spaces — *hypogea*. Many have been found along the Via Portuense, the Via Trionfale, the Via Flaminia, the Via Latina and Via Appia. One of the best examples is at the Christian cemetery of St Sebastian on the Via Appia Antica: there a group of pagan mausolea can be seen which were originally on the surface, dating from the middle of the second century. One of them, the mausoleum of Clodius Hermes built around 160, not only contains niches for urns to hold the ashes of people who had been cremated and sarcophagi for burials but also has an underground extension with simple graves, probably for the family's freedmen. This reflects not only the transition from cremation to inhumation but also the need of even the rich to develop burial crypts.

What of the Roman afterlife? In the *Satyricon*, Trimalchio wanted to build a tomb so that he would live after death. What he meant by that is far from clear. His reading of the will was intended to make his friends and dependents as grateful that evening as they would be after his death. His mock funeral, where he wanted them to speak nicely about him, suggests that in some sense not only his memory but even his personal comfort after death depended on their memory of him. The black humour of the tale is that the design and inscription of his tomb is absurd, unfashionably ostentatious and deceiving — in other words, it will not be him but a figment that will be remembered — and that despite all its magnificence it will still be vulnerable to the casual defilement of a passing stranger. The first thing he wants is that it should be inscribed properly with the correct formula: 'This monument will not pass to the heir.'[7] The disturbing ambiguity of this standard expression is that the tomb is not to be inherited by the beneficiaries of the estate so as to prevent them selling or exploiting it, yet nevertheless it is they, the people who in the past have depended on the deceased's generosity, who will now be the only ones who can guarantee his peace and comfort in death. The standard Roman way of talking of the dead is to use a plural word which has no singular form, the *manes* — the shadowy, undifferentiated mass of the dead. Individual tombs, however, guaranteed personal memory and, in some way, individual survival.[8] In some sense, aristocratic Romans continued to have a presence in their funeral masks, displayed in the houses of their descendants and worn at funeral processions, but strikingly these were preserved within the sacred precincts of the city, the *pomerium* — in other words, they belonged in the land of the living.[9] Tombs, by contrast, lay outside the *pomerium* in the realm of the dead and, in some way, ensured personal survival after death.

Roman views about the afterlife were imprecise and varied.[10] They seem to have fused two different ideas.[11] One, clearly ancient idea was that the deceased inhabited the grave and that there they could be

---

[7] *Hoc monumentum heredem non sequitur:* the standard inscription on tombs or graveyards.

[8] Henri Lavagne, 'Le Tombeau, mémoire du mort' in François Hinard (ed), *La Mort, les morts et l'au-delà dans le monde romain* (Caen: University of Caen, 1987) pp. 159–65; see also Michèle Ducos, 'Le Tombeau: *Locus Religiosus*' in François Hinard (ed), *La Mort quotidien dans le monde romain* (Paris: De Boccard, 1995) pp. 135–44.

[9] Florence Dupont, 'Les Morts et la mémoire: le masque funèbre' in Hinard, *La Mort, les morts et l'au-delà* pp. 167–72.

[10] Toynbee *Death and Burial* pp. 33–9.

[11] The best account is still Franz Cumont, *Lux Perpetua* (Paris: Paul Geuthner, 1949) pp. 13–77.

nourished and comforted by family and friends laying down offerings. Roman funeral rites seem to have expressed this as a double birth in a two-stage ceremony, a birth out of the world and then a birth into the afterlife.[12] The other was that the spirits of the dead migrated to the underworld, passing into a shadowy existence where they forgot the mortal life they had lived on earth and now lay beyond the assistance even of a visitor to the underworld such as Aeneas (in book 6 of the *Aeneid*) or Orpheus (in book 4 of Virgil's *Georgics* or book 10 of Ovid's *Metamorphoses*). Despite this radical inconsistency — on the first account the dead needed the help of the living, on the other account they were incapable of receiving it — the two concepts seem to have co-existed in Roman custom and myth and it was in the grave that they came together. The grave was seen as the gate of the underworld, through which the dead person passed to the world of the dead. The unburied, without a grave, could not therefore pass over into the shadow-land of death and were condemned to a restless, distressing existence. The classic example in literature was Aeneas's helmsman, Palinurus, whom Aeneas met as he travelled to the underworld: as he had never been buried, Palinurus could not cross the Styx until his bones were laid to rest on earth.

Among the educated, philosophical opinions ran counter to these ideas. Epicureanism, a materialistic doctrine familiar to any reader of Lucretius's great poem on the nature of things, *De Rerum Natura*, held that death was annihilation; life was material and death was dissolution. It taught the moral lesson that, if there was no afterlife, then people should be indifferent to death. Clearly, many people did believe that death was the end, as can be seen from the not uncommon inscription on tombs: *nf, f, ns, nc*[13] — I was not, I was, I am not, I do not care. Other philosophical theories held that the soul did have an existence in some way independent of the body. Pythagoreanism, for instance, encountered in the pages of Ovid's *Metamorphoses*, held to a doctrine of the transmigration of souls, a form of reincarnation, in which people could look forward to another life after death. Followers of Plato, whether they read him directly in the *Phaedo*, the *Gorgias* or the *Phaedrus*, or indirectly in Cicero's *Somnium Scipionis*, Scipio's Dream, could speculate that the afterlife comprised a judgment on a person's actions, where the

---

[12] This is argued by Anthony Corbeill, *Nature Embodied: Gesture in Ancient Rome* (Princeton: Princeton University Press, 2004) pp. 89–99.

[13] *Non fui, fui, non sum, non curo.*

souls were rewarded or punished for their conduct in life. With such variety of opinion to be found in the elite culture of Rome, it is not surprising that when the philosophical emperor Hadrian speculated about death in his famous, much-anthologised poem *Animula vagula blandula*, he wondered where his dear little soul, guest and comrade of his body, would go — pale, naked and cold — after his death.

Burial customs and the cult of the dead echoed more ancient beliefs. The practice of relatives visiting family tombs with small offerings bringing comfort and refreshment to their dead relatives not only shows the continuing relationship of living and dead but indicates some sense of personal survival after death.[14] Many of the tombs in the *Autoparco* and *Santa Rosa* excavations at the Vatican had holes for relatives to pour honey or some other nourishing liquid down to the deceased. The main commemoration of the dead in the Roman calendar was the Parentalia, lasting from 13–21 February. Ovid, writing about fifty years before Petronius, describes the last and most important day of the festival, Feralia (*Fasti* 2.533–70), when families would honour the graves and appease the souls of their forefathers by bringing small gifts to their tombs. He justifies the modesty of the gifts by observing that the spirits of the dead, the *manes*, ask little, valuing reverence more than a costly gift.

Two things are noteworthy about Parentalia. First, it was intended to bring comfort and peace to the dead. Ovid describes the ceremonies in forbidding and dark terms as a way of placating their spirits; perhaps most Romans thought of it more optimistically as a time of celebration and reunion with loved ones. In other words, in death the usual roles in society were reversed — the father now depended on the reverence of his sons for his peace and security in the afterlife; the rich depended on their heirs; the master depended on his freedmen. Secondly, it was a family festival, a time to visit the family graves. Here Roman attitudes to prestige and virtue, to family and *pietas*, reverence, come together. Everything depended on having children and on being remembered. The dead father or wealthy man was now dependent on the dutiful or affectionate devotion of his children or his heirs; but at the same time it was they — fathers and those who left a legacy — who could hope for the solace in the afterlife that the loyalty of former dependents could bring. Success in this life — children, wealth — was echoed in the afterlife. Hence the importance for the rich of family mausolea, built near the road where

---

[14] Toynbee *Death and Burial* pp. 61–64; Cumont *Lux Perpetua* pp. 29–54.

they could be noticed. What of those however who had no fine tomb, no children to honour their memory, no property to bequeath?

Ovid describes another set of still darker days of the dead in the Roman calendar, the Lemuria, in May (*Fasti* 5.419–44). On these days, the ghosts of the unknown dead were exorcised from the home by the head of the household moving around the house in deepest night throwing beans over his shoulder, commanding the spirits to depart. Ovid confessed himself unsure about the origin or meaning of the ceremony but the restless and dangerous spirits of the night, the *lemures* (from which the name of the animal, the lemur, derives), were clearly perceived as hungry and malevolent. These were presumably the ghosts of the unburied, the forgotten, the unappeased and unnourished who haunted the realm of the living and who needed to be warded off and driven away.

To have no marked grave and to be remembered by no one was the fate of slaves, the poor and the childless. There were thousands upon thousands of them. The corpses of the destitute were thrown in communal pits, *puticuli*,[15] to rot along with ordure and refuse and the remains of animals — a humiliating, inhuman end which probably reflected the squalid conditions in which they had lived. Notices in the city asking people not to dump rubbish also specified that they should not dump corpses.[16] It has been estimated that there were at least 1,500 unclaimed corpses in Rome that needed to be disposed of in this way each year; in addition there must have been huge numbers of the pathetically poor and slaves whose final destination was the *puticuli*.[17] The fact that it was a not uncommon custom to free a slave as he or she was dying so that they could be given a proper funeral[18] suggests that the remains of slaves were usually unceremoniously dumped like garbage. The grimmest of Horace's *Satires* (1.8) describes the mass grave adjacent to the ramparts of the Esquiline hill, where a slave would deliver the bodies of his fellow slaves in

[15] Varro *De Lingua Latina* 5.25 refers specifically to the pit beyond the wall at the Esquiline hill.

[16] Hopkins *Death and Renewal* pp. 207–11; see also Valerie M. Hope, 'Contempt and Respect: the Treatment of Corpses in Ancient Rome' in Valerie M. Hope and Eireann Marshall (eds), *Death and Disease in the Ancient City* (London: Routledge, 2000) pp. 104–27.

[17] John Bodel, 'Dealing with the Dead: Undertakers, Executioners and Potter's Fields in Ancient Rome' in Hope and Marshall *Death and Disease* pp. 128–51.

[18] Jean-Christian Dumont, 'La Mort de l'esclave' in Hinard *La Mort, les morts et l'au-delà* pp. 173–86.

cheap boxes and where bankrupts and wastrels would also end up; the whole site had been disfigured by whitening bones until it was cleared and landscaped by Horace's patron Maecenas. Writing about 30 BC, forty years before Ovid and nearly a century before Petronius, Horace said that the graveyard had been marked out by a pillar bearing the words that Trimalchio wanted inscribed on his tomb: this monument will not pass to the heir. At the huge, stinking open pit where the only remains of the penniless were flung, those words had a bitter irony.

Though these massive pits were designated as graveyards and were thus protected under religious law, there was no way that the deceased could be comforted by surviving family and friends or their memory preserved. It was only a tiny minority of people whose remains were housed in a monumental tomb and a small minority, though impossible to estimate how small, whose ashes were laid in a *columbarium*. The great majority vanished into these communal pits; and though there is archaeological and literary evidence for them from the late-republican and early-imperial periods, there is simply no way of knowing whether such pits were still used from the second century onwards or how else the bodies of the poor were disposed of.

THE ORIGIN OF CATACOMBS

One overpowering reason can be adduced for the appeal of Christianity in the third and fourth centuries: its attitude to death. Christians spoke confidently of an afterlife and of resurrection. They believed in the absolute value and the personal survival of every individual. Gradually, they enshrined that belief in the vast warren of underground cemeteries they dug around the city of Rome where the Christian dead could be laid reverently in peace. For the poor, the childless and slaves, being welcomed into this community not only in life but also in death was profoundly attractive. If the alternative was the *puticuli* (or whatever replaced them in the second and third centuries) and nameless oblivion among the *manes* or, much worse, restless and unappeased craving among the feared *lemures*, the promise of eternal life for the Christian individual, and its expression in this world as a decent funeral and a marked grave in a catacomb, must have had an appeal that was hard to resist.

There is no more eloquent evidence of the solidarity of the Christian community and its belief in the unique and eternal importance of each of its members than the catacombs.[19] About sixty Christian catacombs and smaller underground burial places have been found on all the arterial roads feeding into the city of Rome, amounting to hundreds of miles of underground corridors dug between the early years of the third century and the middle decades of the fourth. Hundreds of thousands of bodies, impossible to estimate accurately but perhaps totalling about three quarters of a million, were buried there in that century and a half. The fate of the dead in the *puticuli* reflected the living conditions of the destitute in Rome — poor, nasty, brutish and short, but never solitary. So too the catacombs reflected the aspirations of the church — a fellowship of people, cared for as individuals and yet united as a community who expected to share in a general resurrection. It is no accident that the network of Christian cemeteries developed just as the church organised the city into seven diaconal districts[20] and claimed responsibility for 1500 widows and poor people.[21] A church that invested so much effort on the welfare of the needy and commanded the allegiance of a broad spectrum of the population of the city proclaimed that that unity extended on beyond the grave into a shared life in heaven.

The Christians were not alone in this view of life and death. Their beliefs were derived from their Jewish heritage. It is no surprise then that the Jewish community in the third and fourth centuries also dug catacombs as communal cemeteries for their dead.[22] Of course there are fewer of them, about six in all, and they are not at all as extensive as their Christian counterparts, but the same sense

---

[19] The best account, with lavish illustrations and excellent plans, is Vincenzo Fiocchi Nicolai, Fabrizio Bisconti and Danilo Mazzoleni, *The Christian Catacombs of Rome: History, Decoration, Inscriptions* (Cristina Carlo Stella and Lori-Ann Touchette (trans); Regensburg: Schnell and Steiner, 1999); James Stevenson, *The Catacombs: Rediscovered Monuments of Early Christianity* (London: Thames and Hudson, 1978) is still useful. The best short introduction is L. V. Rutgers, *Subterranean Rome: In Search of the Roots of Ancient Christianity in the Catacombs of the Eternal City* (Leuven: Peeters, 2000). For a detailed survey with plans of all the main catacombs, see Pasquale Testini, *Le Catacombe e gli Antichi Cimiteri Cristiani in Roma* (Bologna: Cappelli, 1966).

[20] *LP* 1, 148.

[21] Eusebius *HE* 6.43.11.

[22] Toynbee *Death and Burial* pp. 237–39 and Rutgers *Subterranean Rome* pp. 146–53 offer brief accounts of them; Harry J. Leon, *The Jews in Late Ancient Rome: Evidence of Cultural Interaction in the Roman Diaspora* (Peabody, Mass: Hendrickson, 2nd ed, 1995) offers a detailed survey on pp. 45–66, a description of sepulchral inscriptions on pp. 122–34 and a consideration of their art on pp. 195–228. L. V. Rutgers, *The Hidden Heritage of Diaspora Judaism* (Leuven: Peeters, 2nd ed, 1998) pp. 45–71 reinforces arguments that they should be dated to the third and fourth centuries.

of solidarity in death as in life and of hope in resurrection and life after death inspired them. They date from the same period as the Christian catacombs.[23] The earliest Jewish cemeteries, such as the Vigna Randanini catacomb on the Via Appia Antica (between the great Christian catacombs of St Callistus and St Sebastian), were not originally planned as one coherent whole. Instead, they began as a number of distinct underground burial chambers, *hypogea*, with their separate entrances on the surface, which were gradually extended and united as one network. Others, such as the two catacombs on the Via Torlonia along the Via Nomentana, not far from the important Christian catacomb of St Agnes, were dug out systematically from the start as one organised complex. The grave inscriptions reveal the strong sense of Jewish identity and of participation in the life of the Jewish community and yet also of integration into the society and culture of Rome.

It seems likely that Christians, and probably Jews, practised inhumation before it became common in pagan society. Minucius Felix, writing arguably in the first half of the third century in Rome, put into the mouth of a critic of Christianity the argument that Christian burial was based on a foolish distaste for cremation: their belief in resurrection surely did not mean that it was any harder for the burnt ash to be reconstituted as a body than the decomposed corpse. The Christian protagonist replies that that is not their reason for burying the dead, they simply prefer the ancient way.[24] For the discussion to have had any force, some distinction in burial practices must have existed. But before the underground cemeteries were dug, Jews and Christians presumably buried their dead in graveyards along with everyone else. Christian graves have been found alongside pagan ones in the Vatican cemetery. The fine sarcophagus of Marcus Aurelius Prosenes, who died in 217 after a successful career in the service of the Emperor Commodus, only reveals his Christian faith in a discreet inscription on its upper right side.

As the Christian communities grew and the practice of inhumation became normal, Christians began to develop their own cemeteries. In North Africa in the early third century, Tertullian wrote about protests against Christian cemeteries, which suggests that they were new.[25] At

---

[23] See L. V. Rutgers, *The Hidden Heritage of Diaspora Judaism* (Leuven: Peeters, 1998) pp. 45–71.

[24] Minucius Felix *Octavius* 11; 34.

[25] *Ad. Scapulam* 3.1.

about the same time Origen referred to Christian cemeteries in Alexandria.[26] In Rome, the earliest cemeteries were probably private initiatives at the end of the second century. This is suggested by the names of some of the oldest—Domitilla, Priscilla, Praetextatus, Bassilla and Trasone. They probably had a good deal in common with the old *columbaria* which grand families would build to house the ashes of their freedmen: an effort by people of means to provide burial crypts for themselves and their less prosperous fellow-Christians. *Hypogea* were extended underground in irregular and unplanned excavations, sometimes unearthing older *hypogea* and incorporating them into the labyrinth of tunnels, as for instance in the earliest phase of the Vibia catacomb.[27] The Domitilla catacomb provides important but elusive evidence of the absorption and transformation of what were originally independent, pagan *hypogea* into an extensive Christian underground cemetery in the first half of the third century.[28] The work was made easier if the tunnellers, the *fossores*, could exploit already-existing excavations — an old quarry at St Sebastian on the Appian Way, for instance, or disused water tunnels at Priscilla on the Via Salaria. The earliest Christian cemeteries were therefore haphazard and erratic not only in their foundation but in their shape underground.

They were called cemeteries, using the Greek word *koimētēria*: sleeping rooms or dormitories. This was a distinctively Christian word reflecting a distinctively Christian belief in the afterlife. Those who were buried there were said to have 'fallen asleep in Jesus' (1 Thess. 4.14). The common name for the subterranean cemeteries of Rome, catacombs, originally applied only to one of them, St Sebastian, which was built at a place called *catacumbas*. This is often construed to mean 'at the hollows';[29] it is equally likely that it was the name of an inn with a signboard depicting a couple of small boats.[30] The fact is that it is a

[26] *Homilae in Ieremiam* 4.3.16.

[27] Testini *Le Catacombe* pp. 152–53.

[28] Umberto Maria Fasola *The Catacombs of Domitilla and the Basilica of the Martyrs Nereus and Achilleus* (Philippe Pergola (ed); Christopher S. Houston and Fausto Barbarito (trans); Città del Vaticano: Pontificia Commissione di Archeologia Sacra, 3rd ed, 2002) pp. 13–16; Testini *Le Catacombe* pp. 52–55.

[29] E.g. Fiocchi Nicolai *The Christian Catacombs* p. 9; Rutgers *Subterranean Rome* p. 43.

[30] Antonio Ferrua *The Basilica and the Catacomb of Saint Sebastian* (Nicholas Reitzug (trans.); Città del Vaticano: Pontificia Commissione di Archeologia Sacra, 2nd ed, 2006) p. 11; *kymbē* is the Greek for a drinking cup and a small boat, so *kata kymbas,* 'at the boats' or 'at the cups' would be an appropriate name for a tavern — though why an inn so near Rome should have a Greek name remains unexplained.

very odd name and no one can be sure why the area was called by it. Only at the end of the Middle Ages did the term catacomb come to be applied to all the underground cemeteries in Rome.

Private individuals soon found that they could not satisfy the desire for Christians to be buried together, in Christian cemeteries. Excavating catacombs was very expensive and there were large numbers of the poor looking for a decent burial. Second and third-century Christians boasted of the generosity with which they looked after their own poor and needy. Inevitably, that provision of welfare included burial of the dead. Tertullian, for instance, described a monthly collection for all the needs of the Church:

> One day each month, each person, if he wants to, contributes a small donation, but only if he wants to: there is no compulsion, everything is voluntary. These gifts are like a bank deposit of devotion. They are not taken out and spent on banquets, drinking sessions and eating houses but rather to support and bury the poor, to supply the needs of destitute girls, boys and parents or of the old confined to their homes or those who have been shipwrecked. If there are any down the mines or exiled to the islands or in prison on account of their faithfulness to God's Church, they become the nurslings of our community of faith.[31]

Tertullian's main point seems to be that membership of the Christian church did not depend upon paying a subscription, so that though it may have looked to an outsider like a burial society[32] it was in fact something quite different. But he also makes the point that the church looks after the needy. It was not only the church in North Africa that had undertaken responsibility for the burial of the poor. An early sign of a centralised organisation in Rome for the funding and administration of cemeteries is to be found in the *Apostolic Tradition* (40):

> No one should be charged heavily for burying someone in the cemeteries, for they are the property of all the poor, though a workman's fee should be paid to the man who digs and the cost of the tiles should be paid. The bishop should provide for those who are in the cemetery from what is offered to the church, so that there should be no heavy cost for those who come to the cemeteries.

The earliest example of a communally owned and administered Christian cemetery in Rome was probably the section of the St Callistus catacomb called Area 1 built at the end of the second

---

[31] *Apology* 39.5–6.
[32] Robert L. Wilken *The Christians as the Romans Saw Them* (New Haven: Yale University Press, 1984) pp. 31–47 suggests that the Romans must have regarded early Christianity as some sort of funeral *collegium*.

century.[33] On the surface, an area of land 250 feet by 100 feet was fenced off. Underground, two parallel galleries were linked by a series of connecting passages forming a grid pattern. It was planned as a whole and was designed so that it could be extended further. All the early burials were in identical horizontal cavities, *loculi*, lining the walls of the passages. Only in about the year 235 were five richly-decorated small rooms, *cubicula*, constructed off the galleries to house *a mensa* tombs, where the grave was covered with a lid resembling a table top. One of the *cubicula* was the Crypt of the Popes, which eventually contained the graves of nine bishops of Rome. This cemetery was presumably the one assigned to the care of the deacon Callistus by Zephyrinus at the start of the third century.[34] The fact it was called 'the cemetery' suggests it was the first to be owned and run by church officials.

Callistus, however, was not buried in his own catacomb but in the Calepodio cemetery on the Via Aurelia Vetus, another early example of a communal catacomb arranged as a series of small galleries branching out from two parallel tunnels, rather resembling a comb.[35] Again, the early graves in these corridors were all simple *loculi*. From the same date, the first decades of the third century, dozens of irregularly ordered galleries were excavated at the catacomb of Priscilla, housing thousands of *loculi*. In the corridor near the entrance, there were several grander tombs with marble sarcophagi, but the sheer size of the catacomb if not its irregular shape suggests centralised funding.[36] One of the best examples of a cemetery containing scarcely anything but *loculi* is the catacomb of Novatian on the Via Tiburtina which contains graves that can be securely dated by their inscriptions to 266–70. An inscription declares that Gaudentius the deacon made the tomb for the martyr Novatian.[37] As there is no record of a cult of a martyr called Novatian but the theologian and anti-pope was said to have died as a martyr,[38] this looks as though it is his burial place. There is only one *a mensa* tomb, that of the martyr Novatian himself. The rest are almost all austerely simple. The earliest datable epitaphs are from 266, several of them are in Greek and several are crudely

---

[33] Testini *Le Catacombe* pp. 61–69.

[34] Hippolytus *Ref.* 9.12.14.

[35] Testini *Le Catacombe* p. 145.

[36] Ibid., pp. 69–75.

[37] ICUR VII, 20334.

[38] Socrates *Historia Ecclesiastica* 4.28.

inscribed.[39] Others date from the early to mid-fourth century.[40] Some epitaphs are complex, suggesting a later date and elevated social status. But the catacomb is devoid of paintings and has only a couple of separate *cubicula*, one of which contained three sarcophagi.

Forming a very marked contrast with the starkness of the catacomb of Novatian is the Crypt of the Popes in the St Callistus cemetery.[41] In about 235, a *cubiculum* was constructed off one of the galleries. On the wall facing the entrance was an *a mensa* tomb, cut into the soft tufa rock and covered with a flat lid. This was presumably the founder, perhaps donor of the *cubiculum*, but no inscription survives to identify whose sepulchre it was. Given that otherwise only bishops of Rome, other bishops and clergy were buried there, the *cubiculum* must from the outset have been intended as the burial place of the church hierarchy. The project can therefore be seen as part of bishop Fabian's reconstruction of the organisation and discipline of the Roman church. The first to be buried there in a simple *loculus* was Antherus, who died in 236. His epitaph, in Greek letters, recorded simply: *Anteros Epi* (for Antheros Episcopos: bishop Antherus).[42] Sometime afterwards, Pontian's body was repatriated from Sardinia and buried there. The epitaph, again in Greek lettering, describes him as *Pontianos Episc Mrt* (for Pontianos Episcopos Martys: bishop Pontian martyr).[43] Fabian himself was buried there in 250; as he had died in prison as a victim of Decius's persecution, he too was described as a martyr.[44] The epitaph of Lucius (d. 254)[45] has also been found in the crypt. Its whole aspect was changed in 258 with the burial of Sixtus, captured at the cemetery and martyred on 6 August. The niche above the *a mensa* tomb was adjusted to hold his sarcophagus.

In the following century, the *cubiculum* was transformed into a chapel: the door was heightened and widened, two light shafts were opened in the roof to illuminate the centre of the room and the altar, two spiral columns were installed to help mark out the area in front of Sixtus's tomb as a sanctuary. It had clearly become a shrine. In about

[39] ICUR VII, 20335–8.

[40] ICUR VII, 20340–2.

[41] Antonio Baruffa *The Catacombs of St Callixtus: History, Archaeology, Faith* (William Purdy (trans); Vatican City: Libreria Editrice Vaticana, 3rd ed, 2006) pp. 52–67.

[42] ICUR IV, 10558.

[43] ICUR IV, 10670.

[44] ICUR IV, 10694.

[45] ICUR IV, 10645.

the 370s, Pope Damasus placed two marble slabs bearing inscriptions of his own composition engraved in the fine, distinctive lettering of the stone-carver Furius Dionysius Filocalus. The one on the front of Sixtus's tomb is probably Damasus's best-known poem *Hic congesta iacet*, while on the right-hand wall he put his poem describing Sixtus's martyrdom.

Already, then, by the middle of the third century, Rome was encircled by Christian cemeteries. To the west, serving the densely working-class area of Trastevere, was the Calepodio catacomb on the Via Aurelia. To the south, on or near the Via Appia were Domitilla, Praetextatus, Callistus and Vibia. To the east, on the Via Tiburtina was the Ciriaca catacomb where Laurence was buried in 258 and the catacomb of Novatian, presumably serving his church. To the north east, on the Via Salaria Nova were the catacombs of Priscilla and Trasone; on the Via Salaria Vetus was the catacomb of Bassilla. They served the local Christian communities in the different regions of the city. From early, haphazard extensions of *hypogea* built at private initiative and expense, they grew into large, planned networks of tunnels which were clearly beyond the resources of private individuals to excavate or maintain. How far they were administered and funded locally, by the deacons responsible for seven districts for example, can only be a matter of speculation but such a large enterprise as the construction and development of these catacombs does suggest considerable overarching control of funds. It is more than likely that the expansion of the catacombs in the first half of the third century, rather than reflecting a Christian community divided according to the districts in which they lived, contributed considerably to the development of episcopal authority and the central administrative machine of the church in the city.

A DIADEM OF MANY GEMS

When Valerian chose to attack the church in 257–58, one of his main targets was the cemeteries. It would have been impious to destroy them, but he attempted to close them to Christian visitors. In other words, he wanted to stop Christians burying their dead there and visiting their graves. This indicates the importance of cemeteries in the functioning of the Christian community. A century later, Julian, the last pagan emperor, observed in a famous passage: 'it is their philanthropy to strangers, their care for the graves of the dead and the pretended holiness of their lives that have done most to increase atheism,'[46] by which, of course, he meant Christianity. Belief in the resurrection, respect and devotion to the dead, the assurance of a decent funeral and a marked grave and a remembrance, all of these were powerful factors drawing people into the Christian church.

Though Christians did not use the standard name for a graveyard, a *necropolis*, their cemeteries well suited that description. They were indeed cities of the dead, in which all slept together in a solidarity they had hoped to enjoy in life, united in a common citizenship with a dignity and order that many of them had not known in the teeming bedlam of the streets of Rome. With the galleries for streets and the open chambers off them for squares, the catacombs expressed the unity of the Christian community and to a very considerable degree its austere equality. The catacombs were never a place for the living to take refuge but they were a place where the living could gather in union with their dead in prayer and ritual meals. But above all, in an age when the Christians had few or no buildings of their own on the surface, they were an eloquent statement of the Christian under-standing of death, encircling the vast, noisy, dangerous, filthy and glorious city of Rome.

It was inevitable that when Valerian's persecution was abandoned, the catacombs would expand once more. The ones built in the first half of the third century were extended and new ones were developed. According to the *Liber Pontificalis*,[47] when Dionysius was bishop of Rome (260–69) he set up the parish system in the city and placed the cemeteries under the control of the presbyters. This seems to be the point at which the central clerical control of the catacombs was finally established, a natural reaction to their attempted closure by Valerian. The names of the catacombs are, again, significant. No longer are they named after an original donor. Instead, they could be named after a place or a martyr or simply a distinguishing feature. The most famous place name was *catacumbas*, the cemetery later called St Sebastian on the Appian Way. The simplest distinguishing feature was size, as in the *Coemeterium Maius* (the major cemetery). The cemeteries named after martyrs — Agnes, Laurence, Gorgonius — reveal intense devotion to martyrs and the desire for burial near their tombs. What these names suggest is that these cemeteries were corporate enterprises. St Callistus remained the principal burial place of the popes, with a new area being opened up at the end of

---

[46] *Ep.* 22.
[47] *LP* 1.157.

the century and the beginning of the fourth to hold the tombs of Popes Gaius (283–96), Eusebius (308) and Miltiades (311–14).[48] An inscription records that the deacon Severus had obtained permission from Pope Marcellinus (296–304) to build a double cubiculum for himself and his family. It is the earliest example of the bishop of Rome being described as pope.[49] Another papal cemetery was the Novella on the Via Salaria, planned by Pope Marcellus.[50] It seems likely, therefore, that some cemeteries were specifically papal and others were administered by presbyters.

Catacomb construction was always constrained by the circumstances of the site but one highly efficient plan, resembling a fish's skeleton or a gridiron, was used repeatedly: a long gallery with offshoots on each side spaced only a few yards apart, giving maximum intensive use of space. Very good examples are the lower level of Panfilo on the Via Salaria Vetus and the lower level of Priscilla on the Via Salaria, dated to the beginning of the fourth century. Others with the same economical plan were areas X, B and Z of Saints Marcellinus and Peter, the Staircase of 1897 area of Domitilla, the anonymous catacomb at the Villa Pamphilj on the Via Aurelia Vetus and the catacomb Ad Duas Lauros. These galleries house thousands of simple *loculus* burials; Ad Duas Lauros, for instance, had 11,000 tombs. The late third and early fourth centuries were not only the high point of Christian burial in the catacombs but also an era of intensive, planned development. At the very least, the *fossores*, the sappers who dug the tunnels, were copying each others' best efforts. It is not unlikely that the repeated use of the same plan is evidence of centralised planning and coordination of resources.

The fishbone pattern continued to be used in the first half of the fourth century: the lower levels at Praetextatus, the lower level of the Staircase of 1897 area at Domitilla, the lowest level at San Ermete, the lower level of Giordani, the two vast regions at St Agnes behind the martyr's shrine. As they grew in size, the catacombs were going deeper, with lower levels dug underneath the earlier tunnels. Where the earlier layers had often stretched in different directions somewhat haphazardly, the lower levels were more rigidly planned, using space more efficiently, evidently anticipating growing demand. Ancient

---

[48] Baruffa *Catacombs of St Callixtus* pp. 93–105.

[49] Ibid., 107–9; John Moorhead '"Papa" as Bishop of Rome' *JEH* 36 (1985) pp. 337–50.

[50] *LP* 1, 164.

Rome had never seen anything like this: a huge network of almost identical cemeteries offering a secure resting place as a member of a vast family, the Christian church.

People wanted to be interred near a martyr, of whom there were probably over two hundred buried in the catacombs.[51] Martyrs' graves can be identified by the density of burial near them: there are a large number of graves in the floor as well as in the walls near a martyr's tomb and often a special crypt called a *retrosanto* was constructed behind the tomb to provide further space for burials. Clearly, it was a privilege to be interred near the saints, a privilege for which people were willing to pay. In the cemetery of Priscilla, for instance, next to the entrance to the *cubiculum* of St Crescentius, an inscription records that Felicissimus and Leoparda had a *bisomus*, a *loculus* to hold two bodies.[52] In Callisto, Serpentius bought a *loculus* from the *fossor* Quintus near the crypt of St Cornelius (*ad sanctum Cornelium*).[53] Near the tomb of St Gaius also in Callistus (*in Callisti at domn[um] ... Gaium*), a husband bought an *arcosolium* for his wife Iovina.[54] A particularly good example of a fine *retrosanto* crypt housing three large *arcosolia* was built in the second half of the fourth century behind the tomb of the martyr Gaius; its walls and floor were covered in multi-coloured marble, and the floor was decorated with geometrical designs. On the wall of the entrance passage, the artist placed a picture of himself and the message, 'Iconius fashioned and whitened this place in ten days.'[55] This pressing desire to be near the martyrs was expressed too in graffiti asking for their intercession. 'St Sixtus, remember in your prayers (*in mente habeas in horationes*) Aurelius Repentinus.'[56] 'Holy spirits, remember Marcianus, Successus, Severus and all our brethren.'[57] 'Martyrs, holy, good and blessed, help Cyriacus.'[58]

This dramatic extension of catacomb systems was accompanied by the emergence of social distinctions among the graves. With that came the appearance of Christian art. Since most of the bodies were

---

[51] Agostino Amore *I Martiri di Roma* (Rome: Antonianum, 1975) surveys the martyrs associated with each catacomb.

[52] ICUR IX, 25165.

[53] ICUR IV, 9441.

[54] ICUR IV, 9924.

[55] ICUR IV, 9542.

[56] ICUR IV, 9521.

[57] ICUR IV, 9522.

[58] ICUR X, 26350.

removed once the catacombs ceased to be the main cemeteries of the Christian community, the galleries today look stark, their empty *loculi* strikingly uniform. From archaeological evidence, however, it seems that the sealed *loculi* were in fact cheaply and modestly decorated to relieve their anonymous uniformity. Many bore no inscription, suggesting that the family and friends of the deceased were illiterate; the slab closing the *loculus* could only therefore be singled out by some other decoration. Some had coins or pieces of glass studded into the plaster. Fairly commonly — hundreds of examples have been found — the base of a glass container bearing a religious image was stuck in the plaster. These might have been the broken pieces of vessels used for a funerary meal when the deceased was buried. In a small way, these shiny embellishments distinguished the grave and attracted the notice of visitors making their way down the galleries. Given how common it was to ornament even the simplest *loculi*, it is not surprising that richer people took the opportunity of constructing considerably more eye-catching tombs.

Given the fundamental attitude that wealth was there to be used generously and, though dangerous in excess, was not in itself a bad thing, it comes as no surprise that, as the catacombs grew in size and importance in the second half of the third century, social distinctions began to be seen in the kind and location of tombs. Though the overwhelming majority of the tombs were slots in the walls of the tunnels, *loculi*, distinguished only by simple inscriptions, in the late-third and fourth century richer people began to have tombs that were marked out either by the design of the grave or their location.[59] Larger graves were constructed with a table-top surface crowned by an arch — an *arcosolium* tomb. These could be located in the tunnels along with the *loculi* or be placed in specially constructed chambers off the tunnels, burial rooms called *cubicula* which could often be highly decorated with wall paintings.

For instance, in Regio X of Marcellinus and Peter, which is an early example of the fishbone plan, four small burial chambers, *cubicula*, three of which were painted, open off the tunnels. These were designed for grander tombs, perhaps to house the graves of a family buried together. At about the same time, similar areas were developed elsewhere in Marcellinus and Peter, in Callistus and in Domitilla

---

[59] See Philippe Pergola, 'Sepultures privilégiées de la catacombe de Domitille à Rome' in Yvette Duval and Jean-Charles Picard (eds), *L'Inhumation privilégiée du IVe au VIIIe siècle en occident* (Paris: De Boccard, 1986) pp. 185–87.

to provide *cubicula* for more affluent burials.[60] They contained *arcosolia* tombs and eventually they could house elaborately carved sarcophagi, with sculptures rivalling the finest non-Christian work. Undeniably, these were tombs that were intended to impress visitors with the wealth, as well as the faith, of the deceased. Not only did the conversion of members of the wealthier classes lead to the provision of more elite burials with their fine décor, but the reverse was also true: the availability of finely decorated burial chambers played an important part in the conversion of the Roman elite to Christianity.[61] The crucial question, however, is what was the relationship of the *cubicula* burials with the humbler *loculi* in the galleries outside.

One advantage of the *cubicula* was that they provided space for people to gather for the reverential commemoration of the dead. There is some archaeological evidence of tables and niches in the galleries of the catacombs suggesting that the Christians gathered there to celebrate funeral banquets not unlike those eaten by their pagan friends at their family graves. Much more substantial evidence of such banquets survives in the *cubicula*, which of course would have been far more convenient for such a gathering. At the end of the third century, for instance, remarkable *cubicula* were constructed in Regio I of St Agnes and the oldest section of the Coemeterium Maius, with benches, stools and niches carved out of the rock; the work in both places is so similar as to suggest that the same teams of *fossores* were responsible for both. The image common in wall paintings of people eating a meal might well refer to these funerary feasts.[62] These meals were an important aspect of the solidarity of the community, not only expressing the family unity of Christians but probably providing opportunities for the wealthier to share a meal with the poor.[63]

---

[60] Regio Y in Marcellinus and Peter, the area of Gaius and Eusebius in Callistus, the upper level of the Hypogea of the Good Shepherd in Domitilla and the area of Miltiades in Callistus.

[61] P.-A. Février, 'Une approche de la conversion des élites au IVe siècle: le décor de la mort' *Miscellanea Historiae Ecclesiasticae*, VI, *Congrès de Varsovie 1978* (Bruxelles: Publications universitaires de Louvain, 1983) pp. 22–45.

[62] P.-A. Février, 'Le culte des morts dans les communautés chrétiennes durant le IIIe siècle' *Atti del IX Congresso Internazionale Cristiana, Roma, 21–27 settembre 1975*, I (Studi di Antichità Cristiana, 32; 2 vols; Città del Vaticano: Pontificio Istituto di Archeologia Cristiana, 1978) vol. 1, pp. 11–274; Elisabeth Jastrzebowska, 'Les scènes de banquet dans les peintures et sculptures des IIIe et IVe siècles' *Recherches Augustiniennes* 14 (1979) pp. 3–90.

[63] P.-A. Février, 'A propos du repas funéraire: Culte et sociabilité: "In Christo Deo pax et concordia sit convivio nostro"' *Cahiers Archéologiques* 26 (1977) pp. 29–45.

The *cubicula* do not give the impression of being separated off, areas for the exclusive use of the wealthier folk whose relatives were interred there: rather they seem to play a role as meeting spaces, or 'chapels', for the benefit of all. Their position along the galleries, juxtaposing simple and grander burials randomly, suggests a close relationship between them. At the higher levels, they were lit by skylights open to the surface, providing an important source of light into the tunnels. The art of the *cubicula* is largely public and common-place, not private and personal. An interesting exception is the *Cubiculum of Five Saints* in the catacomb of St Callistus, dating from the early fourth century, which has the names of six people described as being in peace, five of whom appear to be celebrated with portraits in a posture of prayer.[64] A fairly limited range of images is repeated frequently, suggesting that the wall paintings had a straightforward catechetical function relevant to everyone. Trades are depicted in some wall paintings, as they are in some epitaphs — greengrocers, bakers, barrel sellers, wine merchants, barge transporters and, above all, the *fossores* who excavated the catacombs. These must refer to the graves nearby but they do not determine the decoration of the whole *cubiculum*. Furthermore, there is no sign in the inscriptions that the occupants of the *cubicula* were regarded as the patrons of the people buried in the *loculi*. In other words, social distinctions were recog-nised in the variety and location of graves but the wealthier tombs were of benefit to all without any claim to public acknowledgement for the munificence of the dead or their families to the others buried in the catacomb.

It is thus unusual to find areas where the only the rich seem to have been buried, at a distance from ordinary folk. In Callistus, the Regione di Sotere, dating to the middle years of the fourth century, has a quite distinctive network of *cubicula* and *arcosolia* facing each other in architecturally impressive spaces with vaulted or domed ceilings. In Praetextatus, the Spelunca Magna, Regio B, is made up of a few galleries which show a regular setting of *cubicula* and *arcosolia*. Here, graves of the senatorial aristocracy have been found, the Annii, the Postumii and the Insteii,[65] suggesting that this section was marked out as a privileged area for the upper classes. While their very rarity shows that there was usually a much closer relationship between grander and humbler burials, they do illustrate the way that fourth-

---

[64] ICUR IV, 9770; Baruffa *Catacombs of St Callixtus* pp. 109–10.
[65] For the inscriptions: ICUR V, 14016, 14132, 14155, 14445.

century Christianity could mirror the social structures of society. One factor contributing to the segregation of grander sepulchres was access: special staircases were built to allow people to visit these areas.[66] It is possible therefore that there were private entrances to these parts of the catacombs, for the use of the wealthier families. In a sense, their position was therefore different from the old social gradation found in a typical necropolis on the surface: the elite tombs there had always been nearest the road, where they could most easily be visited and admired by all, while poorer graves were positioned further back or further up the hill. These elite sections of the catacombs represent a different a sort of privilege: the privilege of private seclusion.

In 1955, the discovery of a new catacomb on the Via Dino Compagni on the Via Latina revealed a unique example of private privilege.[67] Dating from the middle years of the fourth century, it consisted of a series of magnificently painted *cubicula* linked by unpainted corridors. To the archaeologists, the overall impression of passing from one room to another in this catacomb was that of visiting an art gallery. It was evidently a private catacomb for a group of families, built and decorated over the course of a couple of decades. The chambers were architecturally elaborate, with vaulted ceilings, columns, cornices and gables. In these splendid rooms, fine *arcosolia* tombs and sarcophagi housed the bodies of the rich. In the corridors were modest *loculi*, where presumably family dependents and slaves were buried. In all, there were 325 tombs, containing about 400 bodies.

Here the Roman social order was strikingly in evidence. Owned and administered by the wealthy, the catacomb had room for a limited number of their dependents. Freed from the control of the church authorities, the owners had decorated their catacomb according to their own taste so that they could include a very large number of scenes found nowhere else in the Roman cemeteries: the expulsion of Adam and Eve from Eden, Lot fleeing from Sodom, the drunkenness of Noah, the blessing of Ephraim and Manasseh, the crossing of the Red Sea, the Pillar of Fire, the vision at Mamre, Jacob bringing the children of Israel into Egypt, Moses receiving the commandments, the Angel standing in Balaam's way, Samson killing

[66] Pergola 'Sepultures privilégiées' pp. 186–87.
[67] For a lavishly illustrated description, see Antonio Ferrua, *The Unknown Catacomb: A Unique Discovery of Early Christian Art* (Iain Inglis (trans); New Lanark: Geddes and Grosset, 1991).

the lion and striking the Philistines with the jawbone of an ass and chasing foxes into the Philistine fields, Christ between Peter and Paul, the soldiers casting lots for Christ's robe. In the feeding of the 5,000, Christ is portrayed as a child. In other catacombs, the scenes used for decoration and instruction followed a more restricted and predictable repertoire. Very little can be said with certainty about the function and choice of catacomb decoration, but it is not impossible that in catacombs under the direct supervision of the church authorities a limited and well-known set of images was used repeatedly for catechetical purposes whereas in this private catacomb a wider range of biblical scenes could be illustrated for a select clientele.

Far more mysterious than this unique sequence of biblical scenes is the appearance in some of the *cubicula* of paintings of episodes from pagan mythology. There are several depictions of Hercules — slaying the Hydra, with the apples of Hesperides, with his patron Minerva and bringing back Alcestis from the underworld. What are these doing in a Christian catacomb? They are clearly further evidence that this was a private cemetery, out of the control of the church authorities who would not have tolerated such images in a public catacomb. It is true that Orpheus — a Christ-like figure rescuing his beloved from the Underworld — seems to feature twice in catacomb art. He is apparently depicted in a third-century *cubiculum* in Callistus and in a late fourth-century *arcosolium* in Marcellinus and Peter. It has to be admitted that portrayals of the youthful Orpheus and the beardless Christ are inevitably similar. But the very rarity of such pagan images elsewhere in the catacombs makes these pictures of Hercules in the Via Dino Campagni extremely striking. One explanation has been that Hercules was regarded, like Orpheus, as a Christ-like figure. In other words, this is an example of Christianity assimilating a pagan myth.[68] But the selection of scenes does not seem sufficiently Christological to make this theory plausible. Another view is that the key picture is of Hercules bringing Alcestis back from the underworld; again a pagan myth has been assimilated to Christianity, this one having a strong resurrection motif. Perhaps this was intended to stress that a husband and wife would meet again in the afterlife.[69] This theory cannot adequately account for the other scenes portrayed

[68] Josef Fink, 'Herakles als Christusbild an der Via Latina' *Rivista di Archeologia Cristiana* 56 (1980) pp. 133–46.

[69] Beverly Berg, 'Alcestis and Hercules in the Catacomb of Via Latina' *Vigiliae Christianae* 48 (1994) pp. 219–34.

here from the life of Hercules. The simplest explanation is that the catacomb included pagan burials which were commemorated with their own pictures.[70] There is some other slight evidence of pagan burials elsewhere in catacombs but again, if this view is correct, it emphasises how distinctive this private catacomb was from those under the authority of the church leadership. It makes very good sense to suppose that some of the families who contributed to this private catacomb were of mixed religion and that they would want to be buried together in the family vault. That pagans burials either scarcely ever happened elsewhere in the catacombs or were never celebrated with pagan religious symbolism is an indication of the firm control exercised over the other Christian cemeteries.

By the middle years of the fourth century, the catacomb network had nearly reached its fullest extent. The complex at St Callistus, for example, which was made up of several previously distinct cemeteries, eventually amounted to over twelve miles of tunnels on four levels. People continued to be buried in the catacombs during the fifth century but by then they were being superseded by graveyards within the city. The old taboo against being interred within the sacred limits of the city gave way to an entirely new Christian attitude to burial and bodies so that it was increasingly common for Christians to be buried inside the city walls. The catacombs had expressed a belief in the solidarity of the living with the dead, all united together in the Christian community which made up the Body of Christ, which was very different from pagan attitudes to the afterlife and the polluting danger of the corpse.

Between the fourth and eighth centuries, the catacombs became places of pilgrimage or even tourism. There is a celebrated short description from the pen of St Jerome of his visits to the catacombs as a student in the late 350s: 'crypts, dug deep in the earth, their walls on either side lined with the bodies of the dead … here and there, the light, not coming in through windows but filtering down from shafts above, relieves the horror of the darkness'.[71] Damasus, who was pope between 366–84, was responsible for a great deal of work on martyrs' shrines, ornamenting them with epitaphs composed by him in verse recording their martyrdoms. The catacombs were ceasing to be remembered as cemeteries of the ordinary faithful and were

---

[70] Mark J. Johnson, 'Pagan-Christian Burial Practices of the Fourth Century: Shared Tombs?' *JECS* 5 (1997) pp. 37–59.

[71] *Commentarii in Ezechielem* 40.5.

venerated instead as shrines of the saints. In 441, Pope Leo the Great could remind his congregation in Rome of how thousands of blessed martyrs, emulating the triumph of Peter and Paul, 'encircle our city in purpled serried ranks, shining out, and crown it with a diadem twined together from the beauty of many gems'.[72]

The eighth century was a period of depredation and decline, as the catacombs were ravaged by Lombard invaders. Eventually in the eighth and ninth centuries, the remains of the dead were re-located from most of them into churches within the city,[73] providing a vast source of small relics which eventually found themselves in altars and reliquaries all over the world. The catacombs were sealed up, abandoned and forgotten until they were rediscovered and explored in the late sixteenth century and then again more extensively and professionally in the mid-nineteenth century.

THE ORIGINS OF CHRISTIAN ART

When a *loculus* was sealed up, a brief inscription was often incised on the plaster recording the name of the person buried inside. Eventually, it became common to add a short message of farewell. It also became common for the *fossores* to inscribe a symbol along with the person's name. A fish was very popular, probably recalling the Gospel stories of Jesus likening those called by his disciples to a catch of fish. The deceased was therefore someone caught by the LORD in his net. It would also remind people of Jesus feeding the five thousand, which in turn would recall the eucharist — thus, at the same time, the fish stood for Christ. It is not uncommon to find the Greek word for fish, *icthus,* written out:[74] it is an acronym for 'Jesus Christ, God's Son, Saviour' (*I*esous *Ch*ristos *Th*eou *Hu*ios *S*oter). This very simple image, so easily and quickly drawn on the damp plaster, was therefore very rich in meaning.

Other persistently recurring symbols include the cross; an anchor, symbolising hope and safety; a dove, symbolising peace and God's covenant with humanity; a phoenix, symbolising rebirth; a swastika, symbolising prosperity and creativity; the cross flanked by the first and last letters of the Greek alphabet, alpha and omega, showing

---

[72] Tractate 82.6.

[73] Richard Krautheimer, *Rome: Profile of a City, 312–1308* (Princeton: Princeton University Press, 1980) pp. 112–13, 134–36.

[74] For instance, an early third-century inscription: ICUR II, 4246.

that Christ sums up all history; a P for *pace*, in peace; the first two letters in Greek of the title Christ, *Chi* and *Rho*, in a great variety of forms; wreaths celebrating victory. These images were potent in their simplicity. Some were specifically Christian; they could only be understood by someone already well informed about Christian belief. Others, such as the dove or the phoenix, were recognisable to anyone. The *fossores* were therefore both utilising the stock figures of non-Christian art and forging a new symbolic imagery for the Christian faithful.

Something similar happens with the early depictions of Christ.[75] Christ is often presented as the Good Shepherd, with a lamb or a ram on his shoulders. The Christian significance of the image seems unmistakeable but it bears a striking resemblance to an extremely common non-Christian artistic motif, the ram-bearer (the *kriophoros*), a young man in rural costume carrying a ram on his shoulders as the personification of philanthropy and the simple joys of country life. In other words, the Christians took a commonplace image and gave it their own, distinctive meaning. Similarly, when Christ was depicted as a teacher, he was portrayed as a philosopher, scroll in hand. Christ the healer was equipped with a staff with which he touched the sick to perform a miracle. These were part of the standard imagery of every-one's art. This seems undramatic enough; if a teacher had to carry a scroll or a healer had to have a staff to be identified in a picture, it was natural that that was how the Christians should have presented Christ. It is extremely unusual to find a more daring assimilation of pagan religious or mythical imagery into a portrayal of Christ. The couple of pictures where Christ looks like Orpheus with his lyre could also be seen to resemble King David singing the psalms. The most unusual is to be found in the Vatican Necropolis, very near the monument to St Peter. Tomb M has a depiction of the Sun God as a youthful charioteer but the beams emanating from the Sun God are patently in the form of a cross — so this is commonly taken as a picture of Christ as Apollo.

Christ tended to be presented as youthful, neither the powerful, bearded Christ of the Byzantine icon nor the suffering Christ of much later western art. It is not easy to evaluate the importance of Christ's youth in these pictures. He seems to be the young man who restores youth to others, so his youth is symbolic of rebirth and restoration. At

---

[75] Mary Charles-Murray in Jeffrey Spier, *Picturing the Bible: the Earliest Christian Art* (New Haven: Yale University Press, 2007) pp. 51–63.

the same time, his youth is a reminder of uncorrupted innocence, of God's first creative purpose. Is the viewer expected to see in his youth the Son, the image of the Father, who discloses the unknowable and unseen and ageless God? Does his youth therefore carry a trinitarian significance, pointing beyond itself to the Father? What is fairly clear is that, in these very early wall paintings of the third and early fourth century, Christ is not depicted as an imperial figure, peering impassively down on his earthly subjects. Christ is not the rival of Caesar. Rather, the very speed with which a fresco sketch had to be made on the plastered wall adds to the impression of his slender vitality, his grace and ease in movement and even his apparent vulnerability.

The range of scenes from both Old and New Testaments deployed in catacomb art in the third and early fourth centuries is fairly limited.[76] From the middle years of the third century in the cemetery of Callistus can be found: the baptism of Christ, the adoration of the Magi, the raising of Lazarus and the miracle at Cana. From later dates can be found: the multiplication of the loaves and fishes, various healing scenes including the blind man, the paralytic and the woman with the issue of blood, and Jesus's encounter with the Samaritan woman. What seems to be the earliest depiction of the Virgin and Child can be found in the Priscilla catacomb, dating from the middle years of the fourth century. These, along with the Good Shepherd, form the staple of the New Testament repertoire until fourth-century sarcophagi begin to depict scenes from the passion of Christ such as his betrayal and arrest and trial before Pilate, surrounding a cross. The absence of portrayals of the crucifixion before the fifth century is striking.

New Testament scenes tend to be outnumbered by ones from the Old Testament. This illustrates well the Christian claim to be the fulfilment of all God's promises and revelation throughout the history of the Old Testament. It also indicates that much of the imaginative furniture of the early Christians, and therefore of the sermons they heard and the expositions of the faith they were taught, dwelt on the Old Testament prefigurations of Christ's revelation in the New Testament. By far the commonest was the story of Jonah. Jonah is shown being tossed over the side of the boat, being spat up by the whale that had swallowed him or else resting on dry land — all images of Christ's death and resurrection. Another very common scene was Noah in the ark, an image of salvation. Moses striking the rock in the

[76] Robert M. Jensen in Spier *Picturing the Bible* pp. 65–85.

wilderness, releasing a spring of water for his people, was an image of Christ the saviour, while Daniel in the lions' den or the three young men in the fiery furnace were images of the triumph over death in resurrection. Susanna was a reminder of God's vindication of innocence, as was the sacrifice of Isaac with its specific Christological reference to Christ's death.

The simplicity of the art allows for fluidity and multiplicity of meaning. Themes of creation and recreation, salvation and mercy, healing and justice are juxtaposed and overlap in ways that would have given ample scope either for meditative consideration or for catechetical exposition. A good example of the potency of these images is another very common picture, that of the banquet. While banquet scenes have been seen as probably referring specifically to the funerary meals celebrated to commemorate the dead,[77] the range of allusion was no doubt deliberately very wide: the meals Christ shared with his apostles, above all the Last Supper; the eucharist; the Christian love feast, the *agape*; the heavenly banquet.

These frescoes are almost always to be found on the walls of *cubicula* or in the arch of an *arcosolium* tomb. In the *cubicula*, the paintings therefore could occasionally form a sequence with an overall meaning. A good example in the catacomb of St Callistus is the decoration of the five small chambers called the *Cubicula* of the Sacraments, dated to the start of the third century.[78] Here a series of images alludes to baptism and the eucharist. Moses striking the rock to bring forth water in the desert is portrayed several times. Jonah is presented in four different places, one of which is the entire cycle showing him thrown into the sea, swallowed by the whale and then left on the seashore. There are depictions of the baptism of Christ, the scene where Jesus promises the Samaritan woman living water and the healing of the paralytic at the pool of Bethesda. There are several representations of a man fishing and the earliest picture of the baptism of a Christian. All of these have a strongly baptismal theme. Other paintings are eucharistic. The multiplication of the loaves and fishes is depicted as a meal, while the sacrifice of Isaac is closely related to what seems to be explicitly a eucharist. Furthermore, there are three paintings of the Good Shepherd; this image has eucharistic resonances if considered in the light of the psalm, 'The LORD is my

---

[77] Jastrzebowska 'Les scènes de banquet'.
[78] Baruffa *Catacombs of St Callixtus* pp. 79–84.

Shepherd', for there the Shepherd provides a banquet and a cup that runs over (Ps. 22 [23].5).

Perhaps it is surprising that the frescoes do not more often constitute coherent series of related pictures, for the *cubicula* frequently had an overall decorative plan which resembled the interior decoration of Roman houses. Some had an architectural design, with the walls divided into a lower range painted to resemble marble and a higher range covered in paintings, while the ceiling was decorated with geometrical figures intended to convey an ethereal, heavenly effect. Others followed the shift in domestic decoration towards a less architectural, brighter design with whitened walls broken up by thin red or green lines to create areas in which a wide variety of pictures could be painted. These often contained floral designs, suggesting a garden in bloom.

For Christian art to have developed, the Christians needed a place and a reason to paint. The catacombs in Rome provided them with their first large opportunity to discover and develop the visual arts. For the most part, the style of the pictures and very often the detail too looked exactly like contemporary non-Christian paintings. Jonah resting after his deliverance from the whale, for example, looks strikingly like the sleeping Endymion of myth — a naked youth, in the same pose, with much the same features. A non-Christian visitor, if ever such a person penetrated the subterranean passages, would have found the overall design of the *cubicula* and the feel and colouring of the paintings reassuringly familiar. On closer inspection, however, the visitor would have been puzzled. Without a fairly good grasp of the central message of Christianity and the biblical stories that expressed it, no outsider could make sense of the paintings. For all their formal similarity to the standard art of the world around them, the catacomb paintings are remarkable evidence of the different imaginative world of belief that the Christians inhabited.

CHRISTIAN VOICES

About 40,000 inscriptions survive from the catacombs. Since about three-quarters of a million people were buried there, this is in fact a small proportion. The exploration of the few catacombs untouched by the ravages of time or the devotion of later generations suggests that the majority of graves were unmarked. The inscriptions that survive are thus those of the literate and, given that marble inscriptions have a much better chance of enduring than plaster ones, probably reflect a disproportionately large number of the more affluent Christians. Nevertheless, turning the pages of the ten large volumes in which they have been collected and annotated, the *Inscriptiones Christianae Urbis Romae*, the reader hears the voices not of the tiny minority of early Christians who wrote works which have survived but of ordinary folk, sometimes barely literate, speaking in the raw emotions of grief and hope summoned up by the loss of relatives or friends.

We find their names. Open the index listing the names of the four cemeteries on the Via Nomentana and the Via Salaria and glance at random:[79] Callityche, Calligona, Calligonus, Calliope, Callipodia, Callistratus, Calocaerus, Calpurnia Prisca, Camasius, Campanus, Candida, Candidiana, Candidianus, Capitolinus, Caprius, Cara, Carissima, Cassiana, Castoria and Castorius her son. There are thousands of them from those cemeteries alone. The vast majority have names that would pass unremarked in the Rome of the third or fourth centuries. There are 385 names in Greek inscriptions. Few have names overtly linking them with Christianity: five called John in Latin and two in Greek; two called Paul in Latin and one in Greek; eight called Peter; five called Maria; two Stephens; four Susannas; one Thomas; two called Timothy in Greek. A few others have names that indicate their faith: four women were called Adeodata and one man Adeodatus ('given by God'); one man was called Quoddeusdedit ('whom God gave'). There are enormous numbers, however, who have a double name of which part is Aurelius or Aurelia — Aurelius Acutianus, Aurelius Emilius, Aurelius Agapitus and so on. Some of these are the freedmen of the imperial household, carrying the imperial name to show their dedication to their former owner; most are the immigrants to Rome who gained the citizenship as a result of Caracalla's decree of 212 and commemorated his beneficence by taking the imperial name. The personal name of the majority is a simple Latin one — Aurelius Felix or Florentius or Fortis. At least two have specifically Christian names, Aurelius Petrus and Aurelia Susanna, suggesting that they were born to Christian parents. Some are Greek — Epafras, Heliodorus, Zosias, Zenon. Some suggest more exotic origins — Eufrates or Babylonias.

A search through the indexes of the other volumes of the *Inscriptiones Christianae* confirms that this picture is typical. Imperial freedmen figure prominently. There are many more people with apparently pagan names such as Hermes, Hercules, Aphrodite,

[79] ICUR VIII.

Apollo or Achilles than people with biblical names. Very few appear to be named after martyrs. There are some who have names expressive of Christian faith, such as Renatus ('reborn'), Benedictus ('blessed') or Redemptus ('redeemed'). A few have names which speak of their origin: Proiectus or Proiecticius ('abandoned') or Stercorius ('found on the dung heap'). These are presumably people exposed as infants, abandoned by their parents to die but rescued by Christians.

Few names suggest exalted social rank. Almost everyone has just one name. Many appear to be the names of slaves and immigrants. Almost all in the third century are utterly laconic, just recording a name, sometimes adding *in pace*: in peace. Almost all reveal the popular Latin of the streets — with the letter *b* replacing *v* (*bibit* instead of *vivit*— 'he lives') or *e* replacing *ae*. Some are barely literate. Some are surprisingly grand. An early example of a slave's burial is from the catacomb in the Via Salaria Vetus: an unusually lengthy epitaph, that of Marcus, who lived eighteen years, nine months and five days. He was a slave attached to the imperial tailoring department (*inter bestitores*) and was described as *Caputafricesi* — that is, he was a student in the school for imperial servants on the street called Caput Africae, climbing the Caelian Hill from the Colosseum.[80] His education there was clearly a matter of great family pride. His tombstone was set up in the catacomb of San Ermete by his father, Alexander, who was a slave of the two Augusti, who must have been Septimius Severus and Caracalla (198–211).[81] Another example, from the catacomb of St Sebastian, dating to roughly the 220s, set up by his parents Earinus and Potens, remembers Atimetus, a slave born in the emperor's household, who lived eight years and three months. The inscription is decorated with a fish and an anchor.[82]

Gradually, as the epitaphs on the graves became more expansive in the late third and fourth centuries, they began to reveal the occupations of the dead. A few were lawyers, notaries, doctors, clerks of the grain administration and teachers. The epitaph of Deuterius, for instance, reported that he was 'an interpreter of the poets (*vates*) and teacher of both languages' (Latin and Greek).[83] Rather more common were the bricklayers, cleaners, dyers, seamstresses and shoemakers

[80] Samuel B. Platner and Thomas Ashby, *A Topographical Dictionary of Ancient Rome* (Oxford: OUP, 1929) pp. 98–99; Eva Margareta Steinby, *Lexicon Topographicum Urbis Romae* (6 vols; Rome: Edizioni Quasar, 1993–9) vol. 1 p. 235.

[81] ICUR X, 27126.

[82] ICUR V, 12892.

[83] ICUR IV, 10888.

who made up the great anonymous bulk of the population. *Fossores* tended to commemorate themselves, understandably, in inscriptions or in paintings. One epitaph included a picture of Eutropus, a sculptor, along with his son, engaged in making a sarcophagus.[84]

All ranks of the clergy are well represented. In the best, austere style many simply record that the deceased was a priest: 'Iulianus Presbyter',[85] or a partial inscription, 'Presbyter in pace'.[86] A Greek inscription records 'Dionysius, doctor, presbyter'.[87] We find an exorcist, Paul, burying his wife or daughter Martyria — both strikingly Christian names.[88] The lengthy verse inscription of the deacon Severus, dating from the end of the third or very beginning of the fourth century, records how he constructed a *cubiculum* in the catacomb of St Callistus with the permission of Pope Marcellinus and there buried his very dear daughter Severa.[89] One epitaph amounted to a short obituary of an acolyte from the third quarter of the fourth century, installed by his brother who was a priest:

> Annius Innocentius, acolyte, lived for twenty-six years. He often laboured on journeys by ecclesiastical command. Indeed he was sent twice to the provinces in Greece and often to the regions of Campania, Calabria and Apulia. He died on his last mission, to Sardinia. His body was brought back here. He sleeps in peace on VII Kal Sept. His brother, the presbyter Annius Vincentius, with whom he worked well, made [this tomb].[90]

Here we find a papal diplomat, from the noble family of the Annii, a trusted young man of marked abilities, presumably a Greek speaker, who might have risen high in the Roman clergy. The transfer of his body from Sardinia back to Rome for burial is a sign of his elevated social status. His brother, the priest Vincentius, died in 366 and was buried in the same cemetery.[91]

In the epitaph of Annius Innocentius, we hear the confident voice of the Roman aristocracy, recording distinguished service to the Church just as other members of the family might have commemorated service in the imperial government. The brief obituary provided by his brother would have sounded eminently respectable to non-Christian

---

[84] ICUR VI, 17225.
[85] ICUR IV, 9944.
[86] ICUR IV, 10354.
[87] ICUR IV, 9483.
[88] ICUR IV, 10026.
[89] ICUR IV, 10183.
[90] ICUR IV, 11805.
[91] ICUR IV, 11763.

friends. They would have admired too the sentiments expressed in inscriptions from grateful freedmen to their mistresses: 'For Petronia Auxentia, in peace, most noble woman, well deserving, who lived for thirty years, her freedman made [this tomb]';[92] 'DM For Marcia Rufina, a worthy mistress of the house, the freedman Secundus made [this tomb]'.[93] That last inscription is not at all unusual in the catacombs in including the standard pagan formula on Roman graves 'DM', *dis manibus,* to indicate its sacred status. Though DM had become a formula devoid of religious content, the social relations of freedman and former owner — deference, respect and gratitude — are as vivid here as in any Roman epitaph.

Were all Christians confined by the conventions of class? One epitaph, from a tomb in the upper complex of the Domitilla catacomb set up for Flavia Speranda by her husband, Onesiforus says this:

> For Flavia Speranda, holiest, unequalled wife, mother of all, most noble lady, well deserving, who lived with me twenty-eight years, eight months, without anger, Onesiforus her husband made [this tomb].[94]

'Most noble lady' — *clarissima femina*; inscribed on the tomb as *cf.* — is the title of a woman of senatorial rank. Onesiforus is a Greek name of no distinction. But has the inscription been correctly recorded? If it has, then here we have the memorial of a long and happy marriage between an aristocrat and a commoner.

It might have been an unconventional marriage, if the inscription has been read correctly, but the sentiments Onesiforus expressed were typical enough. The phrase 'without anger' (*sine bile*) is quite conventional.[95] Similar expressions are 'without any discord',[96] 'without bitterness',[97] 'without blame and with all tenderness'[98] 'without any complaints.'[99] Husbands tend to praise their wives for their sanctity and their simplicity, for their prudence and diligence; wives tend to praise their husbands for meekness, affability, goodness, integrity and sweetness towards everyone. Onesiforus described his wife as 'unequalled' (*incomparabilis*). This was a popular adjective for beloved spouses: in the Novatian cemetery on the Via Tiburtina,

[92] ICUR IV, 10085.
[93] ICUR IV, 9415.
[94] ICUR III, 7599.
[95] ICUR III 7497; 13338; 14245.
[96] ICUR VI 15625.
[97] ICUR III, 8175.
[98] ICUR VII, 17765.
[99] ICUR III, 9170; V, 13130; 15273; VIII, 23101.

for instance, Valentina buried her unequalled husband Eusebius, who lived forty-one years and eight days;[100] a wife who gave no name but just announced that she was his only wife set up a tomb to the unequalled Vitalis.[101] It is not uncommon for inscriptions, however, to describe the deceased spouse as the equal or partner, using the related word *compar*. 'I Marcus made for us, Karisia most beloved partner, an eternal home'.[102] Sharing a grave expressed this unity in death: 'I Gallicanus made a double grave (*bisomum*) for me and my lady, most holy wife Fatalis'.[103] Friends too might want to be buried together. A damaged inscription records that Januarius wanted to be buried along with his friend, whose name was probably Severinus.[104]

Infant mortality must have been extremely high in ancient Rome. In one gallery of the Panfilo cemetery, for instance, there were 111 graves, of which 83 were for children, only five of whom had epitaphs. The inscriptions recording the death of children are often among the most revealing of personal hope and loss. The grave of Iunius Acutianus, aged about ten, says: 'in this tomb which you see, rests someone witty (*facetus*), though a boy in age, a lamb snatched into heaven and given to Christ'.[105] A boy of seven, Dalmatius, was described by his grieving father as a 'very sweet son, full of genius and common sense' who was a quick learner of Greek as well as Latin but who died after an illness of three days.[106] A boy called Augustine who died aged 15 years and three months, was mourned by his mother for his singular piety, the innocence of his life and his marvellous wisdom. His parents must have been of different faiths and he had chosen his mother's religion; it was she who constructed the tomb.[107] One grave simply recorded the names and the dates of death of the baby Felicitas and the boy Secundio, who died in the same month and were buried together.[108]

The lives of some babies were recorded in scrupulous detail. Aurelius Asclepodiotus lived one year, two months, three days and

[100] ICUR VII, 20412.
[101] ICUR VII, 20531.
[102] ICUR III, 6499.
[103] ICUR III, 7574.
[104] ICUR IV, 9408: Genuarus placuid se uniter poni cum amicum suum sibi rinu.
[105] ICUR IV, 11328.
[106] ICUR I, 1978.
[107] ICUR IV, 11823.
[108] ICUR VII, 20417.

two hours.[109] Cepasia lived eight months and twenty five days.[110] Cyriaca lived two years and ten months.[111] Dulcitius lived two months and twenty-four days.[112] Fanius Paulus asked his little son, Fanius Leo, who died aged two years, three months and twenty-one days, to pray for his brothers.[113] It was quite common to ask for the children's prayers: 'Lucernius, you went before your time; you are in peace; keep your parents in mind'.[114] Some children's deaths had been long anticipated. These words were put into the mouth of a boy, Discolius: 'Here I rest, free from all anxiety; what I awaited has happened; when the coming of Christ occurs, I shall rise in peace'.[115] Parents were sometimes buried with their children. Bonōsē set up a tomb for her son, Bonōsos, with an inscription in Greek saying that they would sleep in our LORD God Christ. It is striking that the son was named after his mother.[116] Another Greek inscription in the same catacomb, the upper level of the Domitilla cemetery, simply recorded 'Prima, with her own daughter, sleeping in our LORD God'.[117]

Some epitaphs say explicitly what must have been true of others, that the deceased had been baptised before death. The baby Apronianus, for instance, who died aged one year, nine months and five days, was commemorated with this inscription: 'much loved by his grandmother, when she saw he was destined to die, she prayed to the church that he might leave life on earth a believer (*fidelis*)'.[118] Tyche died aged one year, ten months and fifteen days, on the day she was baptised.[119] This confidence that baptism was the gate to eternal life is shown in the epitaph of a woman called Julia: 'I had my birth in Rome; if you ask my name, it was Julia; I lived faithfully with my husband Florentius to whom I left three living sons; having just received divine grace, I was taken into peace as a neophyte'.[120]

[109] ICUR III, 7456.
[110] ICUR III, 7491.
[111] ICUR III, 7527.
[112] ICUR III, 6660.
[113] ICUR III, 7576.
[114] ICUR VII, 20454.
[115] ICUR IX, 25102.
[116] ICUR III, 8039.
[117] ICUR III, 8068.
[118] ICUR VIII, 23087.
[119] ICUR IX, 25562.
[120] ICUR IV, 11927.

Another epitaph records Felix, who lived 23 years and ten days: 'he departed from this life a virgin and a neophyte, in peace'.[121]

Shaping everything — the trust in the power of baptism, the expression of continuing bonds of affection, the desire to be buried together, the quiet confidence in the power of prayer of and for the dead, the recognition of the equality in death of even the youngest child, the aspiration to be buried near the martyrs — was belief in resurrection. The deacon Severus, whose family vault in the cemetery of St Callistus had been constructed with the permission of Pope Marcellinus, commemorated his daughter Severa:

> Severa, sweet to her parents and to her servants, on the VIII Kal Feb gave back her soul which the LORD had decreed to be born in the flesh with wonderful wisdom and character. Her body is buried here, quiet in peace until she shall rise again through him who, by his holy spirit, took her soul chaste, pure and forever inviolable. The LORD will give it back again with spiritual glory. She lived nine years, eleven months and fifteen days. Thus she passed from this life.[122]

---

[121] ICUR IV, 12459.
[122] ICUR IV, 10183.

Chapter 5

CONSTANTINE

The emperor Carus was killed, they said, by a bolt of lightning. Accidents happen, but assassination at the hands of his praetorian prefect, Aper, would be more typical of the fate of late third-century Roman rulers. Carus had only been emperor for a year but had taken his army, triumphantly, deep into Persian territory when death suddenly claimed him in the summer of 283. The army began the long march home, nominally under the command of his younger son, Numerian, but in reality led by Aper. By November 284, they were approaching the coast of Bithynia but no one had seen Numerian, enclosed in his litter, for days. When the rumours that he was dead proved true, Aper was arrested and the senior officers chose one of their number, a man of very humble origins from Dalmatia, Diocles, as their new emperor. At a parade of the whole army, he accepted the acclamation of the troops and then, with his own hand, killed Aper in front of them all.

This could have been yet another gory incident in the bloodstained history of imperial succession in the second half of the third-century but, by extraordinary luck and outstanding talent, Diocles was to give the empire military success and security, political stability, constitutional reform and a measure of economic stability. Transforming his name to the more noble-sounding Diocletian, he appealed to the ancient values of Rome. At the same time, he was typical of his generation in that he was a career soldier from the Balkans who rose to the top by skill and hard work. But he was also one of the most creative figures in Roman history. He was the first emperor ever to retire. He devoted himself to his garden and died in his bed.

On anyone's account, Diocletian's reign was a turning point. Its most momentous innovation was the establishment of a new system of imperial government which allowed for a division of power and a peaceful succession. The empire was too big for one man; the emperor could not fight on the Danube and in Mesopotamia and be a political presence in Italy or Asia Minor all at once. Emperors had already begun to deal with the challenge by sharing power with their sons — Gallienus, for instance, had been made co-Augustus by his father Valerian, left behind to govern the West while Valerian campaigned in the East. Diocletian's predecessor, Carus, had appointed both his sons as Caesar, junior emperors. Numerian's murder opened the way for Diocletian to become head of the army and emperor, and the defeat of the elder son in Italy early in 285 left him undisputed master of the Roman world. In 285, Diocletian appointed a Caesar who could shoulder some of the responsibilities of government. He chose a fellow senior officer who had served on the Persian campaign, Maximian. The following year, 286, he elevated him to the rank of Augustus and probably adopted him as his son. Maximian campaigned on the Rhine frontier while Diocletian supervised operations in the East. In 293, each Augustus adopted a junior colleague as Caesar, Diocletian in the East appointing Galerius and Maximian in the West appointing Constantius.

The empire was now therefore ruled by a college of four imperial figures, a system of government called the Tetrarchy. Adoption and marriage relationships established the quartet as one imperial family. Broadly speaking, they distributed the empire between them with four major capitals — Sirmium for Diocletian, Antioch for Galerius, Milan for Maximian and Trier for Constantius — but their courts were highly mobile and there were no rigid boundaries between their territorial responsibilities. In no sense was the empire divided. It was still firmly one empire with one coordinated policy. It was simply that its imperial administration was redesigned to recognise its size and complexity. This was very different world from that of Pliny at the beginning of the second century, when the empire was still a collection of largely self-governing provinces belonging to the most powerful city state in history.

Achievements came quickly. Revolts in Mauretania and Egypt were suppressed. Incursions across the Danube were repelled. Constantius invaded and reclaimed Britain from another local commander who had attempted to establish a separate empire. After an initial defeat, a successful war was waged against the Persians which brought a final peace settlement in February 299. Simultaneously, currency reform and tax reorganisation addressed some of the deep-seated economic problems faced by government and people as a result of the costly crisis of the third century. Provinces were divided into smaller units and then grouped into a dozen dioceses, each governed by a *vicarius*. Troops in the provinces were put under the command of military officers called *duces*, so that the governors' responsibilities were purely civilian. That these developments remain in the vocabulary of Europe — diocese, duke — eighteen centuries later indicates that Diocletian should be remembered as one of the great administrative reformers of history.

On the 20 November 303, Diocletian, accompanied by his fellow Augustus Maximian, went to Rome to mark his twenty years in power. His only visit to the city, it illustrated both its symbolic significance and its political unimportance. This was a celebration on a colossal scale: in addition to Diocletian's twenty years, they commemorated ten years' rule of the two Caesars and furthermore the tetrarchs were awarded a joint tiumph to laud all their victories.[1] In other words, it was Rome that was chosen to celebrate the mature success of the Tetrarchy. Unfortunately, the visit was not a success. Diocletian found the freedom of speech in the city — whether heckling by the crowd or insufficient deference from the nobility — intolerable.[2] Annals written fifty years later recorded that there was a disaster at a circus event when 13,000 spectators were killed when part of the building collapsed.[3] For a man of Diocletian's religious outlook, this was worse than tragic: it was inauspicious. He cut the visit short, moving on to Ravenna to assume the consulship for the new year. While the festivities must have been the greatest that Rome had seen since those of Philip the Arab in 248, the old who remembered the millennial games might have reflected on the sufferings of the empire since then and wondered how, despite the achievements of the last twenty years, Diocletian's celebrations had gone so catastrophically wrong.

Diocletian did not intend to meet the fate of his predecessors over the previous century. He did not want to end his reign as the victim of an assassin's knife. When he went to Rome, it is not unlikely that plans were being laid for the future, for a dignified retirement and an orderly handover of power. The boldness of such a move cannot be overstated. No emperor had ever abdicated. For nearly a century, none of his predecessors could have felt sufficiently secure to vanish into private life, the empire passing quietly into the hands of his chosen heirs. Diocletian's decision to retire was finally made after a

---

[1] Recorded by the Chronographer of 354: MGH Chron. Min. 148.

[2] Lactantius *De Mortibus Persecutorum* 17.1–3.

[3] Chronographer of 354: MGH Chron. Min. 148.

grave illness that prostrated him during the winter of 304–305. On the 1 May 305, at the precise spot in Bithynia where he had accepted the imperial office twenty-one years before, he abdicated, along with his colleague Maximian. The Caesars, Constantius and Galerius, were elevated to the rank of Augustus and two new Caesars were named. Everyone had expected that the sons of the retiring Augustus and his successor would be the ones promoted. Maximian had an adult son, Maxentius. Constantius had an adult son, Constantine. Both seemed ready for the imperial purple but Diocletian had one last surprise.[4] The two men appointed were close associates of the other new Augustus, Galerius. Maximinus Daia was his nephew and Severus was an old military colleague: these were the new Caesars. This indicates where power lay within the Tetrarchy and, of course, it was an arrangement that was not going to last. Neither Maxentius nor Constantine was going to let power slip from his hands. Diocletian retired, permanently, to a massive palace at Split on the Dalmatian coast where its ruins still speak of his grandeur. Maximian's retirement proved less permanent: he was to move across the political chess board again, once this settlement of 305 was checked.

It was Diocletian's reformist government, at its strongest, which launched the greatest persecution of Christians in the ancient world. Their motives were fundamentally religious. Animated by a spirit of pagan piety, they sought to convert dissidents back to the old religion and to eradicate Christianity forever. The regime had a strongly religious tone: early in their joint reign, Diocletian took the title Iovius (Jupiter) and Maximian assumed the name of Herculius — both gods with deep Roman associations. When Constantius and Galerius joined them to form the Tetrarchy, they took the titles of Herculius and Iovius also.[5] It is not unlikely that over sixty years of war with the Sassanid kings of Persia had affected Roman attitudes. One of the ingredients in the success of the Sassanids was their religious zeal; perhaps Diocletian was following suit. Pagan intellectuals were also writing with a new hostility to Christianity. In the closing decades of the third century, they felt it was a religion worth taking seriously enough to attack at length. Porphyry, for instance, wrote a long treatise in fifteen books against the Christians, arguing that the

---

[4] Lactantius gives a vivid description of Constantine's being physically brushed aside and Maximinus Daia's being brought forward: *De Mort Persec* 19.2.

[5] Consequently, the western and eastern emperors are sometimes described as the Herculian and Jovian dynasties respectively.

profession of Christianity merited the death penalty. Traditional religious sentiment, philosophical pagan opinion and political pragmatism all pointed towards a fresh assault on Christianity as a major obstacle to unity of hearts and minds across the empire.

Fifteen years of consolidation, 284–99, had brought security and peace and effectively saved the empire. These achievements allowed Diocletian to feel strong enough to embark on a steady policy of purging the Roman world of religious dissidents.[6] The first to be targeted were the Christians in the imperial court and in the army in 299. Then in 302 came an attack on the Manichees, an alien and secretive version of Christianity that taught a radically dualist understanding of the world: the leaders were singled out and then their followers. In 303, they turned on the Christian leaders and finally, in 304, they attacked ordinary Christians. It bears all the hallmarks of a coherent strategy. The purge began in the army, which was the embodiment of the state and its religion. Diocletian felt safe to clear out the Christians from the ranks and risk the unrest that might accompany such an act because of the peace with Persia, finally agreed in February 299. Then the emperors turned on the least liked religion in the world — Manchaeism. Then, finally, the people who had defeated their predecessors for too long — ordinary Christians.

The first edict against the Christians was issued from the imperial court at the eastern capital, Nicomedia, on the 23 February 303. It decreed that all churches and any house in which the Christian scriptures were found should be destroyed; all copies of the scriptures and liturgical books were to be surrendered and burnt and sacred vessels confiscated; all meetings for worship were prohibited. Christians who refused to conform lost their right to bring actions in the courts and forfeited their status if they belonged to the privileged classes, making them subject to torture. Members of the imperial civil service were to be reduced to slavery. That very day, the church in Nicomedia, visible from the palace windows, was demolished. A few months later, a second edict was issued ordering the arrest of the Christian clergy. The prisons were soon so full that a third edict came out in the autumn of 303, offering pardon to prisoners if they offered sacrifice.

---

[6] See P. S. Davies, 'The Origin and Purpose of the Persecution of AD 303' *JTS* 40 (1989), pp. 66–94, which places the 303 persecution in a wider perspective and thus makes it part of Diocletian's, not just Galerius's, programme; for full accounts of the persecution, see Timothy D. Barnes, *Constantine and Eusebius* (Cambridge, Mass: Harvard University Press, 1981) pp. 3–27; Stephen Williams *Diocletian and the Roman Recovery* (London: Batsford, 1985) pp. 153–85.

It looked like an amnesty but in fact it subjected people to torture who had hitherto only endured incarceration. The fourth edict had a much wider scope: promulgated early in 304, it demanded that all inhabitants of the empire should sacrifice to the gods.

It seems that only the first edict was implemented in the West. In other words, the persecution was far more severe in the eastern provinces. The pages of Eusebius's *Ecclesiastical History* and *Martyrs of Palestine* and Lactantius's *Deaths of the Persecutors* provide vivid, eye-witness accounts of the macabre apparatus of oppression deployed by the Roman state across the eastern empire. Though Eusebius admitted there were countless defections,[7] the overall concern of both writers was to stress the courage of Christian resistance and the large numbers who endured torture and death. They both depict Galerius as the major instigator of the persecution but also acknowledge that Maximinus Daia, his nephew and Caesar and later Augustus in the East, had a ferocity all his own. In fact, the anti-Christian offensive opened up the first policy disagreement between the tetrarchs and, arguably, contributed to the breakdown of the system.

The full programme of persecution was only implemented in the eastern provinces under the control of Diocletian and Galerius and, after 305, under Galerius and Maximinus Daia. It is thus not surprising that the Christian historians who lived through the persecution believed that the policy stemmed directly from their leadership. In the West, Maximian and his Caesar Constantius did not share the same appetite for persecution. Constantius was responsible for Britain, Gaul and Spain. He destroyed church buildings but did not kill people.[8] Maximian ruled Italy and North Africa. In Africa, he found strong resistance to the requirement to surrender the scriptures and church vessels and the law was enforced vigorously. From the martyrdom accounts that survive of the period, Maximian's officials were clearly ready to sentence recalcitrant Christians to death. But this opened up yet another dispute about what was and was not acceptable behaviour for Christians in their relations with the pagan world. The African view was not necessarily shared by others, who did not regard the demand to hand over the sacred books and vessels as something to be defied to the point of death. It opened too the old question about what should be done to those who had handed them over, the *traditores*: how serious was their sin? This effectively caused

---

[7] *HE* 8.3.1.

[8] Lactantius *De Mort Persec* 15.7; Eusebius *HE* 8.13.13; *Vita Constantini* 1.13.

a major schism within North African Christianity, separating the hard-line majority of African Christians, labelled Donatists by their opponents, from the rest of the Christian world.

The events in Rome in 303 are lost in what must have been a deliberate act of ecclesiastical amnesia. It is clear that the bishop, Marcellinus, complied with the edict and handed over the scriptures. This became a rebuke thrown in the faces of the Catholics nearly a century later by the Donatists in North Africa.[9] Augustine strenuously denied the accusation that Marcellinus, along with his presbyters Miltiades, Marcellus and Silvester, had surrendered the scriptures and burned incense as simply incredible.[10] The three presbyters were all in their turn to become bishop of Rome and Augustine was, presumably, quite right to say that it was incredible that all three had been implicated with Marcellinus in acting as *traditores*. But Marcellinus himself, however, probably was a *traditor*. His failure could not be entirely expunged from the memory of the Roman church. The *Liber Pontificalis*, written centuries later, reported that Marcellinus had offered incense and then repented before 180 bishops and was martyred soon afterwards.[11] This makes no sense: the first edict did not require the offering of sacrifice and, had Marcellinus died as a martyr, his name would have appeared in the very early calendars of martyrs' days[12] and Augustine would not have failed to register the point in his lengthy polemics against his Donatist opponents.

Whatever the circumstances and motives of Marcellinus's act, its consequences were grave. He appears to have been forced to stand down, dying the following year and leaving the Roman church with a three-year interregnum. For a church which boasted confessors and martyrs such as Pontian, Fabian, Cornelius and Sixtus among its bishops, this was a failure which risked the loss of a great deal of moral prestige. Arguably, it was to weaken the papacy for over a decade.

MAXENTIUS IN ROME

When Diocletian announced his abdication and proclaimed the new dispensation of the tetrarchs that May morning in Bithynia in 305,

[9] As can be seen from Augustine *Contra Litteras Petiliani* 2.92.202.
[10] *De Unico Baptismo* 16.27.
[11] *LP* 1.162–3: Duchesne accepts the veracity of the account.
[12] For the earliest Roman calendar, see MGH Chron. Min. 71.

he did not realise that he was also giving notice of the demise of the system. The Tetrarchy seemed so secure: a college of four emperors bound by the strongest ties of marriage and united policy. In fact, its strength was Diocletian's personality. Without him, personal rivalries and hereditary expectations pulled the constitution of the Tetrarchy apart. Diocletian made a fundamental mistake in thinking that the sons of Maximian and Constantius would watch others promoted over their heads and allow the balance within the imperial quartet to move so decisively in Galerius's favour. Both Maxentius in Italy and Constantine with his father in Gaul were waiting for their opportunity.

The settlement of 305 could not withstand the death, just over a year later, of the new Augustus of the West, Constantius. He died while visiting his northernmost territories in Britain. His troops in York at once proclaimed his son as the new Augustus but Constantine was cautious enough to claim only the title Caesar. The official western Caesar, Severus, in command of Italy and North Africa, was acknowledged as Augustus by the surviving senior tetrarch, Galerius, who recognised Constantine's title of Caesar. But Severus simply could not establish his position. Rome rose against him, furious at the plans of Galerius to tax the city.[13] With the support of the mob, the praetorian guard, who were also enraged that Galerius planned to disband them,[14] chose Maxentius as the ruler of Rome. This act, more than any other, undermined the Tetrarchy for the city of Rome still conferred a profound aura of legitimacy upon its ruler. Realising that he would not be left in peaceful occupation of the city for long, Maxentius brought his father, the former Augustus Maximian, out of retirement to bolster his regime. Maximian was an able general. The legitimate Augustus of the West, Severus, marched on Rome but there were massive desertions to Maximian, who was popular with the troops. Severus could not take Rome. He withdrew to Ravenna where he was besieged by Maximian and finally coaxed into surrender. Promised his life, he abdicated, was brought to Rome and then forced to commit suicide. A further attempt to re-establish legitimacy was made by Galerius, who invaded Italy in a futile attempt to depose Maxentius and his father. Out-fought by Maximian, he withdrew from Italy and left the West to look after itself.

This was exactly the political instability and civil war that the Tetrarchy had been intended to extinguish for ever. It was a time of

---

[13] According to Lactantius *De Mort. Persec.* 23.5; 26.1–2.
[14] Lactantius *De Mort. Persec.* 26.3.

opportunity for the cunning and the determined and the strongest and most determined of the players was Constantine. Maximian abandoned his son, Maxentius, and joined Constantine. He thought he would be the power broker; he was wrong. A summit was held at Carnuntum on the Danube in 308. Diocletian emerged briefly from retirement and extolled the beauty of the cabbages he grew at Split to his old colleague Maximian. A settlement of sorts was agreed: Maximian was to go back into retirement; Constantine was to be the western Caesar; a new Augustus, Licinius, was appointed to replace the dead Severus. But Maxentius, whom they did not acknowledge, was secure in Italy and regained control of North Africa. The agreement was nonsense without these western heartlands. The eastern Caesar, Maximinus Daia, furious at being overlooked, had persuaded his uncle, Galerius, to give him too the title of Augustus; Galerius found himself obliged to award the same title to Constantine. In 310, Maximian emerged from retirement once more in a final bid to seize power in the West. Constantine, with astonishing speed, demolished his insurrection in Gaul and required that this exit from the stage should be final; he killed himself.

Though Maxentius was not recognised by the other rulers of the Roman world, his position looked unassailable. His forces had defeated Severus; they had driven Galerius out of Italy; they had regained control of North Africa. He had the loyalty of his troops and no longer needed the patronage or generalship of his father, Maximian. His coup had been popular in Rome because Galerius had planned to tax the city, which had begun to enjoy again the outpouring of imperial munificence. Central Rome had suffered in a great fire in 283[15] — the Forum[16] including the Senate House,[17] the Forum of Caesar,[18] the Basilica Julia,[19] the Theatre of Pompey,[20] the Porticus of Pompey[21] and the Graecostadium[22] were among the bigger buildings damaged or destroyed. Maximian, his father, had undertaken a major building programme. The city had seen very little substantial building in the third century apart from Aurelian's

---

[15] Recorded by the Chronographer of 354: MGH Chron. Min. 148.
[16] TDAR 234; LTUR 2, 342.
[17] TDAR 144; LTUR 1, 333.
[18] TDAR 226; LTUR 2, 305–6.
[19] TDAR 79–80; LTUR 1, 177.
[20] TDAR 517; LTUR 5, 37.
[21] TDAR 428–29; LTUR 4, 148–49.
[22] TDAR 248; LTUR 2, 372: there is no evidence it was rebuilt.

huge but ominous project of building a new circuit of walls in the 270s, much of which still stand today.[23] The repairs after the fire, as well as restoring the city's prestige, must have represented a massive injection of funds into its economy. The regime boasted its success and its largesse with one of the biggest monuments in Rome, the Baths of Diocletian,[24] which could accommodate about 3,000 bathers, finished only a little over a year before Maxentius's accession to power. It is therefore unsurprising that Maxentius continued this policy of imperial building as the public face of his regime.[25] He built baths on the Palatine[26] and a building that might well have been a temple in honour of his son, Romulus, in the Forum.[27] On a bigger scale, he rebuilt the massive Temple of Venus and Roma, the biggest in Rome[28] and initiated another huge monument, the Basilica Nova,[29] transforming the appearance of the Forum.

Maxentius realised that Rome itself was his strongest card. The city, protected by the Aurelian walls, was impregnable. More than that, it afforded him the glamour and the holiness which had drawn Diocletian there so unsuccessfully in 303. His regime appropriated Romanitas for itself.[30] Coins were struck with the image of Romulus and Remus and the legend *Conservator Urbis Suae* (preserver of his city). The temples of Romulus and of Venus and Roma were particularly significant monuments in the heart of the city: Romulus, the city's legendary founder from whom Rome took its name; Venus, the goddess who had brought Aeneas to Italy and was held to be the city's protectress; Roma, the genius of the city itself. Maxentius's cultivation of Romanitas can be contrasted with Diocletian's impatience and frustration during his visit to the city in 303. Galerius never visited Rome (Lactantius speculated that, as he had had no idea of its size, he had underestimated the difficulty of besieging it when he invaded Italy, and reported that he talked not of the Roman but

[23] TDAR 348–50; LTUR 3, 290–99.

[24] TDAR 527–30; LTUR 5, 53–58.

[25] For a full account, see John Curran, *Pagan City and Christian Capital: Rome in the Fourth Century* (Oxford: Clarendon Press, 2000) pp. 54–63; see also Theodora Heres, *Paries: A Proposal for a Dating System of Late-Antique Masonry Structures in Rome and Ostia* (Amsterdam: Rodopi, 1982) pp. 101–06.

[26] TDAR 530; LTUR 5, 60.

[27] TDAR 450; LTUR 4, 210–11.

[28] TDAR 553; LTUR 5, 121–23.

[29] TDAR 76–78; LTUR 1, 170–73.

[30] See Mats Cullhed, *Conservator Urbis Suae: Studies in the Politics and Propaganda of the Emperor Maxentius* (Stockholm: Paul Åströms Förlag, 1994) pp. 45–67.

of the Dacian empire[31]). In other words, out of the wreckage of the Tetrarchy, Maxentius was able to paint his eastern rivals as foreign and un-Roman while he boasted his own fidelity to the ancient ideal of the city. Rome was again an imperial capital and Maxentius's imperial status was largely based on its pride and its hopes.

There was a clearly religious dimension to Maxentius's regime but he tolerated the Christians. While the full force of the persecution that had been launched in 303 was still being applied with ferocity in the East, it ceased altogether in the West with the abdication of Maximian in 305 and the accession of Constantine and Maxentius in 306. Constantine offered peace to the Christians in his dominions at once and, shortly after coming to power, Maxentius made a formal announcement of toleration.[32] This allowed a bruised and humiliated church in Rome to elect a successor to the *traditor* bishop Marcellinus. During the three years since his resignation or deposition, the church had been entangled in very similar problems to those caused by the Decian persecution in 250–51. The evidence is fragmentary and elusive and it is not now possible to reconstruct in any detail what seems to have been a ferocious dispute. The man chosen as the new bishop, Marcellus,[33] was a rigorist who provoked a strong reaction among those who had lapsed in the persecution and were now doing penance, as his official memorial inscription set up over sixty years later recorded:

> Because this truth-telling ruler preached to the lapsed that they should weep for their crimes, he was a bitter enemy to all these wretched people. From this, furious anger and hatred followed and discord, quarrels, sedition and slaughter destroyed the covenants of peace.[34]

What Maxentius wanted was peace. Unrest among the Christians was not helpful to his regime. He therefore exiled Marcellus when he had been bishop for only a little over a year. He died shortly afterwards and his body was brought back for burial in the catacomb of St Priscilla. Removing Marcellus, however, did not solve the problem. The next bishop, Eusebius,[35] apparently elected in the spring of 308, looked for a more lenient approach to the lapsed but was challenged

---

[31] *De Mort. Persec.* 27.5, 8.

[32] Eusebius *HE* 8.14.

[33] *LP* 1.164–66.

[34] The memorial insciption of Damasus is the major source for his intransigence and banishment in the face of opposition. See Antonio Ferrua, *Epigrammata Damasiana* (Vatican City: Pontificio Istituto di Archeologia Cristiana, 1942) 40.

[35] *LP* 1.167.

by a rigorist, Heraclius, who seems to have been the leader of an opposition faction. Again, within six months of Eusebius taking office, Maxentius intervened, banishing both Eusebius and Heraclius to Sicily. Eusebius did not long survive his exile. His body was brought back and interred in the catacomb of St Callistus.

Again, the events are known only through his official memorial tablet set up by Pope Damasus over sixty years later:

> Heraclius forbade the lapsed to lament their sins; Eusebius taught these wretched people to weep for their crimes. The people were split into parties as the furious anger built up: sedition, slaughter, war, discord and quarrels. Immediately, both were expelled by the barbarity of the tyrant. Although the ruler kept the covenants of peace intact, he endured exile joyfully, under the LORD's judgment. On the littoral of Sicily, he left the world and this life. For Eusebius, bishop and martyr.[36]

What is remarkable here is that Maxentius was caught up in the role of imperial arbiter in the church's affairs. Though the action of sending bishops off into exile resembled the persecuting policies of his predecessors in the 250s, and was described as such in these monumental inscriptions, his motives were quite different. He had made a formal declaration of toleration. He found himself drawn into the internal imbroglios of the Christian church. There is a sliver of evidence to suggest that he was not unwilling to play such a role. The church historian Eusebius said that he 'began by making a pretence of our faith in order to gratify and flatter the Roman populace'.[37] This is a very odd statement, out of keeping with the rest of Eusebius's account of his character and government, which he presented in very black terms in order to heighten the contrast with the man who would overthrow him, Constantine. It can be argued that Maxentius wanted to be seen at least as the patron of the Christian church and perhaps even hinted at more.[38]

One significant argument against this view of his being pro-Christian is that he did not restore the property of the church until 311. To cease persecution but not make restitution of confiscated property for five years looks like clear evidence of an ambivalent attitude towards

---

[36] Ferrua *Epigrammata Damasiana* 18.

[37] *HE* 8.14.1.

[38] Daniel De Decker, 'La Politique religieuse de Maxence' *Byzantion* 38 (1968), pp. 472–562 argues that he was a Christian and that his support of pagan cults was not unlike that of Constantine; though the case might be overstated, the suggestion that Constantine resembled Maxentius far more than his propaganda could acknowledge and continued his policies is very attractive.

the Christians. But what was this property? It does not seem that the catacombs were closed, despite the legislation of 303: the exiled popes seem to have been brought back for burial without any difficulty. The *Liber Pontificalis*, which often mixes historical details with a great deal of unreliable information, reported that Marcellus had organised the twenty-five *tituli*, effectively the parishes of the city, as 'dioceses for the baptism and repentance of many converts from paganism and the burial of martyrs'.[39] In other words, in 307 Marcellus had made a further step beyond that taken by his predecessor Dionysius forty years before in establishing the parish system. That suggests that, at an early stage of Maxentius's regime, church buildings were in Christian hands. Arguably, on coming to power and seeing a new bishop elected, Maxentius had restored the buildings to the church; alternatively, and rather less probably, they had never been closed. In other words, the property that Maxentius did not restore until 311 was probably money and sacred vessels rather than buildings.

The failure to return the moveable property might have said more about the church than about Maxentius. Despite official toleration, the church was torn apart by internal disputes. Two bishops in succession, Marcellus from the end of 306 to the beginning of 308 and Eusebius for about six months in 308, had failed to establish order and regain control. After the removal of Eusebius, the church was again leaderless for about three years. To whom then should the property have been restored and how should it have been administered? Handing over a significant sum of cash and sacred vessels to a leader or leaders acknowledged by some but not by others could only have inflamed the dispute. Only in the summer of 311 was a new bishop, Miltiades, elected who did succeed in establishing himself firmly in office. Significantly, he was credited with introducing the practice of sending pieces of the consecrated bread (the *fermentum*) from the eucharist he celebrated to all the churches in the city as a sign of unity.[40] Soon after Miltiades's election, Maxentius restored the church's confiscated properties. Augustine recorded, in his disputes with the Donatists, how Miltiades had sent two deacons with letters from Maxentius and the praetorian prefect to the urban prefect, the head of the city's administration, to reclaim the church's property.[41]

---

[39] *LP* 1.164.

[40] *LP* 1.168–69.

[41] Quoting the anecdote as part of his defence of Miltiades against the charge of having been a *traditor*. Augustine *Breviculus Collationis* 3.18.34; *Contra Partem Donati Post Gesta* 13.17.

Maxentius might therefore have been sympathetic enough to the church not merely to offer toleration but to act as umpire in one of the most savage and disrupted periods in its history, removing bishops whose policies caused bitter division and holding the church's funds until stability could be restored.

One other tantalising suggestion has been made to add to this picture of Maxentius as the first imperial patron of the Roman church. He constructed a magnificent villa, temple, mausoleum and circus complex at the place called 'in catecumbas'[42] on the Via Appia, south of Rome.[43] This was in keeping with the imperial style of palace-building in the new capitals of the tetrarchs. The temple was dedicated to Romulus, in memory of his dead son. The circus could accommodate about 10,000 people. Visitors were expected to see in the circus the emperor's traditional role as sponsor of the games and source of largesse for the people, in the temple the appeal to the ancient genius of eternal Rome and in the mausoleum a confident statement about the future of the dynasty. Just across the Via Appia stood the Christian catacomb of St Sebastian. A basilica, an enclosed surface cemetery in a distinctive circus shape, was built there in the early fourth century. Significantly, the *Liber Pontificalis* does not attribute it to Constantine. The masonry of which it was built matches that of the circus and mausoleum opposite, suggesting that it was constructed by Maxentius at the same time, in about 310.[44] This would reveal Maxentius as a supporter and patron of the Christians who wanted to associate his new palace complex with their adjacent pilgrimage and burial site. It would make it the oldest of the Roman basilicas, the model for those built a few years later by Constantine. It would also mean that Constantine's policy of lavishing magnificent basilicas on the Roman church was in continuity with the policy of Maxentius, a fact that neither Constantine, nor the Roman church, wanted posterity to remember.

---

[42] Chronographer of 354, 'fecit et circum in catecumbas': MGH Chron. Min. 148.

[43] LTUR Sub. 4, 49–59.

[44] See Heres *Paries* pp. 341–44; for a full review of the evidence and bibliography, see Elzbieta Jastrzebowska, 'S. Sebastiano, La Più Antica Basilica Cristiana di Roma' in Federico Guidobaldi and Alessandra Guiglia Guidobaldi (eds), *Ecclesiae Urbis: Atti del Congresso Internazionale di Studi sulle Chiesi di Roma (IV–X secolo), Roma, 4–10 settembre 2000* (3 vols; Città del Vaticano: Pontificio Istituto di Archeologia Cristiana, 2002) vol. 2, pp. 1141–55.

CONSTANTINE AND THE END OF THE TETRARCHY

The map of the Roman world in 311 looked rather different from its appearance ten years earlier. There were now five rulers who divided the world between them — Constantine in the far West, ruling Gaul, Spain and Britain; Maxentius ruling Italy and North Africa; Maximinus Daia ruling Syria and Egypt; Licinius in control in Pannonia; and Galerius ruling the rest of eastern Europe and Asia Minor. Though the other four refused to acknowledge Maxentius, in most respects they carried on as though the health of the tetrarchic constitution was as robust as ever. In fact, these five emperors eyed each other with the wariness born of fear and craving. They had failed to restore the system at Carnuntum in 308. They also knew that Galerius was gravely ill and that, with his death, it would collapse.

Galerius had been pursuing the persecution of Christians in his territories with undiminished enthusiasm. The fact that there had been no persecution of Christians in the West for the last five years and that the most severe edicts had never been applied there was of no concern to him, though it was clear enough evidence of the breakdown of the tetrarchic system. Surprisingly, in April 311, probably mindful that his own death was near, he issued an edict of toleration. It was an enormously important document. It admitted the complete failure of the policy:

> Among the arrangements which we are always putting in place for the benefit of the state, we had tried to establish everything in conformity with the ancient laws and public discipline of the Romans. This was also our aim for the Christians, who had abandoned the way of life of their forefathers, so that they should return to right opinions. Self-will and foolishness had somehow taken possession of them so that instead of following the ancient usages, which perhaps their own forefathers had established, they followed their own judgment and made up their own laws and drew together various groups of people in different places. After the publication of our edict that they should undertake the observance of the ancient practices, many of them were subjected to danger and many were dispossessed. Since, however, very many persisted in their determination and we can see that they were neither paying reverence or offering worship to the gods nor were they worshipping their own God, we have decided, with our customary clemency in showing pardon to all, to extend to them our indulgence to permit them once more to be Christians and to establish their meeting places once more, provided they do not offend against good order. We intend to indicate to magistrates by another letter what they should observe. Thus it will be the duty of the Christians, in accordance with this indulgence of ours, to pray to their God for our welfare and that of the state and for their own, so that the state may continue to be safe everywhere and they might live in peace in their homes.[45]

[45] Lactantius *De Mort. Persec.* 34.

This text reveals the pagan piety which had inspired the persecution and which now compelled its cessation: while it would have been best for the Christians to observe the Roman practices, it was better that they should pray to their own God for the common welfare than that they should offer no worship at all. Galerius cannot bring himself to admit the intensity of the oppression inflicted on the Christians; he avoids any reference to executions, speaking instead of Christians being put in danger or dispossessed, thereby minimising the scale and the shame of his failure. But with the realism of a dying man, he knew that the empire would have to give formal recognition to the practice of Christianity. Though there is no indication in the text that he ordered the restitution of the church's confiscated properties, he had signed a magna carta of Christian liberties which made continuing persecution no longer normal but eccentric.

When Galerius died shortly afterwards — a hideous death according to Lactantius, who was pleased to report the details[46] — the two eastern emperors sprang to seize his territories. Licinius secured eastern Europe; Maximinus Daia took Asia Minor; their dominions were separated by the Bosphorus. Licinius observed Galerius's last edict and extended toleration to the Christians. Maximinus Daia showed greater resolve and continued with persecution in the East.[47] As the ruler of the whole of the eastern empire where the bulk of the Christian population lived, Maximinus Daia could still inflict massive damage on the Christian church, but now it was his policy, rather than that of those who condoned Christianity, which seemed out of step.

The situation on both sides of the world was fragile: war seemed imminent. Licinius was preparing to attack Maxentius but Constantine moved first. He invaded Italy before Licinius could act and showed strategic brilliance in his lightning advance south. Maxentius withdrew behind the walls of Rome but his hold on the city was not sure enough to withstand a siege. He was unpopular with all classes of society. The expense of his massive building projects had forced him to introduce the taxation, the fear of which had first brought him to

---

[46] *De Mort. Persec.* 33.

[47] According to Lactantius, he prevented the building of churches or the worship of God and people who refused to offer sacrifice were blinded or mutilated and all meat in the palace was slaughtered by pagan priests, *De Mort. Persec.* 36.3–37.2; Eusebius substantiates this and adds that he had the fictitious *Acts of Pilate* displayed in public and taught in schools to undermine Christianity and executed a number of Christians including bishop Peter of Alexandria, *HE* 9.2.1–7.16.

power.[48] There had been a catastrophic riot after a soldier was killed, leading to the butchery of 6,000 people by the army.[49] His attempted seduction of the Christian wife of the urban prefect (the head of the city's administration), who preferred suicide to compliance with his desires, must have alienated members of the senatorial elite and the Christian church.[50] At the games to celebrate his accession on 27 October 312, Maxentius faced the jeering of the crowd who shouted that Constantine could not be beaten.[51] The following day, he left the city and offered battle to Constantine's army, who had painted a Christian symbol on their shields.[52] Defeated and driven back, Maxentius was drowned in the Tiber with the collapse of the Milvian Bridge. The following day, 29 October 312, Constantine entered Rome, styling himself the liberator of the city.

Constantine's occupation of Rome was a superb symbolic coup but it was not enough to secure his position. At once, he set about forging an alliance with Licinius. Between them they ruled Europe and it was in the interests of both to isolate Maximinus Daia in the East. In February 313, he and Licinius met in Milan, sealed their treaty with the marriage of Licinius to Constantia, Constantine's half-sister, and issued an edict of toleration of Christians,[53] the chief practical effect of which was the restoration of Christian property in Licinius's territories. The diplomatic significance of the edict was much greater as it established that the main distinction between the western and eastern halves of the empire lay in their treatment of Christianity. Suddenly vulnerable, Daia offered belated toleration to the Christians in his territories[54] and then launched an assault on Licinius. He was rapidly defeated in the summer of 313 and killed himself. Licinius's power had increased massively as a result of this victory as he became ruler of the whole Roman world from the Balkans to the Middle East and Egypt. Two years after the death of Galerius, the rule of the Roman empire had contracted from five emperors to two.

With the whole Roman world now divided between Constantine and Licinius, it is no surprise that there was another short, sharp

---

[48] Chronographer of 354: MGH Chron. Min. 148.

[49] Chronographer of 354, MGH Chron. Min. 148; Zosimus *Historia Nova* 2.13.

[50] Eusebius *HE* 8.14.16–17.

[51] Lactantius *De Mort. Persec.* 44.7.

[52] *De Mort. Persec.* 44.5: the text is not clear about what exactly the symbol was.

[53] Commonly called the Edict of Milan: Lactantius *De Mort. Persec.* 48; Eusebius *HE* 10.5.2–14.

[54] Eusebius *HE* 9.9a.1–9.

war in 316. Constantine proved unable to drive home his early victories but secured a large slice of Licinius's European territories in the peace agreed in 317. Constantine now had the whole long, dangerous northern frontier to defend — the coastline of Britain, the Rhine and the Danube — and until these borders were secure he could not risk a full-scale war with Licinius. His main capitals were Trier, to command the Rhine, and Serdica (Sofia), to command the Danube. His son, Crispus, whom he appointed Caesar, was entrusted with the defence and administration of the western provinces from Trier while he concentrated on the Balkans. Successful campaigning ensured that by 324 he could contemplate an assault on the East. Licinius's toleration of Christians had worn thin and he had begun excluding them from public service, forbidding synods of bishops, closing churches and perhaps even condoning executions.[55] It gave Constantine a pretext to present himself again as a liberator, as he had done in delivering Italy from Maxentius. It is not unlikely that it also persuaded him of the righteousness and therefore ultimate victory of his cause. He invaded Licinius's European toe-hold in the summer of 324, won a quick victory over Licinius's army and drove him back into the city of Byzantium. Crispus won a naval victory off Callipolis (Gallipoli) making the defence of Byzantium almost impossible and Constantine crushed Licinius's army at Chrysopolis (Scutari). Licinius fell back to Nicomedia and then, having won assurances about his safety from Constantine through the intercession of his wife, Constantia, he abdicated and surrendered. He was executed the following year.

The Tetrarchy's most brilliant child had destroyed it. Constantine had watched great men take their exits and had himself helped a number of them off the stage. Inexorably, his armies secured for him ever-greater power: the western provinces in 306; Italy and North Africa in 312; almost the whole of Europe by 317; the whole Roman world in 324. He had watched the Tetrarchy fail in its attempt to do what no previous emperor had succeeded in achieving: the eradication of Christianity. He not only disassociated himself from that policy, he reversed it. The scale of this revolution can be judged by contrasting two scenes in Nicomedia: the promulgation, in the name of the four emperors, of the decree against the Christians at Diocletian's court in the February of 303 and the abdication of

---

[55] Eusebius *HE* 10.8.1 — 9.3; *Vita Constantini* 1.49 — 54; 2.1–2.

Licinius in the September of 324 when the sovereignty of the whole empire passed into the hands of a single Christian emperor.

CONSTANTINE AND THE CHRISTIANS

There is a sense in which the Tetrachy's success spelled its demise. Its greatest achievement was Galerius's triumph over the Persians in 298, which overturned the Sassanid triumphs of the previous sixty years and guaranteed peace for the sixty to come. Security in Mesopotamia allowed the tetrarchs to make their great assault on Christianity and then to turn on each other in a series of coups and civil wars. But Galerius, the hammer of the Persians, had failed to capture Rome and suppress the regime of Maxentius. As Constantine advanced south towards Rome in his lightning campaign in the October of 312, he must have dwelled on Galerius's failure as he pondered his own strategy. His relief must therefore have been jubilant when Maxentius offered battle north of the city on 28 October rather than oblige Constantine to undertake a lengthy and demanding siege.

On the night before the battle, Constantine dreamed that he had been directed to put the heavenly symbol of God on his soldiers' shields and it was thus bearing some form of Christian sign that his army drove back Maxentius in defeat.[56] This incident is connected with a vision that he reported on oath to bishop Eusebius of Caesarea, in which he saw a cross in the sky with the message 'Conquer with this' (*toutoi nika*), and subsequently in a dream was instructed to have the sign copied and used as his new standard or Labarum.[57] When did the vision take place? It has been plausibly suggested that it occurred after his defeat of Maximian, Diocletian's old colleague who had emerged from retirement against him in 310. There is a report of Constantine seeing a vision of the sun in a panegyric delivered in that year in the aftermath of which Constantine displayed considerable devotion to the sun-god. On this account,[58] Constantine was convinced of his divine destiny as the servant of the one God as a result of a vision in 310 (perhaps a complex solar halo phenomenon) and then reinterpreted the meaning of the vision on the eve of the

---

[56] Lactantius *De Mort. Persec.* 44.3–6.

[57] *Vit Constant* 1.28–32.

[58] See Peter Weiss, 'The Vision of Constantine' *The Journal of Archaeology* 16 (2003) pp. 237–59.

battle with Maxentius that it was the Christian God who summoned him to victory.

As Constantine entered Rome on 29 October 312, probably sharing the curiosity of most of his troops seeing for the first time the most famous city in the world, his soldiers bore a Christian symbol on their shields. Yet there seems to have been a studied ambiguity about Constantine, a malleability about the image he chose to present of himself and his regime. Whether this revealed religious confusion or political pragmatism has long been debated, contributing to a wide range of interpretations of his character and his policies.[59] Though there now seems a consensus in seeing Constantine as a genuine believer in Christianity, whether as a result of a conversion in 312[60] or, less plausibly, from childhood as a result of an upbringing in a Christian family,[61] there is still room for disagreement about his implementation of religious policy. Did he believe he had been commissioned by God to convert the Roman world to Christianity[62] or did he aim at an inclusive, broadly tolerant version of Christianity which could embrace internal disagreement while also sitting comfortably alongside the pagan religious practices of the majority of citizens of the empire?[63]

There are two sides to the question. On the one hand, what did Constantine do for the Christian church? On the other hand, what was his policy towards pagan religion? The evidence for the latter is open to dispute.[64] For instance, his most enduring monument in Rome is his triumphal arch,[65] which was complete by the summer of 315, when he returned to Rome to celebrate his *decennalia*, ten years in power. Though much of its masonry and sculpture was reconstituted from

[59] See Barnes *Constantine and Eusebius* pp. 272–75; Noel Lenski 'Introduction' in Noel Lenski (ed) *The Cambridge Companion to the Age of Constantine* (Cambridge: CUP, 2006) pp. 1–10.

[60] Barnes *Constantine and Eusebius* p. 43.

[61] T. G. Elliott, *The Christianity of Constantine the Great* (Scranton PA: University of Scranton Press, 1996).

[62] Barnes *Constantine and Eusebius* pp. 43; 275.

[63] H. A. Drake, *Constantine and the Bishops: The Politics of Intolerance* (Baltimore: Johns Hopkins University Press, 2000); 'The Impact of Constantine on Christianity' in Lenski (ed) *Age of Constantine* pp. 111–36.

[64] For the evidence and discussion of other interpretations, see Barnes *Constantine and Eusebius* pp. 52–53; Curran *Pagan Capital* pp. 169–81; A. D. Lee, 'Traditional Religions' in Lenski (ed) *Age of Constantine* pp. 159–79.

[65] See Curran *Pagan Capital* pp. 86–90; R. Ross Holloway *Constantine and Rome* (New Haven: Yale University Press, 2004) pp. 19–53.

earlier buildings, it made up a coherent propaganda statement of the new regime: Constantine was depicted as triumphant in war, the liberator of the city, and liberal in peace, the embodiment of the civil virtues; his father, Constantius, was repeatedly displayed, stressing his hereditary legitimacy, while his piety towards the gods was shown in scenes of him offering sacrifice, with particular emphasis on the gods of the sun and the moon. It bears no Christian symbol; indeed, it appears to make a marked appeal to a solar devotion. But nevertheless it is clear that Constantine distanced himself from pagan worship and excluded animal sacrifice from the imperial cult, perhaps even risking unpopularity in Rome at his twentieth anniversary celebrations in 326 for refusing to sacrifice on the Capitol.[66] Then again, he does not appear to have stopped anyone else taking part in cultic sacrifices or to have closed pagan temples.[67] He banned private divination, which he regarded as flirting with dangerous magic, but the ancient tradition of public divination by the haruspices, who read the signs of the future in unusual events, thunder and, above all, the entrails of animals, seems not to have been restricted.

If his attitude to pagan religion could be regarded as distant, his attitude towards Christianity was undeniably enthusiastic. Over the course of his reign, the legal position of Christian clergy was transformed and in other ways the sensitivities of the Christian faith were given some legal recognition.[68] Exemption from taxation and the public duties that fell to members of the class from which magistrates and town councillors were drawn was an important privilege. Bishops were allowed to settle legal disputes between Christians. Slaves could be manumitted in a Christian ceremony. Sunday was marked in the army by the recitation of a special monotheistic prayer and it functioned as a weekly public holiday, a day on which the courts transacted no official business. Crucifixion was abolished, as was the penalty of facial disfigurement (the face being regarded as the expression of the divine image). Property rights for celibates were made easier; divorce was made more difficult.

Some of this is difficult to evaluate. For example, the dedication of the army to God on a Sunday was not explicitly Christian; though Constantine's Christian device was emblazoned on their shields and

[66] Zosimus *Historia Nova* 2.29.1–5.

[67] This key point is disputed. For a contrary reading of the evidence, see Barnes *Constantine and Eusebius* pp. 210–11; 246; 254–55; 269.

[68] See Barnes *Constantine and Eusebius* pp. 50–52.

was borne before them on parade, the prayer they recited addressed the one God who had given them victories but made no mention of Christ.[69] It resembled a prayer with which Licinius's troops fortified themselves as they were about to engage the army of Maximinus Daia.[70] It seems that the alliance of Constantine and Licinius in 313 included some commitment to the active promotion of monotheism, at least in the army. This was not inconsistent with Christianity but it fell far short of its enforcement. It seems fair to say that, in the eyes of Christians, Constantine was a generous patron; from the pagan point of view, he was an advocate of monotheism, known to be a supporter of Christianity, but tolerant of the ancient ways.

CONSTANTINE AND THE CITY OF ROME

Diocletian only visited Rome once; Galerius never got there at all. But in 312 Constantine came to a city that had rediscovered what it was like to be an imperial capital. For six years, the possession of Rome had sanctioned Maxentius's legitimacy and in return he lavished upon it the largesse of an imperial court. Now Rome bolstered not only Constantine's claims to legitimacy but his claim to seniority within the tetrarchic scheme. Though he only stayed for just over two months before he headed north to Milan to negotiate his alliance with Licinius and though he never made the city his effective political capital, he was fully aware of Rome's emblematic significance as the ritual heart of the empire. Thus, in the late autumn and early winter of 312, he set about the task of effacing the memory of Maxentius and claiming his achievements for himself.[71] Presenting himself as the emperor who would restore their privileges, he treated the senate with elaborate courtesy and received in return the title *Maximus*, marking him out as the greatest of the surviving three emperors.[72] He stamped his own image on the ceremonial sacred centre of the city. He transformed Maxentius's colossal Basilica Nova on the north-west side of the Forum into a monument to himself, the Basilica Constantina, housing a massive statue of him as powerful, impassive, with huge, all-seeing eyes. Over the course of time, other large statues of Constantine were erected in the city, at least one of which

---

[69] Eusebius *Vit Constant* 4.20.

[70] Lactantius *De Mort. Persec.* 46.6.

[71] See Curran *Pagan City and Christian Capital* pp. 76–90.

[72] Lactantius *De Mort. Persec.* 44.11 — Maximinus Daia had already styled himself Maximus and was infuriated by Constantine's acquisition of the title.

presented him holding a cross or some other distinctively Christian symbol.[73] Fulfilling the role of munificent patron of the people, he undertook important reconstruction work on the Circus Maximus and the building of another set of public baths. When he returned to Rome in the summer of 315 to celebrate the tenth anniversary of his accession, the triumphal arch with its pagan and dynastic imperial decoration was finished and must have played some major part in the festivities. By the time he returned a decade later for his last visit, to commemorate the twentieth anniversary of his accession in the summer of 326, there was a great deal more to see: by then, the whole position of the Christian church in the city had been visibly transformed by his building efforts.

The Roman church had emerged from the persecution of 303–306 shaken and divided. The bishop Marcellinus had been forced to step down. His successors Marcellus and Eusebius had both been exiled by the emperor Maxentius. It was only in the summer of 311 that a bishop was elected who could command the allegiance of his people and re-establish order: Miltiades. Maxentius restored the confiscated properties of the church to Miltiades and, perhaps, even showed his support for Christianity by building a basilica for them at the catacomb of St Sebastian just across the Appian Way from his palace complex. It is no surprise that Constantine wanted to make a major, indeed ostentatious, gesture for Miltiades and the Roman church. It is plausible, from the date commemorated as the dedication of the building, that he handed over land to build a huge basilica for the bishop less than three weeks after entering Rome on 9 November 312: the Lateran basilica.[74]

This was very much a building for the bishop. It had no previous Christian associations, so it was not intended to mark the shrine of a martyr or serve any other pilgrimage purpose. It was a basilica: in other words, it resembled the audience halls and court rooms of the

[73] Eusebius's account of the entry into Rome likens Constantine to Moses and says that his statue 'in the most public place in Rome' held the Saviour's sign in the right hand and bore the inscription: 'By this saving sign, the true proof of courage, I saved and delivered your city from the yoke of the tyrant and moreover I freed the senate and people of Rome and restored them to their ancient fame and splendour' *HE* 9.9.9–11.

[74] For the basilicas built and supported by Constantine, see Curran *Pagan City and Christian Capital* pp. 93–105; Holloway *Constantine and Rome* pp. 57–112; Hugo Brandenburg *Ancient Churches of Rome from the Fourth to the Seventh Century: The Dawn of Christian Architecture in the West* (Andreas Kopp (trans); Bibliothèque de l'Antiquité Tardive, 8; Turnhout, Belgium: Brepols, 2005) pp. 16–108.

city where the magistrates conducted official business or the emperor himself held court. This was not only a church, where services could be held, but was the bishop's public assembly hall, where he could exercise his functions as leader of the church and great man in the city. Given that memories of the recent disruption of the episcopal leadership in Rome were still fresh, this was a forceful statement that the persecution was not only finished but its effects were being reversed. The basilica was massive — 333 feet long and 180 feet wide, with five aisles. Its location at first sight seems strange: on the south-eastern edge of the city near the walls, in a district where only the very rich could afford their mansions, far away from the teeming masses of the Christian poor. It was evidently not intended as the main place of worship of ordinary folk. The advantage of the site, however, apart from placing the bishop in one of the most affluent parts of town and conveniently near the Sessorian Palace,[75] where Constantine's devout mother Helena lived, was that the land was in Constantine's personal hands. A property that had long been part of the imperial treasury, the *Domus Lateranorum*, was near to a palace which had probably belonged to his second wife, Fausta, the *Domus Faustae*, and to the barracks of Maxentius's horse guards, the *equites singulares*, who had gone down fighting with him at the Milvian Bridge. In other words, the building of the basilica was part of Constantine's policy of obliterating the memory of his predecessor, Maxentius, while establishing the bishop of Rome firmly as the beneficiary of his own largesse.

Adjacent to the basilica, Constantine built the baptistery where the bishop performed the baptisms at Easter. This was effectively the cathedral, the main church where the bishop fulfilled his episcopal office. It did not stand as a vast, unadorned shell. A list of the gifts of Constantine, and probably his immediate family, was incorporated into the *Liber Pontificalis*,[76] and it records astonishing bequests of silver and gold together with estates for the upkeep of the building and the bishop. Some kind of silver screen had a five-foot high double image of Christ: facing the congregation, Christ was seated as a teacher, facing the clergy in the apse he was seated on a throne; the screen also bore images of the twelve apostles and four angels. From it, hung a gold lamp weighing fifty pounds which held fifty lights. The lighting

---

[75] Today the church of Sta Croce in Gerusalemme.

[76] See Raymond Davis (ed), *The Book of Pontiffs (Liber Pontificalis): The Ancient Biographies of the First Ninety Roman Bishops to ad 715* (Translated Texts for Historians, 6; Liverpool: Liverpool University Press, 2nd ed, 2000) pp. xxix–xxxv.

of the basilica was particularly lavish: four gold crowns each with twenty lights; a gold chandelier in front of the altar with eighty lights; a silver chandelier with twenty lights; forty-five silver chandeliers in the body of the basilica, each weighing twenty pounds; twenty-five silver chandeliers to the left of the basilica, each weighing twenty pounds; fifty silver candlesticks in the body of the basilica, each weighing twenty pounds. The basilica was fully furnished with altars and sacred vessels of silver and gold. The document also records the long list of estates from all over Italy and North Africa and even Crete for the support of the bishop and the basilica.

Some years later, another enormous basilica was built at the other side of the city, St Peter's. This was primarily intended to be a huge covered cemetery at the site believed to be Peter's grave. Christians wanted to visit and to be buried near the tomb of the apostle and this basilica was built to provide them with a place where they could assemble as pilgrims as well as a graveyard near his tomb. It was not a church in the sense of being a building designed for liturgical worship. When the eucharist was celebrated, a moveable altar was put in place. The crux of the basilica was the place venerated as the apostle's grave, probably since the beginning of the third century,[77] which was the subject of celebrated excavations in the twentieth century. Who built it? The *Liber Pontificalis* attributed it to Constantine and the lavish bequest of estates, many of which were in the east of the empire, does suggest that the project dated from the later part of Constantine's reign but before the empire was divided between his sons. The cemetery on which it was constructed was certainly still in use until about 320 and some of the bricks used to build the basilica appear to bear the name of Constantine's son, Constans. A plausible conclusion therefore would be that Constantine endowed the basilica in the late part of his reign but that the building was completed after his death.[78]

[77] Gaius reports the monuments (*tropaia*) of Peter on the Vatican and Paul on the road to Ostia, Eusebius *HE* 2.25.2

[78] See J. M. C. Toynbee and J. B. Ward-Perkins, *The Shrine of St Peter and the Vatican Excavations* (London: Longmans and Green, 1956). For a recent account of the tomb and excavations, see Holloway *Constantine and Rome* pp 120–55; he reaches the unconventional conclusion that the archaeologists' reconstruction of the monument enclosed inside Constantine's memoria is wishful thinking and what they did find is not to be identified with the tropaeum described by Gaius; Peter, in his judgment, was buried 'in catacumbas' on the Appian way until Cornelius moved the relics to the Vatican in 231; the tropaeum marked the scene of his martyrdom, not the original grave. Brandenburg *Ancient Churches of Rome* pp 66–68 holds by contrast that Peter and

It was an extremely difficult site on which to build, sloping sharply both to north and west as it climbed the Vatican hill. The hill was covered with an ancient cemetery, much of which had to be filled in in order to construct the platform on which the basilica would stand. It was, again, a vast building: about 360 feet long and 212 feet wide, and thus significantly larger than the Lateran basilica, and in front of it was a large enclosed square making the whole building very imposing indeed. Inside, the whole basilica was richly endowed with ornaments and lights. Its focal point was the marble and porphyry monument to St Peter, directly above and concealing the older monument. (The spiral columns, which were a distinctive feature of this monument, were copied by Bernini for the columns of the baldachino over the high altar of the renaissance basilica which replaced the fourth-century edifice in the sixteenth century; the originals were reused in the piers supporting the dome.)

It is possible, though far from certain, that Constantine also built a small basilica at the shrine of St Paul on the road to Ostia. He certainly transformed the tomb of the martyred deacon Laurence on the Via Tiburtina, creating a pilgrimage chapel with access up and down a flight of steps, and he built a very large cemetery basilica adjacent to it with a distinctive rounded end. This was homage to one of the Roman church's best loved saints and must have responded to a popular cult of Laurence in the city. The floor of the basilica was filled with graves, one on top of another, of people who wanted to be buried near the martyr. Further out of Rome, on the Via Labicana, at a place called 'ad duas lauros', the site of the graveyard of Maxentius's *equites singulares*, he built a mausoleum for his mother and a nearby basilica dedicated to the saints Marcellinus and Petrus, again with the distinctive rounded end, another burial church, packed with graves.

Another cemetery basilica and mausoleum complex was constructed at the catacomb where St Agnes, a celebrated young virgin martyr, was buried on the Via Nomentana. Though attributed to Constantine by the *Liber Pontificalis*, it is more likely that it was built by his daughter,

Paul were never buried 'in catacumbas' as there is no trace of a grave; it was instead a pilgrimage site hallowed by the claim that Peter and Paul had lived there; the Vatican was always regarded as Peter's burial place and the tropaeum marked the grave, see *ibid* pp 92–94; the traditional attribution of the building to Constantine has been challenged by Glen W. Bowersock 'Peter and Constantine' in *St Peter's in the Vatican*, ed William Tronzo, Cambridge: CUP (2005), pp 5–15

Constantina.[79] The remains of two other apsidal shaped basilicas of an early fourth century date have been found, one on the Via Praenestina and the other on the Via Ardeatina. Though they were not recorded as imperial projects, they seem to have been built on imperial property. Adding to this list the Basilica Apostolorum at the catacomb of St Sebastian, another apsidal cemetery basilica, brings the total number of these cemetery basilicas to six. All of them are built on imperial land near catacombs on the arterial roads coming out of the city; at least three of them were imperial projects. They all have the same distinctive shape, with a rounded end which some have taken to be reminiscent of a circus but perhaps might more safely be regarded as providing an ambulatory at the end of the basilica for the visitors to process around. The most intriguing of the early fourth-century basilicas is that on the Appian Way at the catacomb of St Sebastian. This marked the site of the holiest cult of them all — that of Peter and Paul. If, as has been suggested, it was the work of Maxentius and was closely associated with his own imperial complex (including a mausoleum) directly across the road, then that might explain why Constantine and his family built this series of basilicas. Constantine was quietly taking over and going beyond his predecessor's policy on this, as on so much else in Rome.

These basilicas were not constructed for the ordinary weekly worship of the Christian populace. The Lateran was a remote but spectacular edifice for major episcopal ceremonies. The others were pilgrimage and burial places, satisfying the need of the people to venerate the tombs of the martyrs and their desire to be buried near them. They acknowledged in brick and stone a new sense of Rome's sacredness, not in the ancient monumental centre but on the outskirts, where the martyrs' graves and the catacombs were to be found. Thus Constantine's patronage favoured not local parish communities but rather the city and diocese of Rome. Of the churches in the city where the ordinary Christians worshipped, nothing is known. Though the foundations beneath Rome's oldest churches have been thoroughly excavated, there is no evidence of churches used by the Christians before the mid-fourth century.[80] One, SS Giovanni e Paolo, is built

---

[79] The mausoleum survives as Sta Costanza, one of the most elegant churches in Rome.

[80] See Brandenburg *Ancient Churches of Rome* pp. 110–13.

on a house which contained a shrine to the martyrs, but it was plainly not a church.[81]

When Constantine occupied Rome in 312, he also became ruler of North Africa. He inherited a bitter schism concerning the succession to the see of Carthage.[82] The bishop acknowledged around the world, Caecilian, did not command the acceptance of the majority of the people at home. This was because the bishop who consecrated him, Felix of Aptunga, was accused of having been a *traditor* in the Great Persecution. A rival bishop, Majorinus, had been consecrated; he was succeeded by Donatus (with the result that his supporters were dubbed Donatists by their opponents). Constantine became directly involved in the dispute because he ordered the restoration of church property in North Africa in the late autumn of 312.[83] To whom should the property be restored? Constantine found that he had become the arbiter of a complex and acrimonious Christian dispute which now became worse. Constantine must have been aware of the schism as he was very clear whom he recognised: he sent money and promised support to Caecilian[84] and ordered that his clergy were exempted from public duties. This did not stave off the inevitable appeals to the governor in North Africa against Caecilian which were forwarded to Constantine.

Within months of taking power in Italy and North Africa, Constantine thus found himself embroiled in a complex ecclesiastical controversy because of his policy of restoring church property and exempting the clergy from public duties. It is not unlikely that Maxentius had anticipated this problem and avoided getting involved in a dispute in Rome by not handing back the church's property until a bishop was securely in place in 311 and refused to restore the property in Africa in order to keep out of the dispute there. Constantine passed the case over to the people best qualified to settle it — the bishops. A council was assembled in October 313 under the presidency of the bishop of Rome: fifteen Italian bishops along with the bishops of Cologne, Autun and Arles gathered with Miltiades in a house provided by Fausta and weighed the arguments on each side. They decided that there was no evidence against Caecilian and confirmed that he was the legitimate bishop of Carthage but

---

[81] *Ibid.*, pp. 155–62.
[82] See Barnes *Constantine and Eusebius* pp. 54–61.
[83] Eusebius *HE* 10.5.15–17.
[84] *HE* 10.6.1–5.

they condemned Donatus for denying the validity of the sacraments performed by Caecilian's Catholic church and therefore baptising any members of that church who joined them. This picked up the argument between Stephen and Cyprian of sixty years before and Donatus and his friends were outraged to find their practice, hallowed by the authority of St Cyprian, condemned. They appealed directly to Constantine, who submitted the matter afresh to a council of bishops he summoned from all over the West to meet at Arles in August 314. Constantine himself attended the council which, inevitably, endorsed the decision of the Roman council of the previous October. The following year, the Donatists produced sworn evidence from the magistrate who enforced the imperial edict in 303 that Felix of Aptunga, the bishop who consecrated Caecilian, had complied and had surrendered the holy scriptures. This was now turning into a legal case for the secular authorities to hear which climbed up the courts until Constantine heard it himself in Milan in October 315, adjudicating once more in favour of Caecilian. By now, rioting had broken out in North Africa and the authorities took a firm line against the Donatists; Donatists, including two bishops, were killed in March 317. Constantine now found himself persecuting Christians, albeit schismatics, and he abandoned the policy, offering them toleration, in 321. Even after they seized the basilica he built for the Catholics in Cirta, Constantine accepted defeat. Donatism would remain the majority church in North Africa for over a century.

This division in the North African church was to be one of the most bitter legacies of the Great Persecution and, in a sense, of Constantine's patronage of the church. The Donatists' opinion of themselves as the true remnant, excluded from government recognition and even persecuted for a time, owed everything to Constantine's role in the affairs of African Christianity. The differences between this dispute and that between Cyprian and Stephen is thus instructive. Constantine set out to reverse the Great Persecution, especially with his programme of building basilicas, his profound respect for the cults of the martyrs and his repeated emphasis on the authority and status of bishops. He clearly fulfilled these aims in Rome where his impact was, probably, overwhelmingly benign but in North Africa he only succeeded in prolonging the effect of the Great Persecution by his attempts to favour the church. That was because the African church was divided in 312 whereas the Roman church had recovered its unity and poise by the time Miltiades was elected in 311. In this, the church might have owed more than it cared to remember to the emperor Maxentius for expelling the two troublesome bishops, Marcellus and Eusebius, and for not restoring the church's properties until after Miltiades was securely in office. Whatever happened in the first decade of the fourth century, and the evidence is undeniably elusive and fragmentary, the church of Rome had again showed extraordinary vigour and vitality.

Further instructive contrasts can be drawn between the experience of the Roman church in the aftermath of persecution and the situation which Constantine met in the East after 324. Alexandria and all Egypt was divided by a schism which resembled that between Catholics and Donatists in Latin North Africa. Melitius of Lycopolis led a church which refused to accept the generous policy of reconciliation for the lapsed offered by Peter of Alexandria. Alexandria was also caught up in a theological dispute which was to transform Christianity, with the presbyter Arius challenging the teaching of his bishop, Alexander (Peter's successor), concerning the eternal generation of the Logos. Arius was not alone. Powerful bishops such as the historian Eusebius of Caesarea and the aristocratic Eusebius of Nicomedia were also hostile to Alexander's teaching. Constantine called a council at Nicaea, the greatest gathering of bishops yet seen, which successfully isolated and condemned Arius and produced a compromise concerning the Melitians, acknowledging their bishops but making them subordinate to Alexander. Constantine had clearly learned lessons from his handling of the Donatists. But over the next ten years he watched the situation unravel. Eusebius of Nicomedia was deposed shortly after Nicaea for continued support of Arius; he was restored in about 328. Eustathius of Antioch, on the opposite side, was deposed and exiled by Constantine to Thrace for the rest of his life. The church in Antioch then plunged into a schism that would continue for over fifty years. In 335, the great Athanasius, successor of Alexander, was deposed for using violence and intimidation against his opponents and Constantine exiled him to Trier the following year — the first of five exiles during his long episcopate of forty-five years. In 336, Marcellus of Ancyra was deposed on doctrinal grounds in his opposition to Arius's ideas. Constantine found himself caught up in a succession of bitter, inter-connected disputes across the East. In Rome, meanwhile, the church forgot its recent past and settled to a long period of consolidation and growth.

CONSTANTINOPLE

Roman history begins in Rome and ends in Constantinople. For eleven hundred years after Constantine and nearly a thousand years after the western empire disintegrated, the Roman empire survived in the East with its capital at Constantinople. It was not extinguished until 1453 when the city was finally captured by the Turks. Constantine founded the new city on the site of Byzantium in 330, six years after he defeated Licinius and became master of the whole Roman world. In doing so, it might seem that he left a remarkable legacy. At the time, perhaps, the new foundation did not seem so important. The East had dominated the empire for generations and emperors had established various capitals for themselves there; Constantinople was simply the direct successor of Nicomedia as the eastern centre of government. Constantine was establishing a new tetrarchic capital, not dissimilar to Serdica, where he spent so much of the seven years between 317 and 324: a small city dominated by the imperial presence and distinguished largely by the ritual buildings of the court.

In one vital way, Constantinople was radically novel. From its inception, it was intended to be a Christian city. Eusebius claimed it was wholly Christian and that there were no pagan images or temples or altars there.[85] Here, as so often in his insufferably sycophantic biography of Constantine, Eusebius was economical with the truth. The pagan historian Zosimus reported that there were temples in Constantinople, even some built by Constantine himself.[86] But Zosimus also acknowledged that Constantine intended the city to be Christian.[87] It lacked the ancient Christian associations and the shrines of martyrs of other cities. Constantine did not endow it with magnificent basilicas to rival those he built in Rome. It had all the usual statuary and decoration, much of it brought from elsewhere in the empire, which inevitably had pagan religious associations. But the crucial thing was that the new city was intended to be different. Everywhere else in the empire, Christians inhabited physical space and followed a calendar determined by pagan religion. However intransigent might have been their views of pagan worship, they had

---

[85] *Vit. Constant* 3.48.

[86] *Historia Nova* 2.31–32.

[87] *Ibid.*, 2.29–30: he attributes the decision to found the city to Constantine's conversion, which he claims followed the execution of his son, Crispus, and the apparent suicide of his wife, Fausta, the full circumstances of which can never be retrieved from the scanty surviving evidence.

to accommodate themselves to the fact that they lived in a pagan world. In Constantinople, if anything, it was the other way around. Paganism was tolerated in a city where Christianity was the public expression of civic life.

For the most part, it was there he resided for the last seven years of his reign and it was in Constantinople, not Rome, that he celebrated his *tricennalia* in 336. It was from there that he set forth on his late campaigns, pacifying again the Danube frontier and then, in 337, embarking on a final war against the Persians. It was perhaps fitting that the last emperor of the Tetrarchy should have died as he advanced steadily to renew the battle with the rival empire which had brought it into existence. He knew he was dying by the time he reached Nicomedia and there he was baptised by Eusebius of Nicomedia, now bishop of Constantinople. He died on Pentecost Sunday, 22 May 337. He had come to see himself as Christ's apostle and so it was equally fitting that he should have died on the day the Twelve were commissioned by the Holy Spirit to go out and proclaim Christ to the whole world. It was fitting too that, when they brought the body back to Constantinople, it was interred in the mausoleum he had constructed adjacent to his church of the Holy Apostles.[88]

The second century had seen Christians struggling to define what Christianity was. The third century was the age when they learned how to live in the pagan city. The fourth century would be the age when Christians learned how to make the city Christian. A tightly-knit community can have long memories. Old people who watched the victory parade of Constantine's troops in October 312 could well remember the events of the 250s and had heard stories from their grandparents stretching back into the previous century. Their own grandchildren would live to see the demise of much of the fabric of pagan religion and the triumph of Christianity as the faith of the majority. The character of Christianity and its position in the world was thus transformed in the space of a few lifetimes and nowhere illustrated that transformation more clearly than the the city of Rome.

---

[88] For the last illness, baptism, death and funeral, see Eusebius *Vit Constant* 4.61–71; for the burial among the Apostles, see *ibid.*, 4.58–60, 71.

BIBLIOGRAPHY

Aland, B., 'Sünde und Erlösung bei Marcion und die Konsequenz für die sog. Beiden Götter Marcions', in *Marcion und Seine Kirchengeschichtliche Wirkung: Marcion and his Impact on Church History*, ed. G. May and K. Greschat, Texte und Untersuchungen zur Geschichte der altchristlichen Literatur, 150, Berlin: W. de Gruyter (2002), 147–57.

Amore, A., *I Martiri di Roma*, Rome: Antonianum, 1975.

Barclay, J. M. G., *Jews in the Mediterranean Diaspora from Alexander to Trajan (323 bce to 117 ad)*, Edinburgh: T&T Clark, 1996.

Barnard, L. W., *Justin Martyr: His Life and Thought*, Cambridge: Cambridge University Press, 1967.

Barnes, T. D., 'Legislation against the Christians', *JRS* 58 (1968), 32–50.

Barnes, T. D., *Constantine and Eusebius*, Cambridge, Mass: Harvard University Press, 1981.

Barnes, T. D., *Early Christianity and the Roman Empire*, London: Variorum, 1984.

Barrett, C. K., *A Critical and Exegetical Commentary on the Acts of the Apostles*, International Critical Commentary on the Holy Scriptures of the Old and New Testaments, 2 vols., Edinburgh: T&T Clark, 1994–8.

Barton, J., 'Marcion Revisited' in *The Canon Debate*, ed. L. M. Macdonald and J. A. Sanders, Peabody, Mass: Hendrickson (2002), 341–54.

Baruffa, A., *The Catacombs of St Callixtus: History, Archaeology, Faith*, tr. W. Purdy, Vatican City: Libreria Editrice Vaticana, 3rd edn., 2006.

Beard, M., North, J. and Price, S., *Religions of Rome*, 2 vols., Cambridge: Cambridge University Press, 1998.

Becker, E.-M., 'Marcion und die Korintherbriefe nach Tertullian, Adversus Marcionem V' in *Marcion und Seine Kirchengeschichtliche Wirkung: Marcion and his Impact on Church History*, ed. G. May and K. Greschat, Texte und Untersuchungen zur Geschichte der altchristlichen Literatur, 150, Berlin: W. de Gruyter (2002), 95–109.

Becker, A. H., and Reed, A. Y. (eds), *The Ways that Never Parted: Jews and Christians in Late Antiquity and the Early Middle Ages*, Tübingen: Mohr Siebeck, 2003.

Benvenuti Papi, A., *Il Diacono Lorenzo tra Storia e Leggenda*, Florence: Edizioni della Meridiana, 1998.

Berg, B., 'Alcestis and Hercules in the Catacomb of Via Latina', *Vigiliae Christianae* 48 (1994), 219–34.

Bévenot, M. *Cyprian:* De Lapsis *and* De Ecclesiae Catholicae Unitate, Oxford Early Christian Texts, Oxford: Oxford University Press, 1971.

Bilde, P., *Flavius Josephus between Jerusalem and Rome: his Life, his Works, and their Importance*, Sheffield: Sheffield Academic Press, 1988.

Blois, L. de, *The Policy of the Emperor Gallienus*, Leiden: Brill, 1976.

Bockmuehl, M., 'Peter's Death in Rome? Back to Front and Upside Down', *Scottish Journal of Theology* 60 (2007), 1–23.

Bodel, J., 'Dealing with the Dead: Undertakers, Executioners and Potter's Fields in Ancient Rome', in *Death and Disease in the Ancient City*, ed. V. M. Hope and E. Marshall, London: Routledge (2000), 128–51.

Bowersock, G. W. 'Peter and Constantine', in *St Peter's in the Vatican*, ed. W. Tronzo, Cambridge: CUP (2005), 5–15.

Boyarin, D., *Border Lines: the Partition of Judaeo-Christianity*, Philadelphia: University of Pennsylvania Press, 2004.

Bradshaw, P. F., Johnson, M. E. and Phillips, L. E., *The Apostolic Tradition*, ed. H. W. Attridge, Hermeneia; Minneapolis: Fortress Press, 2002.

Brandenburg, H., *Ancient Churches of Rome from the Fourth to the Seventh Century: The Dawn of Christian Architecture in the West*, tr. A. Kopp, Bibliothèque de l'Antiquité Tardive, 8, Turnhout, Belgium: Brepols, 2005.

Bremmer, J. N., *The Apocryphal Acts of Peter: Magic, Miracles and Gnosticism*, Leuven: Peeters, 1998.

Brent, A., *Hippolytus and the Roman Church in the Third Century: Communities in Tension before the Emergence of a Monarch-Bishop*, Supplements to *Vigiliae Christianae*, 31, Leiden: Brill, 1995.

Burns, J. P., *Cyprian the Bishop*, Routledge Early Church Monographs, London: Routledge, 2002.

Caragounis, C. C., 'From Obscurity to Prominence: The Development of the Roman Church between Romans and *1 Clement*' in *Judaism and Christianity in First-Century Rome*, ed. K. P. Donfried and P. Richardson, Grand Rapids, Michigan: Eerdmans (1998), 245–79.

Carleton-Paget, J., 'Some Observations on Josephus and Christianity', *JTS* 52 (2001), 539–624.

Clarke, G. W., 'Prosopographical Notes on the Epistles of Cyprian — III Rome in August, 258', *Latomus* 34 (1975), 437–48.

Clarke, G. W. (ed.), *The Letters of St Cyprian of Carthage*, 4 vols., New York: Newman Press, 1984–9.

Corbeill, A., *Nature Embodied: Gesture in Ancient Rome*, Princeton: Princeton University Press, 2004.

Cullhed, M., *Conservator Urbis Suae: Studies in the Politics and Propaganda of the Emperor Maxentius*, Stockholm: Paul Åströms Förlag, 1994.

Cullmann, O., *Peter, Disciple, Apostle, Martyr: A Historical and Theological Study*, London: SCM, 2nd edn, 1962.

Cumont, F., *Lux Perpetua*, Paris: Paul Geuthner, 1949.

Curran, J., *Pagan City and Christian Capital: Rome in the Fourth Century*, Oxford: Clarendon Press, 2nd edn., 2000.

Das, A. A., *Solving the Romans Debate*, Minneapolis: Fortress Press, 2007.

Davies, P. S., 'The Origin and Purpose of the Persecution of AD 303', *JTS* 40 (1989), 66–94.

Davis, R. (ed.), *The Book of Pontiffs (Liber Pontificalis): The Ancient Biographies of the First Ninety Roman Bishops to ad 715*, Translated Texts for Historians, 6, Liverpool: Liverpool University Press, 2nd edn., 2000.

De Decker, D., 'La Politique religieuse de Maxence', *Byzantion* 38 (1968), 472–562.

Donfried, K. P. (ed.), *The Romans Debate*, Edinburgh: T&T Clark, rev. edn., 1991.

Donfried, K. P. and Richardson, P. (eds), *Judaism and Christianity in First-Century Rome*, Grand Rapids, Michigan: Eerdmans, 1998.

Drake, H. A., *Constantine and the Bishops: The Politics of Intolerance*, Baltimore: Johns Hopkins University Press, 2000.

Drake, H. A., 'The Impact of Constantine on Christianity' in *The Cambridge Companion to the Age of Constantine*, ed. N. Lenski, Cambridge: Cambridge University Press (2006), 111–36.

Drinkwater, J. F., 'The "catastrophe" of 260: towards a more favourable assessment of the emperor Valerian I', *Rivista Storica dell'Antichità* 19 (1989), 123–35.

Ducos, M., 'Le Tombeau: *Locus Religiosus*' in *La Mort quotidien dans le monde romain*, ed. F. Hinard, Paris: De Boccard (1995), 135–44.

Dumont, J.-C., 'La Mort de l'esclave' in *La Mort, les morts et l'au-delà dans le monde romain*, ed. F. Hinard, Caen: University of Caen (1987), 173–86.

Dunn, G. D., *Cyprian and the Bishops of Rome: Questions of Papal Primacy in the Early Church*, Early Christian Studies, 11, Strathfield, NSW: St Paul's Publications, 2007.

Dunn, J. D. G. *Jesus, Paul and the Law*, London: SPCK, 1990.

Dunn, J. D. G., *The Parting of the Ways between Christianity and Judaism and their Significance for the Character of Christianity*, London: SCM, 1991.

Dunn, J. D. G *Jews and Christians: The Parting of the Ways, 70–135 CE*, Tübingen: Mohr, 1992.

Dunn, J. D. G. *The Theology of Paul the Apostle* Edinburgh: T&T Clark, 1998.

Dupont, F., 'Les Morts et la mémoire: le masque funèbre' in *La Mort, les morts et l'au-delà dans le monde romain*, ed. F. Hinard, Caen: University of Caen (1987), 167–72.

Duval, Y. and Picard, J.-C. (eds), *L'Inhumation privilégiée du IVe au VIIIe siècle en occident*, Paris: De Boccard, 1986.

Dyson, S. L., *Community and Society in Roman Italy*, Baltimore: Johns Hopkins University Press, 1992.

Edwards, M. J., 'Justin's Logos and the Word of God', *JECS* 3 (1995), 261–80.

Elliott, J. K., *The Apocryphal New Testament: A Collection of Apocryphal Christian Literature in an English Translation*, Oxford: Clarendon Press, 1993.

Esler, P. F, *Conflict and Identity in Romans: The Social Setting of Paul's Letter*, Minneapolis: Fortress Press, 2003.

Fasola, U. M., *The Catacombs of Domitilla and the Basilica of the Martyrs Nereus and Achilleus*, ed. and tr. P. Pergola, C. S. Houston and F. Barbarito, Città del Vaticano: Pontificia Commissione di Archeologia Sacra, 3rd edn., 2002.

Feldman, L. H., *Jew and Gentile in the Ancient World: Attitudes and Interactions from Alexander to Justinian*, Princeton: Princeton University Press, 1993.

Ferrua, A., *Epigrammata Damasiana*, Vatican City: Pontificio Istituto di Archeologia Cristiana, 1942.

Ferrua, A., *The Unknown Catacomb: A Unique Discovery of Early Christian Art*, tr. I. Inglis, New Lanark: Geddes and Grosset, 1991.

Ferrua, A., *The Basilica and the Catacomb of Saint Sebastian*, tr. N. Reitzug, Città del Vaticano: Pontificia Commissione di Archeologia Sacra, 2nd edn., 2006.

Février, P.-A., 'A propos du repas funéraire: Culte et sociabilité: "In Christo Deo pax et concordia sit convivio nostro"', *Cahiers Archéologiques* 26 (1977), 29–45.

Février, P.-A., 'Le culte des morts dans les communautés chrétiennes durant le IIIe siècle', *Atti del IX Congresso Internazionale di Archeologia Cristiana, Roma, 21–27 settembre 1975*, Studi di Antichità Cristiana, 32, 2 vols., Città del Vaticano: Pontificio Istituto di Archeologia Cristiana 91978) vol. 1, 11–274.

Février, P.-A., 'Une approche de la conversion des élites au IVe siècle: le décor de la mort', *Miscellanea Historiae Ecclesiasticae*, VI, *Congrès de Varsovie 1978*, Bruxelles: Publications universitaires de Louvain (1983), 22–45.

Fink, J., 'Herakles als Christusbild an der Via Latina', *Rivista di Archeologia Cristiana* 56 (1980), 133–46.

Fiocchi Nicolai, V., Bisconti, F. and Mazzoleni, D. *The Christian Catacombs of Rome: History, Decoration, Inscriptions*, tr. C. C. Stella and L.-A. Touchette, Regensburg: Schnell and Steiner, 1999.

Goodenough, E. R., *The Theology of Justin Martyr*, Jena: Frommann, 1923.

Goodenough, E. R., *An Introduction to Philo Judaeus*, Oxford: Blackwell, 2nd edn., 1962.

Goodman, M. (ed.), *Jews in a Graeco-Roman World*, Oxford: Clarendon Press, 1998.

Goulder, M. D., 'Did Peter ever go to Rome?', *Scottish Journal of Theology* 57 (2004), 377–96.

Grappe, C., *Images de Pierre aux deux premiers siècles*, Paris: Presses Universitaires de France, 1995.

Gregory, A., 'Disturbing Trajectories: *1 Clement*, the *Shepherd of Hermas* and the Development of Early Roman Christianity', in *Rome in the Bible and the Early Church*, ed. P. Oakes, Carlisle: Paternoster Press (2002), 142–66.

Gruen, E. S., *Diaspora: Jews amidst Greeks and Romans*, Cambridge, Mass: Harvard University Press, 2002.

Guidobaldi, F. and Guidobaldi, A. G. (eds), *Ecclesiae Urbis: Atti del Congresso Internazionale di Studi sulle Chiesi di Roma (IV–X secolo), Roma, 4–10 settembre 2000*, 3 vols., Città del Vaticano: Pontificio Istituto di Archeologia Cristiana, 2002.

Haas, C. J., 'Imperial Religious Policy and Valerian's Persecution of the Church, AD 257–260', *Church History* 52 (1983), 133–44.

Haas, C. J., *Alexandria in Late Antiquity: Topography and Social Conflict*, Baltimore: Johns Hopkins University Press, 1997.

Hall, S. G., 'The versions of Cyprian, *De unitate*, 4–5. Bévenot's dating revisited', *JTS* 55 (2004), 138–46.

Helgeland, J., 'Christians and the Roman Army from Marcus Aurelius to Constantine', *ANRW* 2.23.1 (1979), 724–834.

Heres, T., *Paries: A Proposal for a Dating System of Late-Antique Masonry Structures in Rome and Ostia*, Amsterdam: Rodopi, 1982.

Hinard, F. (ed.), *La Mort, les morts et l'au-delà dans le monde romain*, Caen: University of Caen, 1987.

Hinard, F. (ed.), *La Mort quotidien dans le monde romain*, Paris: De Boccard, 1995.

Holloway, R. R., *Constantine and Rome*, New Haven: Yale University Press, 2004.

Hope, V. M., 'Contempt and Respect: the Treatment of Corpses in Ancient Rome' in *Death and Disease in the Ancient City*, ed. V. M. Hope and E. Marshall, London: Routledge (2000), 104–27.

Hope, V. M. and Marshall, E. (eds), *Death and Disease in the Ancient City*, London: Routledge, 2000.

Hopkins, K., *Death and Renewal*, Cambridge: Cambridge Univerity Press, 1983.

Horbury, W., *Jews and Christians in Conflict and Controversy*, Edinburgh: T&T Clark, 1998.

Hübner, R. M., *Der Paradox Eine: antignostischer Monarchismus im zweiten Jahrhundert*, Supplements to *Vigiliae Christianae*, 50, Leiden: Brill, 1999.

Jaffé, D., *Le judaisme et l'avènement du Christianisme: Orthodoxie et héterodoxie dans la litterature talmudique Ier — IIe siècle*, Paris: Cerf, 2005.

Jalland, T., *The Church and the Papacy*, London: SPCK, 1944.

Jastrzebowska, E., 'Les scènes de banquet dans les peintures et sculptures des IIIe et IVe siècles', *Recherches Augustiniennes* 14 (1979), 3–90.

Jastrzebowska, E., 'S. Sebastiano, La Più Antica Basilica Cristiana di Roma' in *Ecclesiae Urbis: Atti del Congresso Internazionale di Studi sulle Chiesi di Roma (IV–X secolo), Roma, 4–10 settembre 2000*, ed. F. Guidobaldi and A. G. Guidobaldi, 3 vols., Città del Vaticano: Pontificio Istituto di Archeologia Cristiana (2002), vol. 2, 1141–55.

Jay, E. G., 'From Presbyter-Bishops to Bishops and Presbyters: Christian Ministry in the Second Century: A Survey', *The Second Century* 1 (1981), 125–62.

Jewett, R., *Romans: A Commentary*, Hermeneia; Minneapolis: Fortress Press, 2006.

Krautheimer, R., Frankl, W. and Corbett, S. (eds), *Corpus Basilicarum Christianarum Romae*, 5 vols., Cittá del Vaticano: Pontificio Istituto di Archeologia Cristiana, 1937–77.

Krautheimer, R., *Rome: Profile of a City, 312–1308*, Princeton: Princeton University Press, 1980.

Lampe, P., *From Paul to Valentinus: Christians at Rome in the First Two Centuries*, tr. Michael Steinhauser, London: T&T Clark, 2003.

La Regina, A., *Lexicon Topographicum Urbis Romae Suburbium*, 5 vols., Rome: Edizioni Quasar, 2001–8.

Lavagne, H., 'Le Tombeau, mémoire du mort' in *La Mort, les morts et l'au-delà dans le monde romain*, ed. F. Hinard, Caen: University of Caen (1987), 159–65.

Layton, B. (ed.), *The Rediscovery of Gnosticism: Proceedings of the International Conference on Gnosticism at Yale, New Haven, Connecticut, March 28–31, 1978*, Studies in the History of Religion, 41, 2 vols., Leiden: Brill, 1980–1.

Lee, A. D., 'Traditional Religions' in *The Cambridge Companion to the Age of Constantine*, ed. N. Lenski, Cambridge: Cambridge University Press (2006), 159–79.

Lenski, N. (ed.), *The Cambridge Companion to the Age of Constantine*, Cambridge: Cambridge University Press, 2006.

Lenski, N. (ed.), 'Introduction' in Noel Lenski (ed.), *The Cambridge Companion to the Age of Constantine*, Cambridge: Cambridge University Press (2006), 1–13.

Leon, H. J., *The Jews in Late Ancient Rome: Evidence of Cultural Interaction in the Roman Diaspora*, Peabody, Mass: Hendrickson, 2nd edn., 1995.

Levine, L. I., *The Ancient Synagogue: The First Thousand Years*, New Haven: Yale University Press, 2nd edn., 2005.

Lichtenberger, H., 'Jews and Christians in Rome in the Time of Nero: Josephus and Paul in Rome', *ANRW* 2.26.3 (1996), 2142–2176.

Lieu, J., *Christian Identity in the Jewish and Graeco-Roman World*, Oxford: Oxford University Press, 2004.

Löhr, W., 'Did Marcion distinguish between a just god and a good god?' in *Marcion und Seine Kirchengeschichtliche Wirkung: Marcion and his Impact on Church History*, ed. G. May and K. Greschat, Texte und Untersuchungen zur Geschichte der altchristlichen Literatur, 150, Berlin: W. de Gruyter (2002), 131–46.

Lona, H. E. (ed.), *Der erste Clemensbrief* (Kommentar zu den Apostolischen Vätern, 2; Göttingen: Vandenhoek & Ruprecht, 1998)

Macdonald, L. M. and Sanders, J. A. (eds), *The Canon Debate*, Peabody, Mass: Hendrickson, 2002.

Markschies, C., *Valentinus Gnosticus? Untersuchungen zur valentini-anischen Gnosis mit einem Kommentar zu den Fragmenten Valentins*, Wissenschaftliche Untersuchungen zum Neuen Testament, 65, Tübingen: Mohr, 1992.

Markschies, C., *Gnosis: an Introduction*, tr. J. Bowden, London: T&T Clark, 2003.

Mason, S., *Josephus, Judea, and Christian Origins: Methods and Categories*, Peabody, Mass: Hendrickson, 2009.

Mattingly, H., *Coins of the Roman Empire in the British Museum* vol. 3, London: Trustees of the British Museum, 1936.

May, G. and Greschat, K. (eds), *Marcion und Seine Kirchengeschichtliche Wirkung: Marcion and his Impact on Church History*, Texte und Untersuchungen zur Geschichte der altchristlichen Literatur, 150, Berlin: W. de Gruyter, 2002.

McKechnie, P., 'Christian Grave-Inscriptions from the *Familia Caesaris*', *JEH* 30 (1999), 427–41.

Minear, P. S., *The Obedience of Faith: The Purposes of Paul in the Letter to the Romans*, London: SCM, 1971.

Moll, S., 'Justin and the Pontic Wolf' in *Justin Martyr and his Worlds*, ed. S. Parvis and P. Foster, Minneapolis: Fortress Press (2007), 145–51.

Moll, S., 'Three against Tertullian: the Second Tradition about Marcion's Life', *JTS* 59 (2008), 169–80.

Moorhead, J., '"Papa" as Bishop of Rome', *JEH* 36 (1985), 337–50.

Morris, I., *Death-Ritual and Social Structure in Classical Antiquity*, Cambridge: Cambridge University Press, 1992.

Musurillo, H., *The Acts of the Christian Martyrs*, Oxford Early Christian Texts, Oxford: Clarendon Press, 1972.

Nanos, M. D., *The Mystery of Romans: The Jewish Context of Paul's Letter*, Minneapolis: Fortress Press, 1996.

Noy, D., *Foreigners at Rome: Citizens and Strangers*, London: Duckworth, 2000.

Oakes, P. (ed.), *Rome in the Bible and the Early Church*, Carlisle: Paternoster Press, 2002.

O'Connor, D. W., *Peter in Rome: The Literary, Liturgical and Archaeological Evidence*, New York: Columbia University Press, 1969.

Osborn, E., *Justin Martyr*, Tübingen: Mohr, 1973.

Osiek, C., 'The Oral World of Early Christianity in Rome: The Case of Hermas' in *Judaism and Christianity in First-Century Rome*, ed. K. P. Donfried and P. Richardson, Grand Rapids, Michigan: Eerdmans (1998), 151–72.

Osiek, C., *The Shepherd of Hermas: A Commentary*, Hermeneia; Minneapolis: Fortress, 1999.

Parvis, P., 'Justin, Philosopher and Martyr: the Posthumous Creation of the *Second Apology*', in *Justin Martyr and his Worlds*, ed. S. Parvis and P. Foster, Minneapolis: Fortress (2007), 22–37.

Parvis, S. and Foster, P. (eds), *Justin Martyr and his Worlds*, Minneapolis: Fortress Press, 2007.

Parvis, S., 'Justin Martyr and the Apologetic Tradition', in *Justin Martyr and his Worlds*, ed. S. Parvis and P. Foster, Minneapolis: Fortress (2007), 115–27.

Pergola, P., 'Sepultures privilégiées de la catacombe de Domitille à Rome', in *L'Inhumation privilégiée du IVe au VIIIe siècle en occident*, ed. Y. Duval and J.-C. Picard, Paris: De Boccard (1986), 185–87.

Platner, S. B. and Ashby, T., *A Topographical Dictionary of Ancient Rome*, Oxford: Oxford University Press, 1929.

Quentin, H. (ed.), *Commentarius Perpetuus in Martyrologium Hieronymianum*, in *Acta Sanctorum Novembris* 2.2, Brussels, 1931.

Rajak, T., *Josephus: the Historian and his Society*, London: Duckworth, 2nd edn., 2002.

Richardson, P., 'Augustan-Era Synagogues in Rome' in *Judaism and Christianity in First-Century Rome*, ed. K. P. Donfried and P. Richardson, Grand Rapids, Michigan: Eerdmans (1998), 17–29.

Rickman, G., *The Corn Supply of Ancient Rome*, Oxford: Clarendon Press, 1980.

Rives, J. B., 'The Piety of a Persecutor', *JECS* 4 (1996), 1–25.

Rives, J. B., 'The Decree of Decius and the Religion of Empire', *JRS* 89 (1999), 135–54.

Rives, J. B., *Religion in the Roman Empire*, Malden, MA: Blackwell, 2007.

Robinson, J. M. (ed.), *The Nag Hammadi Library in English*, Leiden: Brill, 3rd edn., 1988.

Rutgers, L. V., *The Jews in Late Ancient Rome: Evidence of Cultural Interaction in the Roman Diaspora*, Leiden: Brill, 1995.

Rutgers, L. V., *The Hidden Heritage of Diaspora Judaism*, Leuven: Peeters, 1998.

Rutgers, L. V., 'Roman Policy toward the Jews: Expulsions from the City of Rome during the First Century C.E.' in *Judaism and Christianity in First-Century Rome*, ed. K. P. Donfried and P. Richardson, Grand Rapids, Michigan: Eerdmans (1998), 93–116.

Rutgers, L. V., *Subterranean Rome: In Search of the Roots of Ancient Christianity in the Catacombs of the Eternal City*, Leuven: Peeters, 2000.

Ste Croix, G. E. M. de, 'Why were the Early Christians Persecuted?', *Past & Present* 26 (1963), 6–38.

Ste Croix, G. E. M. *Christian Persecution, Martyrdom and Orthodoxy*, ed. M. Whitby and J. Streeter, Oxford: Oxford University Press, 2006.

Sanders, E. P., *Paul and Palestinian Judaism*, London: SCM, 1977.

Segal, A. F., *Two Powers in Heaven: Early Rabbinic Reports about Christianity and Gnosticism*, Leiden: Brill, 1977.

Selinger, R., *The Mid-Third Century Persecutions of Decius and Valerian*, Frankfurt-am-Main: Peter Lang, 2002.

Sherwin-White, A. N., *The Roman Citizenship*, Oxford: Oxford University Press, 2nd edn., 1973.

Simon, M., *Verus Israel: A Study of the Relations between Christians and Jews in the Roman Empire (135–425)*, tr. H. McKeating, Littman Library of Jewish Civilization, Oxford: Litman Library, 1986.

Sly, D. I., *Philo's Alexandria*, London: Routledge, 1996.

Smallwood, E. M., *Philonis Alexandrini Legatio ad Gaium, Edited with an Introduction, Translation and Commentary*, Leiden: Brill, 1961.

Smallwood, E. M., *The Jews under Roman Rule from Pompey to Diocletian: a Study in Political Relations*, Leiden: Brill, 2nd edn., 1981.

Smith, T. V., *Petrine Controversies in Early Christianity: Attitudes towards Peter in Christian Writings of the First Two Centuries*, Tübingen: Mohr, 1985.

Spence, S., *The Parting of the Ways: The Roman Church as a Case Study*, Leuven: Peeters, 2004.

Spier, J., *Picturing the Bible: the Earliest Christian Art*, New Haven: Yale University Press, 2007.

Stead, G. C., 'In Search of Valentinus' in *The Rediscovery of Gnosticism: Proceedings of the International Conference on Gnosticism at Yale, New Haven, Connecticut, March 28–31, 1978*, ed. B. Layton, Studies in the History of Religion, 41, 2 vols., Leiden: Brill (1980–1), vol. 1, 75–102.

Steinby, E. M., *Lexicon Topigraphicum Urbis Romae*, 6 vols., Rome: Edizioni Quasar, 1993–9.

Stewart-Sykes, A., *Hippolytus: On the Apostolic Tradition*, Popular Patristics Series, Crestwood NY: St Vladimir's Seminary Press, 2001.

Stewart-Sykes, A., 'Bread and fish, water and wine. The Marcionite menu and the maintenance of purity' in *Marcion und Seine Kirchengeschichtliche Wirkung: Marcion and his Impact on Church History*, ed. G. May and K. Greschat, Texte und Untersuchungen zur Geschichte der altchristlichen Literatur, 150, Berlin: W. de Gruyter (2002), 207–20.

Stowers, S. K., *A Rereading of Romans: Justice, Jews, and Gentiles*, New Haven: Yale University Press, 1994.

Taylor, M., *Anti-Judaism and Early Christian Identity: A Critique of the Scholarly Consensus*, Leiden: Brill, 1995.

Testini, P., *Le Catacombe e gli Antichi Cimiteri Cristiani in Roma*, Bologna: Cappelli, 1966.

Thomas, C. M., *The* Acts of Peter, *Gospel Literature, and the Ancient Novel*, Oxford: Oxford University Press, 2003.

Thomassen, E., *The Spiritual Seed: the Church of the 'Valentinians'*, Nag Hammadi and Manichaean Studies, 60, Leiden: Brill, 2006.

Toynbee, J. M. C. and Ward-Perkins, J. B., *The Shrine of St Peter and the Vatican Excavations*, London: Longmans and Green, 1956.

Toynbee, J. M. C., *Death and Burial in the Roman World*, London: Thames and Hudson, 1971.

Tronzo, W. (ed.), *St Peter's in the Vatican*, Cambridge: CUP, 2005.

Veyne, P., *Bread and Circuses: Historical Sociology and Political Pluralism*, abridged with an introduction by O. Murray, tr. B. Pearce, Penguin History, London: Allen Lane, 1990.

Vinzent, M., 'Der Schluß des Lukasevangeliums bei Marcion' in *Marcion und Seine Kirchengeschichtliche Wirkung: Marcion and his Impact on Church History*, ed. G. May and K. Greschat, Texte und Untersuchungen zur Geschichte der altchristlichen Literatur, 150, Berlin: W. de Gruyter (2002), 79–94.

Walker, S., *Memorials to the Roman Dead*, London: British Museum, 1985.

Walters, J. C., 'Romans, Jews and Christians: The Impact of the Romans on Jewish/Christian Relations in First-Century Rome' in *Judaism and Christianity in First-Century Rome*, ed. K. P. Donfried and P. Richardson, Grand Rapids, Michigan: Eerdmans (1998), 175–95.

Watson, F., *Paul, Judaism and the Gentiles: Beyond the New Perspective*, Grand Rapids, Michigan: Eerdmans, 2nd edn., 2007.

Wedderburn, A. J. M., *The Reasons for Romans*, Edinburgh: T&T Clark, 1988.

Weiss, P., 'The Vision of Constantine', *The Journal of Archaeology* 16 (2003), 237–59.

Wiefel, W., 'The Jewish Community in Ancient Rome and the Origins of Roman Christianity', in *The Romans Debate*, ed. K. P. Donfried, Edinburgh: T&T Clark, rev. edn. (1991), 85–101.

Wilken, R. L., *The Christians as the Romans Saw Them*, New Haven: Yale University Press, 1984.

Williams, M. H., 'The Structure of Roman Jewry Re-Considered —

Were the Synagogues of Ancient Rome Entirely Homogeneous?',
ZPE 104 (1994), 129–41.

Williams, M., 'The Structure of the Jewish Community in Rome',
in *Jews in a Graeco-Roman World*, ed. M. Goodman, Oxford:
Clarendon Press (1998), 215–28.

Williams, S., *Diocletian and the Roman Recovery*, London: Batsford,
1985.

Zetterholm, M., *The Formation of Christianity in Antioch: A Social-
Scientific Approach to the Separation between Judaism and Christianity*,
London: Routledge, 2003.

INDEX

(Dates are within brackets)

251